MYLES BEFORE MYLES

828/O BREEN

By the Same Author

THE THIRD POLICEMAN
AT SWIM-TWO-BIRDS
THE HARD LIFE
THE POOR MOUTH
THE DALKEY ARCHIVE
STORIES AND PLAYS
THE VARIOUS LIVES OF KEATS AND
CHAPMAN and THE BROTHER
THE HAIR OF THE DOGMA
FURTHER CUTTINGS FROM CRUISKEEN LAWN
MYLES AWAY FROM DUBLIN

FLANN O'BRIEN
(Myles na Gopaleen)

MYLES BEFORE MYLES

*A selection of the
earlier writings of
Brian O'Nolan*

Selected and introduced by
John Wyse Jackson

The Lilliput Press
Dublin

First published by Granada Publishing 1985
This edition published in 2012 by
THE LILLIPUT PRESS
62–63 Sitric Road, Arbour Hill, Dublin 7, Ireland
www.lilliputpress.ie

ISBN 978 1 84351 264 6

A CIP record for this is available from The British Library

The Lilliput Press receives financial assistance from
An Chomhairle Ealaion / The Arts Council of Ireland

Printed and bound in Sweden by Scandbook AB

Contents

Acknowledgments

Warm thanks are due to Breandán Ó Conaire for translating most of the Irish material, and to Susan Asbee for making available to me the extracts from *At Swim-Two-Birds*; to Tess Hurson, Aibhistín Mac Amhlaigh, Anthony Cronin and very many others for help and encouragement; to Mrs Evelyn O'Nolan for smiling on the project; and to Eoghan and Biddy, Lucy and Julie, and the entire Wyse Jackson family for being themselves. I would also like to thank John Ryan, Peter Costello, and, for the pieces included here by her late husband, Mrs Kathleen Kavanagh.

Introduction

On April Fool's Day 1986, exactly twenty years after the death of the author of this book, there was a strange gathering in Dublin. It was the first international symposium devoted to the life and work of Flann O'Brien. Incorporated into each day's proceedings was an event oddly titled 'Late Evening Criticism', during which delegates and members of what could be called 'Literary Dublin' met, drank Guinness, and then proceeded to criticise each other. One morning, John Ryan, artist, writer and old friend of Flann O'Brien, set off from the symposium with a crocodile of professors, students, Mylesmen and 'corduroys' – Myles na Gopaleen's term for personages of undefined literary pretensions. The object of this pilgrimage was to visit some of the many hostelries where 'your man' had reputedly found inspiration, to look at them, and to soak up, among other things, the ambience. In just such a spirit did the devout penitents of the Middle Ages visit the holy wells of Ireland and partake of the holy liquid therein. It was not until the Holy Hour (when the pubs shut) that the crocodile shuffled, bedraggled but happy, back to the symposium. Flann O'Brien, Myles na Gopaleen and Brian O'Nolan could not have disapproved.

Apart from the celebratory festivities during the three days of the symposium, the emphasis among the more studious delegates was primarily on the novels of Flann O'Brien. This is understandable: a novel must have a beginning (or, in the case of *At Swim-Two-Birds*, three beginnings), a middle and an end; it can be more satisfactorily tackled as a unit, whereas it is not so easy to discuss collections of shorter pieces which by definition lack a collective structure. There is another reason, however. Much of Brian O'Nolan's most interesting and entertaining work has never been published in book form. Most of his writings from the thirties, for example, which include some of his funniest excursions, and which display several nearly unknown aspects of his work, have lain in almost complete obscurity since then, and it is this material which forms the basis of the present collection.

Like Gaul and good sermons, the thirty-five years of O'Nolan's writing life can be divided into three parts. For the first ten years, say, between 1930 and 1940, he was seeking a voice. During the next ten years or so, he had found it. After about 1950, he had become that voice. Throughout, he could write elegantly, intelligently and hilariously, and often with what he once called 'the beauty of jewelled ulcers'. The things that changed were the tone, the style, the language, and the pseudonym, or pen-name.

There are two main reasons for the use of a pen-name. The first is obvious: to provide anonymity for propriety's sake or for professional purposes. As a civil servant, Brian O'Nolan needed to be able to say, as he once did when accused by his superiors of having written an article signed by one 'John McCaffrey', 'I no more wrote that than I wrote those things in the *Irish Times* by Myles na Gopaleen.' The second reason is that the use of a pen-name makes it far easier for some people to write imaginatively and freely, and, indeed, to write well. Try writing to the papers under a false name and you will see what I mean. You will be able to say all sorts of disgraceful things without being accused of believing them.

It is almost impossible to discover from O'Nolan's pseudonymous writings what the man behind them really believed. Pseudonyms were central to his creative impulse. He rarely used his real name, and when he did it was usually in its Irish version, Brian Ua Nualláin, or some variant thereof. Other names that he adopted, apart from Myles na Gopaleen and Flann O'Brien, include Peter the Painter, George Knowall, Brother Barnabas, John James Doe, Winnie Wedge, An Broc, and The O'Blather. The list is by no means complete. It has been said, however, that he began life as who he really was, and ended it as Myles. The whole of Ireland, as well as most of his acquaintances, knew him simply as 'Myles', and he thus gradually lost the freedom of expression that his persona, 'Myles na Gopaleen', had given him. In the later *Cruiskeen Lawn* columns in the *Irish Times*, what

8

'Myles' wrote, Myles believed. Or so people thought. It was probably a response to O'Nolan's realisation of this effect that prompted him to give birth in 1960 to George Knowall, the hectoring polymath of *Myles Away from Dublin*.

In this collection, however, there are few of the acerbities of George Knowall. Brian O'Nolan, here, is above all an entertainer, a 'gas man'. He began his literary career proper with stories and articles, generally humorous in intent, which he wrote in Irish, his first language. (His father had discouraged the use of English at home, and the young Brian is said to have taught himself to read the language – first, by looking at comics, and then, at about the age of seven, by tackling Dickens.) These early Irish pieces, a few of which have been included here, show O'Nolan already trying out ideas and techniques that he was to use in his greatest Irish work, *An Béal Bocht* (*The Poor Mouth*). They were published in the early thirties while he was a student at University College, Dublin. The College magazine *Comhthrom Féinne*, of which he was to become editor for a time, printed his first articles in English, and 'Brother Barnabas', the most important pen-name he used at this time, was celebrated as an oracle and commentator on College matters. Like 'Myles na Gopaleen' ten years later, the eccentric monk practically became a person in his own right, and, indeed, on 30 April 1932 the magazine's gossip column reports that 'Mr B. O'Nualláin was heard speaking to Brother Barnabas in a lonely corridor: "Brian, I had to come back from Baden-Baden." "That's too bad, then."'

At the end of his college career, O'Nolan, together with some friends, notably his brother Ciarán, Niall Montgomery and Niall Sheridan, who was to appear thinly disguised as Brinsley in the novel *At Swim-Two-Birds*, founded *Blather*, variously described by itself as 'The only really nice paper circulating in Ireland', 'Ireland's poor eejit paper', 'The voice from the back of the hall' and 'The only paper exclusively devoted to the interests of clay-pigeon shooting in Ireland.' It was inspired by *Razzle*, an English comic magazine of the period, and contained cartoons, some of them drawn by O'Nolan, silly verse, mock political pieces, short stories, and a host of other miscellaneous pieces which display the warped and imaginative view of things that we

9

have come to expect from O'Nolan. Again, several of the comic devices for which Myles/Flann is known appear in their early forms in the paper, but, that apart, *Blather* remains vastly entertaining still, and a generous selection from its short life is reprinted here.

It is extremely difficult to identify for certain which of the pieces in *Blather* and *Comhthrom Féinne* were actually written by O'Nolan, which were collaborations, and which were the work of other contributors. There was a common sense of humour and style among his friends at the time, and it is likely that there was considerable discussion of what was to go into print. However, what is certain is that O'Nolan wrote most of it, and furthermore that his was the creative guiding force behind all of it. The humour was his own, or he made it his own. The same *caveat* applies, probably to a greater extent, to the section in this collection entitled 'Henrik Ibsen and Patrick Kavanagh'. These letters, written at the beginning of the forties to the *Irish Times*, are a surrealistic exercise in lunacy, in which each contribution sparks off an even more outlandish reply, until finally R. M. Smyllie, the editor, calls a halt. It has been decided to reprint here the best of them, without being unduly concerned as to their true authorship. Evidence, in any case, is minimal. O'Nolan was certainly F. O'Brien, but he may also have been Whit Cassidy, Lir O'Connor, Luna O'Connor, Mrs Hilda Upshott, Judy Clifford and Jno. O'Ruddy. He was probably not Oscar Love, and he was certainly not Patrick Kavanagh. These letters derive much of their entertainment value from their context, and it would be churlish to exclude them on the scholarly grounds of dubious ascription, for their entertainment value is high, and if there was a mastermind behind them, it was none other than...

The present book closes with Brian O'Nolan's verse translations from the Irish. He would not have claimed a great deal for them, I suspect, but they have a lightness of touch that does not diminish their impact, and have none of the pomposity of most Irish verse translations. All O'Nolan's work contains a similar playful unexpectedness. Often this quality hides deep seriousness, outmanoeuvring reality in order to show what makes it appear to be so real. Sometimes, as in the bulk of this collection, the playfulness is for its own sake. And a very good sake it is, too, as the gentleman from Japan used to say. Cheers!

JOHN WYSE JACKSON
Fulham, March 1988

1

The Student

'Tell me this, do you ever open a book at all?'
At Swim-Two-Birds, p. 10

The earliest known piece of published writing by Brian O'Nolan is a little poem written during his schooldays at Blackrock College, Co. Dublin. When it was written is impossible to say, as it appeared when O'Nolan was already an undergraduate at University College, Dublin, but it bears evidence of his having opened perhaps too many books at too early an age. Its title is the school's motto:

> AD ASTRA
> Ah! when the skies at night
> Are damascened with gold,
> Methinks the endless sight
> Eternity unrolled.

The verse is almost unique among O'Nolan's creative writings in that it shows none of his characteristic irony. It is tempting to imagine what the poet Patrick Kavanagh would have remarked if the poem had circulated through the Dublin pubs in later years. Still, O'Nolan never forgot about eternity.

Soon after entering University College, Dublin he became involved in the chief debating society, known to all as the 'L. & H.'. He later wrote two accounts of his time there:

Memories of the Literary and Historical Society, UCD

The Society met in term every Saturday night at seven thirty p.m. in a small theatre upstairs in 86 St Stephen's Green. Impassive as that granite-faced building looks to the present day, it was in the early thirties derelict within and was in some queer way ostracised from the college apparatus. And when the L. & H. met there, there was unholy bedlam.

The theory of the procedure was that the Society met to debate a pre-publicised motion, usually under the auspices of a visiting chairman. But before that item was reached in a night's work, time had to be found for the transaction of Private Business. So private was this business that in my own time the fire brigade had to be sent for twice and the police at least twelve times. Four people were taken to hospital with knife injuries, one man was shot, and there is no counting the number of people hurt in free-for-alls.

And there is no possible way of dealing here with the far more spectacular tragedies arising from people getting sick by reason of too much drink. Still . . . the Society bravely carried on. The roars prefaced by 'Mr Auditor, SIR!' were uttered by certain guttersnipes who are today the leaders in politics, the law, other professions and even journalism. One should not look too closely at the egg while it is hatching. That fable of the ugly duckling is still vivid.

Once a meeting got under way, many people were under the impression that the heavens were about to fall. The situation was one of a sort of reasoned chaos. During Private Business it was customary for the Auditor to scream to make himself heard and rule sundry questioners out of order. Apart from the jam-packed theatre itself, the big lobby outside and a whole staircase leading to it were peopled by a mass of insubordinate, irreverent persons collectively known as The Mob. Their interruptions and interjections were famous and I was myself designated (as I say it without shame) their leader.

Were we bad old codgers, notwithstanding those days of disorder and uproar?

Well, I don't think there was much wrong with us. If something has to go down on the charge-sheet, say that we were young. It's a disease that cures itself.

14

From The centenary history of the Literary and Historical Society, University College Dublin, 1855–1955

An invitation to write a few notes on my own day in UCD and the L. & H. – roughly from 1929 to 1934 – revealed that one effect of university education seems to be the distortion or near-eradication of the faculty of memory. I retain only the vaguest notion of how important rows arose, what they were really about and how they were quenched, whereas some sharp images in the recollection relate to trivial and absurd matters: but perhaps that is a universal rather than a university infirmity.

Architecturally, UCD reminds me of a certain type of incubator, an appropriate parallel – full of good eggs and bad eggs and 'gluggers'. I entered the big Main Hall at an odd hour on the second day of Michaelmas term 1929, looked about me and vividly remember the scene. The hall was quite empty. The plain white walls bore three dark parallel smudgy lines at elevations of about three, five and five-and-a-half feet from the tiled chessboard floor. Later I was to know this triptych had been achieved by the buttocks, shoulders, and hair oil of lounging students. They had, in fact, nowhere else to lounge, though in good weather many went out and sat on the steps. Before I left College, a large 'students' room' had been provided in the semi-ruinous remnant of the old Royal University premises, which is still behind the UCD façade; this room was destined to become the home of really ferocious poker schools. The ladies had a room of their own from the start. The only other amenity I can recall pre-1930 was a small restaurant of the tea-and-buns variety which provided the sole feasible place *intra muros* for the desegregation of the sexes. Later a billiards table was conceded, possibly in reality a missionary move to redeem poker addicts. Lecture theatres were modern and good, the lectures adequate though often surprisingly elementary, and it was a shock to find that Duggie Hyde spoke atrocious Irish, as also did Agnes

15

O'Farrelly (though the two hearts were of gold). Skipping lectures while contriving a prim presence at roll-call became a great skill, particularly with poker and billiards men.

The Republican versus Free State tensions were acute at this time, but one other room was set aside for the non-academic use of students; it was a recruiting office for a proposed National Army OTC. When it opened, a body of students led by the late Frank Ryan, then editing *An Phoblacht* and himself a graduate, came down with sticks and wrecked the joint. And there, I can't remember whether anybody was identified and fired for that!

The President for my span was Dr Denis J. Coffey, a stand-offish type and a poorish public speaker, but a very decent man withal. He lived only round the corner but never came or went otherwise than in a cab. That may seem odd now, but at that time it was the minimum requisite of presidential dignity. Many will recall the hall porters of that and preceding eras – Ryan and his assistant Jimmy Redmond, made in the proportions of Mutt and Jeff. Ryan was the real Dublin man, thin and tall with bad feet, a pinched face behind costly glasses and adorned with a moustache finished to points like waxed darning needles. Jimmy was more plebeian and ordinary-looking, and often more useful. Both, alas, are long dead. I hope Peter recognised two of his own trade.

The students' many societies, of which the L. & H. was the principal one and the oldest, held their meetings in a large building at 86 Stephen's Green. In my day it was a very dirty place and in bad repair, in the care of an incredible porter named Flynn whose eyes were nearly always closed, though not from an ocular complaint or mere sleep. If I am not mistaken, lighting was by gas, and it was in this 86, in an upstairs semi-circular lecture theatre that the L. & H. met every Saturday night. It was large as such theatres go but its seating capacity could not exceed two hundred, whereas most meetings attracted not fewer than six hundred people. The congestion, disorder and noise may be imagined. A seething mass gathered and swayed in a very large lobby outside the theatre, some sat on the stairs smoking, and groups adjourned to other apartments from time to time for hands of cards. Many students participated in the Society's transactions from the exterior lobby by choice, for once inside there was no getting out unless one was a lady student staying in

16

one of the residential halls run by nuns, who imposed a ten o'clock curfew. The mass exit of these ladies always evoked ribald and insulting commentary. A particular reason why many remained outside was the necessity to be free to make periodical trips to the Winter Palace at the corner of Harcourt Street, a pub where it was possible to drink three or four strong pints at sevenpence each.

This most heterogeneous congregation, reeling about, shouting and singing in the hogarthian pallor of a single gas-jet (when somebody had not thought fit to extinguish the same) came to be known as the mob, and I had the honour to be acknowledged its president. It is worth noting that it contained people who were not students at all. A visitor would probably conclude that it was merely a gang of rowdies, dedicated to making a deafening uproar the *obbligato* to some unfortunate member's attempts to make a speech within. It was certainly a disorderly gang but its disorders were not aimless and stupid, but often necessary and salutary. It could nearly be claimed that the mob was merely a severe judge of the speakers. In a document he issued in connection with his own candidature for the auditorship, here is what Cearbhall Ó Dálaigh wrote about them:

> I have no faith in quack-police remedies in dealing with the Mob. Any good speaker can subdue them. It is his pleasure, pride and triumph. I consider the lack of courtesy in other parts of the House equally annoying and unfortunately not eradicable at the hands of good speakers.
>
> I believe that the men at the door – some of them better intellectually than our speakers – will respond to an appeal given in a gentlemanly way and backed by personality.
>
> The crowded House is the soul of the L. & H. It makes the gathering electric.

I agree with that last sentence absolutely. The Commerce Society also held weekly debates in the same theatre and, granted that they had not the indefinable advantage of owning the Saturday nights, the debates were distressingly orderly, prim, almost boring. The same was more so when the *Cumann Gaelach* met to debate in Irish, and be it noted that L. & H. members were also speakers in both those other societies. The mob,

17

however, was on duty *qua* mob only on Saturday nights, though many individual members were to be seen wolfing cakes at the teas which societies often gave before a meeting. The Society now meets in the big Physics Theatre in Earlsfort Terrace. There is no mob now – the *mise en scène* is impracticable – and I have no doubt at all that the Society has deteriorated, both as a school for speakers and, more important, the occasion for an evening's enjoyment.

If my judgment is not faulty, the standard of speaking was very high on the average. There were dull speakers, some with hobby horses, politicians, speakers who were 'good' but boring, but there were brilliant speakers too. The most brilliant of all was J. C. Flood. He was an excellent and witty man, with a tongue which could on occasion scorch and wound. Long after he had become a professional man of the world, he found it impossible to disengage himself from the Society. Another fine speaker I remember was Michael Farrell and, God bless my soul, I amassed some medals myself.

The man I admired most was the late Tim O'Hanrahan, a most amusing personality and a first-class debater on any subject under the sun.

That the Society is really an extra-curricular function of the university organism is shown by the great number of the members of my day (and, of course, of other days) who were to attain great distinction in legal and parliamentary work. The Irish gift of the gab is not so spontaneous an endowment as we are led to believe: it requires training and endowment, experience of confrontation with hostile listeners, and, yes – study.

Not only was the L. & H. invaluable to the students in such matters, but it could teach the visiting chairmen a thing or two. Determined chairmen who tried to control the mob found they were merely converting disorder into bedlam, while timid chairmen learnt the follies of conciliation, and the beauty of a mean between weakness and pugnacity.

I can attempt no statistical survey here, for it would be like what somebody called a net – a lot of holes tied together. But a few names were prominent enough to be securely lodged in my mind. The Auditor in office in 1929–30, when I entered the Society, was Robin Dudley Edwards. He was of striking appear

18

-ance (still is, I hope) and enhanced his personality by appearing nowhere, never, winter or summer, without an umbrella, an implement even then completely out of fashion. To Edwards the umbrella as to Coffey the cab. He was a good speaker and a very good Auditor.

A big change began to come about in 1931–2, when Cearbhall Ó Dálaigh was elected. The last time I saw this ex-Auditor, he was seated on the bench of the Supreme Court. Apart from his College activities, he was in those days writing articles in all manner of outside publications, all contentious and reeking with politics – a sort of primitive Myles na Gopaleen. The country was on the brink of the Fianna Fáil age and Ó Dálaigh was backing that movement so strongly, in speeches and in print, that the election involved political alignments. He had a successful reign in the Society. I note from the printed programme of his year that of the eighteen debates – I exclude six impromptu debates – eight were on political themes.

The next Auditor was the editor of this book.[1] He was elected the hard way. The cost of membership of the Society was one shilling, but I can think of no power or privilege membership conferred other than the right to vote at the auditorial election. When the 1932–3 votes were counted, it was found that the new Auditor was Richard P. Dunne, a law student.

R. P. Dunne was a strange and interesting character, and an able speaker. Having made up his mind to be Auditor, he had himself elected treasurer of the Society in John Kent's year and gradually made members of many people he regarded as his friends, even if they had never attended a meeting of the Society in their lives. The result of the election flabbergasted many people. An Electoral Commission was set up and a committee of these appointed to make recommendations. One recommendation they made was that membership should not carry the vote until the member's second year, but the main thing is that the Commission upset the election of Dunne. On the re-election Meenan was declared Auditor.

The session 1932–3 was of some importance, for it was then I decided it was time for myself to become Auditor. My opponent

[1] James Meenan.

19

was Vivion de Valera. The Fianna Fáil Party was by then firmly established, heaven on earth was at hand, and de Valera gained by this situation. I believed and said publicly that these politicians were unsuitable; so I lost the election.

As an Auditor, I would give de Valera, as in marking speeches, eight out of ten. The affairs of the L. & H. were cluttered with too many politicisms, objectionable not because politics should have no place in student deliberations, but simply because they bored. Perhaps I am biassed, for it was to be my later destiny to sit for many hours every day in Dáil Éireann, though not as an elected statesman, and the agonies entailed are still too fresh in my memory to be recalled without emotion.

The next Auditor was Richard N. Cooke who had in a previous year been auditor of the Commerce Society. Cooke was a good and forceful head man, lively and persuasive as a speaker. A superb domed cranium lent a sort of emphasis to his most trivial arguments. It was about this time, I think, that the Society's membership was rising rapidly, due to the missionary work of interested persons who saw themselves as contenders for the auditorship in the future.

In 1935–6 Desmond Bell was elected, and the year may be said to mark the end of my own association with the College and the Society. In my irregular attendances at meetings, where into my speeches there was now creeping a paternal intonation, I found Bell an active and able Auditor though as a speaker, he was inclined to indulge in 'oratory'.

I am afraid this brief sketch gives little hint of the magic those years held, at least for me. Like any organisation of any size, there must be many officers who work hard and quietly in its many departments, and for little recognition or thanks. A lot of responsibility lay on the committees elected every year. The only programme of debates I have is for 1931–2, *consule* Ó Dálaigh, and shows included on the committee T. Lynch, BA (now County Solicitor for Clare), Donnchadh L. Ó Donnchadha (now a District Justice), Joe Kenny (now County Registrar for Waterford), and Una O'Dwyer, one of the few ladies who distinguished themselves in the Society. But I make no attempt to enumerate all the names that deserve honour for all the work they did in maintaining and fortifying the venerable Literary and Historical

Society. As many of them were destined to do in the bigger world later, they influenced the life of the whole College in their day. Modestly they may say with Virgil: *Quae regio in Terrace nostri non plena laboris*!

By 1931 O'Nolan was writing under a number of pseudonyms for the student magazine, *Comhthrom Féinne* (Fair play). Among his first contributions was another, somewhat different, account of the L. & H.:

The 'L. & H.' from the earliest times

BY 'BROTHER BARNABAS'

At the risk of saying something very commonplace, we must begin by stating that the Literary and Historical Society is an institution of unparalleled antiquity. The fact has been suitably stressed by succeeding auditors, year after year, by way of warning to the Janitor-Philistines, but that does not deter me from reiterating it here in the select seclusion of these columns. The 'L. and H.' is an institution unconscionably ancient, and every loyal child thereof should be sufficiently versed in its tenets and history to defend it alike from the broadside vocalism of the obstructionist, and the more insidious attacks of the non-believer from without the fold.

Accordingly, the excerpts printed below should be committed to memory, care being taken when reciting them, to pronounce all proper names with the slight sing-song intonation current in the latter part of the Stone Age. These excerpts are compiled from the original Minutes, which stretch back far beyond the Palaeolithic Age. All the spellings have been modernised, and the text has been extensively revised with a view to the Amendment (Censorship of Publications) Act.

Date . . .[1]

Curious semi-legible references to 'members' tails'. Chairman 'takes the bough'. Debate illegible. Auditor unknown.

Date . . .

Auditor reads several stones on the interesting subject, 'Is Civilisation a Failure?' Subsequent motion to build a home for decayed ex-auditors with the manuscript is rejected on humanitarian grounds.

Date . . .

Member ejected for cracking a joke 'in the worst possible taste' during private business.[2] Insistent non-member, Mr Yhaclum, has his tail pulled and is ejected. Egg of dinosaur thrown by disapproving bystander. Debate and further proceedings illegible.

Date . . .

New Auditor, Mr Tnek. Is suspected of having glass eyes, as he continues to fix one part of the house with a gaze of unnatural dog-like devotion, or alternatively, a glare of fanatical fish-like hatred. He takes things quietly.[3] Delivers Inaugural Address with tail exposed and wagging nervously.[4] Makes an unexpected witty retort towards the end of his auditorship, and is burnt on a pyre of crude paraffin wax.

The Minutes for several centuries subsequently have been irreparably damaged by Phœnician settlers, who have used the stones for the sharpening of bronze weapons. One curious word – 'Neoinín-clog'* – is still plainly legible on many slabs. It is

---

[1] Parts of the Minutes here are illegible, owing to the vandalism of Erse writers several centuries later, who covered the granite Minute-stones with crude 'Ogham' notchings.

[2] Curiously enough, this joke will appear singularly innocuous to the modern mind; it runs: Why is a bud like a sud? Because one raps the batto and the other baps the ratto!

[3] This is ambiguous, perhaps deliberately so.

[4] This is obviously the origin of the present beautiful custom of delivering the Inaugural Address in 'tails', a custom which has been revered and respected by the gentleman Auditor throughout the ages.

* Trans. Daisy-Bell [ed.].

probably the Erse title of a pagan love saga, a double-cycle of which is known to have existed.

The next legible set of Minutes, in a much better condition, are scratched on stout elephant-hide.

Date AD 198

Auditor, Mr F. McCool, B.Agr.Sc. Mr McCool, speaking first in Irish and continuing in English, said he wished to draw the attention of members to a reference in the Minutes of previous – very previous – meetings, to 'members' tails'. Speaking for himself, he did not like it. These Minutes, unless they were altered or destroyed, would remain to embarrass and humiliate the members of the future, the members of generations still unborn; more especially those who aspired to match supremacy of intellect with dignity of carriage. He therefore proposed that all incriminating Minutes be dumped in the sea at Dollymont (now Dollymount), where a mammoth skating rink could be constructed. Speaking, then, in his official capacity, he had no hesitation in accepting the motion.[5]

Mr Yaf, B.Naut.Sc., who was suspected to be a Viking, and spoke with a curious foreign accent, said he was interested in international peace, and he wished to object. To place *all* the incriminating Minutes in the sea would lead to a phenomenal increase in coastal erosion all over the world. To the best of his recollection, he had never met the word 'skating' or 'rink' in any of the many books he had read, and he was therefore reluctantly compelled to condemn the thing or the practice, or whatever it was. He courteously thanked the house.

Mr Oisin, D.Litt.Celt., speaking in metres too intricate to be recorded, said that he also wished to object, but on grounds much more pertinent than those of Mr Yaf. He himself was of a studious disposition, having never laughed in his life, and after studying his family tree for nine years he had come to the conclusion that no ancestor of his ever had a tail – never had and never would have! (Cheers.) The Auditor's reasons for des-

---

[5] This extraordinary breach of procedure demonstrates the antiquity of the vice of flouting the constitution and all rules of debate, so frequently the last refuge of the half-wit Auditor throughout the ages.

troying the Minutes were obvious. *His* reasons for retaining them were more obvious. He now proposed that a Select Committee of Enquiry be set up, which was to subject the antecedents of every member to the most rigorous scrutiny; that those whose ancestors were found to have had tails be compelled to carry something to represent the fact, preferably a black tail-like rain-shade.

The motion was adopted.

The next most important name of those among the ex-Auditors, who also won fame in other spheres, is that of Mr D. D. McMurrough,[*] BA (Legal and Polit. Sc.). The Minutes are rather brief.

Signature of Mr Adam, B.A.O., the Auditor who introduced women to the Society.

'Riotous scenes marked an interesting debate on the subject: "The more we are together, the happier we will be," Henry VIII. Deo Grat. Rex. a chieftain from a neighbouring island, in the chair. The Chairman, in a neat summing up, said he was sure that Ireland had turned the corner and entered a period of great progress and prosperity, now that the dark and evil days of insular seclusion were a thing of the past. Ireland could now take her place among the nations of the world. (Cheers.) He congratulated the Society on their very able Auditor, whom he had met at an Inter-debate in France.'

Several sets of Minutes, covering the gap between the foregoing and the next available notes, which are inscribed on fossilised goat skin, are in the course of being deciphered.

---

[*] Dermot McMurrough: King of Leinster, 12th century [ed.].

Date . . .
Auditor: Mr G. R. Fawkes, B.Sc. Mr Fawkes, in thanking the members for electing him, said he would endeavour to make the Society go with a bang. He had pleasure in nominating his friend, Mr Tresham, to take his place during his temporary absence in London. He was going to attend an Inter-debate at Westminster, the mother of Parliaments, *muryaa*, and they could bet he would be at the bottom of a very far-reaching motion there. He would ask the gentlemen at the door to stop letting off squibs; his nerves were bad enough, God knows.

Strangely enough, there is no trace of an Inaugural Address by Mr Fawkes.

'Brother Barnabas' was the first of O'Nolan's invented *personae*, and his activities were chronicled many times in subsequent issues:

Graduate cut to ribbons by express-train

BRILLIANT NEW INSURANCE
SCHEME
FREE GIFTS FOR READERS

Another milestone (writes Brother Barnabas, our Special Commissioner) has been reached in the romance of *Comhthrom Féinne*, Ireland's National University Magazine. Our Gigantic Free Insurance Scheme, quietly inaugurated over the weekend, has been an instantaneous and nationwide success, and shows every promise of going from strength to strength. Letters of congratulation have poured in from all parts, whilst suggestions (all of which shall receive our sympathetic consideration) as to extending the scheme to cover all the exigencies of University life have been received by the score. Once again we emphasise that there is nothing to pay; there are no wearisome rules; no tedious conditions. You simply fill in the coupon, tear it into two sections,

post one to us and hand the other to your pet Seller; that is all.[1]
Register now and enjoy real peace of mind.

The first reader to benefit under this novel scheme was Mr Bewley Box, a well-known graduate in the faculty of Science. It appears that Mr Box, being a penniless Communist, had set out on the day of May the first last to walk home from Dublin to Cork along the railway line and thus show his contempt for a capitalist company by refusing to use its system of transport. He walked all day and well into the following night. At approximately 5.49 a.m. on the morning of May the second, when some two hundred yards from Limerick Junction Station, apparently after he had been accepted by the North Signal Cabin, he was struck between the fifth and sixth vertebrae of the spinal column by a GSR train bearing several tons of the *Irish Independent* and the *Irish Times*, (dep. Kingsbridge 3.55 a.m.). Mr Box, realising with admirable presence of mind that a mile-long cattle-train was due in two hours, endeavoured to drag himself from the metals with the aid of his one remaining limb: but before he had time to put his ingenious plan into operation, he was struck by the *Irish Press* train (dep. Kingsbridge 4.0 a.m.) which came thundering through the night just then, and Mr Box was literally reduced to match-wood. The deceased was calm and collected to the last, the collection occupying four trained paper-spikes from Stephen's Green, who were rushed to the spot, some twelve hours. Funeral Private.

Interview with next-of-kin

Our representative, Brother Barnabas, was very courteously received by the grief-stricken mother in a decent and neat little parlour at 13A Cuff Alley, Cork.

'We suppose,' said our representative, speaking from force of habit, in the plural, 'that you are very disturbed over this terrible holocaust?'

'Well, yes,' said Mrs Box, smiling through her tears, 'more or less. The money will come in very useful. £10,000 is a lot, and I'll

---

[1] It is also necessary to pay the Proprietors of *Comhthrom Féinne* a lump sum. Details on receipt of PO for 2/6.

be able to give Peggy and Tommie a good schooling. I can buy the wee house I've been dreaming about for so long, and I can keep what's left as a nest-egg. And I can put up a decent marble gravestone to himself, who collected the last souvenir of the last Cork tram. Well, well. It's a hard life!'

'Ah-ha!' said our representative, 'So your husband's dead, too. Well, Mrs Box, you must be lonely and heart-broken, and if you should ever think of sharing the toils and the troubles of your good life with some one else, I . . .' (*Here the interview lapses into the purely personal and ceases to interest our general readers.*)

The Management of *Comhthrom Féinne* will pay over to Mrs Box the sum of £10,000, after certain legal formalities, etc., have been completed.

Other claims

£100 – Mr X, undergraduate, strained neck and impaired nerves, and general symptoms of 'Backstairs Anaemia.' (Major Subject – 'Irish.').

£10–200 claims of strained aural nerves due to listening for overdue bell.

THIS WEEK'S PRIZE OF FIVE SHILLINGS
(For the Most Interesting Claim)
AWARDED TO MR Z. (Ballyjamesduff)
**(Two feet severed at ankles – Mowing machine
mishap at harvesting)**

£50 – Two claims. Rush for morning papers in Gentlemen's Smokeroom.

£50–150 Claims. Sore shoulder. From putting shoulder to wheel before Examinations.

Arrangements are being made to extend our Free Insurance Policy to cover Failures of students in Gambling, Horse-betting, Failures at all Examinations, Tests, Studentships, etc. Fill up your coupon now. (You will find it on page five of cover.)

27

Free gifts for readers

To mark the inauguration of this Giant Free Insurance Scheme, unparalleled in the history of Irish National journalism, Brother Barnabas has decided to present readers with free balloons, embellished with appropriate quotations from Chaucer and Eoghan Ruadh O Suileabháin to readers of *Comhthrom Féinne*. In order to qualify for this unique and interesting gift (which, by the way, considering the vast number of theories and principles relative to Physics which it exemplifies, should be of special interest to students of the Science faculty), readers, when met by Brother Barnabas, must be carrying a copy of *Comhthrom Féinne*, conspicuously carried folded twice under the arm, a birth-certificate, copies of references from head of school or college or institution attended, a roll of Gaeltacht hand-woven tweed, a copy of *Ulysses* by James Joyce or Lord Tennyson, a complete set of snooker-balls, a BA Hons. degree parchment, a tastefully arranged basket of home-grown tariff-free cut-flowers, a copy of an Oath of Allegiance to Brother Barnabas, four penny buns from the College restaurant, ten Irish-made coal-hammers, a copy of Morphi's *Games of Chess*, a set of new Dublin-made brow-knitters, a red flag, and a small green-coloured urn containing the ashes of the last issue of the *National Student*.

(SPECIAL NOTE TO THE WEAK-CHESTED. – For the convenience of those who are debarred from weight-lifting by doctor's orders, the proprietors of *Comhthrom Féinne* have made elaborate arrangements for the supply of Irish-made barrows, to be hired at a nominal rate. A special army of clerks have been engaged for some weeks past in minutely studying the College Rules, and they have failed to find the slightest trace of any ordinance forbidding barrow-wheeling in the Main Hall. The less developed of our readers, therefore, may join in the fun with the rest. Good luck!)

Poet Lionel Prune is not eligible to compete.

Lionel Prune appeared on several occasions. His similarity to W. B. Yeats, then the grand old man of Irish poetry, is scarcely accidental:

28

Mr Lionel Prune comes to UCD

INTERVIEW WITH OUR
SPECIAL REPRESENTATIVE

As I passed through the Main Hall last week I saw, reclining languidly against the Commerce Society's Notice Board, a stranger of eminent aspect. Taking out my copy of *Dialann an Mhic Leighinn*[1] I quickly noted down details of his appearance in Ogham Shorthand around the margins of pages 77 and 78. He was tall and willowy, and groaned beneath a heavy burthen of jet-black hair long untouched by tonsorial shears. His eyes were vacuous but yearning and looked out on the world through a pair of plane lenses. These latter were held erect on his nose by the device known as *pince-nez* and from the edge of one of them a thick black ribbon descended flowingly to his right-hand lapel buttonhole. A slight trace of black moustache drooped cloyingly from his protruding upper lip. His neck was embellished by a flame-red tie. He wore a great nigger-brown overcoat which stretched well below his knees. His right hand toyed with a walking stick and his left with a bulky dispatch case.

After this brief survey I recognised him in a flash. It was Lionel Prune the distinguished modern poet of the younger school! Remembering the great paper I represented I took my courage in both pockets and approached him diffidently.

'Yes' he murmured, in reply to my nervous questioning, 'I am Lionel Prune. I have attended the lecture halls, corridors and library of UCD incognito for some weeks past with the aim of getting a carefree and insouciant atmosphere into my work. I shall probably do a BA degree in Summer.'

'Splendid!' (said I becoming more bold). 'And what are your impressions of College?'

'I have scribbled one or two little things' he replied, catching hold of my third waist-coat button and shooting up his coat sleeve he read the following from his cuff:

[1] Student's Diary.

29

O TEMPORA!
College in a hustle
'Neath the April sun,
Ryan's-bell rings for lecture,
And the Co-eds run.
Chatter on the steps,
From which the breezes are waftin'
Aroma of strong thundercloud,
And mild Sweet Afton.

Then a lull of quiet,
And a cloud across the sun,
Fags and brown pipes vanish,
There's an armistice of the tongue,
As through the College gateway
A black cab passes
Twixt snap-dragons and shrubberies
And 'Pleasekeepoffthegrass's.'

'Note the staccato rhythm (he went on) the air of fervid nothingness followed by the dramatic *dénouement*. Compare it with the smooth flowing rhythm of this little cameo which flowed from my platignum yesterday:

APPROPINQUAT
Up to the College
The Flood advances,
Softly and swishingly.
Up he prances,
His locks
Are combed
With excessive care
To hide a spot
That
          is bare
      of hair.

How simple, but how impressive! In a perfect picture without a word wasted it exposes the hollowness of modern thought!'

'Ye-es' I said doubtfully, 'but what do you think of modern tendencies in Art?'

He pulled out his Ingersoll. Fresh-scrawled across the face were the following delicate lines –

30

Back in the grey beginning,
True Beauty married Art,
But Mister Charles Donnelly said
'I'll soon this couple part.
And the reason I am anxious
This union old to end,
Is that Art may marry Anarchy
The Poet's Friend.'

'Very sleek I call that (went on Mr Lionel Prune caressingly) but this is also apropos.' And he read from the back of his watch.

AT THE DOG SHOW
Behind the doors of your prison cage,
Thou lookest on man with baleful eyes.
Bark gently! Hide thy Kerry rage,
Or else thou wilt not win a prize.

Dost thou feel blue in there confined
With bars more strong than Hadrian's Wall.
Oh! triumph of matter over mind!
But thou'lt be free though the heavens fall.

'Of course, of course,' I said soothingly, 'Art has been caged cramped and must be free.'

'Let's go and have a cup of coffee (said Mr Lionel Prune). But stay I haven't a coin to spare . . . You'll pay? Good.' And he began to carol blithely and nonchalantly.

'Where's the booze? Where's the booze?
Oh! my bold billiard man,
With your long barrelled cue and your chalk.'

'But the ladies (he interjected suddenly). Ah the ladies of your College! How they twist and tug at a poet's very heart-strings. They are wonderful. Yes I have written of them. Listen!' (He read from a tram ticket.)

IN THE LIBRARY
'Creak! Creak! Creak! on your boxwood chairs! I see
You lady students though you don't give a hoot for me.
All well for John at his counter,
For him you all have your say.

31

Oh well for Mr O'N—ll
For when he speaks
You're quick to obey.

'I lost my heart to one of them (went on Mr Prune confidently), but (he added firmly) she must never know. I don't know how it happened, but I think it was her pipe. Listen to this:

HER DEAR DADAN DUDEEN
'Did you ever hear tell of Coy Corkey,
She lives between Dublin and Dalkey,
From the fumes of her pipe,
If you're wise you'll escape,
For fatal's the pipe of sweet Corkey.'

'In the next thirty-nine verses I go on to – but no, I must not speak of her to such as you.'

He looked at me pityingly and there was a long pause towards the end of which Mr Prune wrote feverishly with a half an inch of pencil on the back of a plate.

'There,' he said at last, and I read:

THE COLLEGE RESTAURANT
Abandon Hope? Who says abandon hope.
Nil to spare
And um.
I will enter here.
'A small coffee please!' The hours roll by
The world is young but I am dry
And as I sit and wait and wait
My feelings I am loath to spake.'

'What about the Literary and Historical Society,' I ventured when our coffee came at last.

'I have here,' he said modestly, fumbling in his dispatch case, 'what is probably the greatest thing I have accomplished.' And he read for me:

Oh! Literary and Historical Society,
(Wangli Wanglos Wanglorum)
Who will your auditor be
I ask with curious propriety.
(Wangli Wanglos Wanglorum).

32

Who – will – he – be?
  Sh-h-h-h-h!
Are you Meenan to say Dunne,
(Wangli Wanglos Wanglorum).
Will lynch the candid Hanly,
Come! Come! It's not Done
(Tangli Tanglos Tanglorum).
Will – you – be – down – troddyn.
  Sh-h-h-h!

I was amazed at the keen insight into our mere College affairs which the great man showed. But I noticed a subtle change come over him after drinking his coffee. The buoyancy vanished from his manner. He seemed to become a little irritable. Still he read me from the back of an envelope this ode after the manner of *Piers Plowman*.

VAE VICTIS!
Oh! College Rugby Club! Oh! College Rugby Club!
You warded off Wanderers wonderfully.
You manxed up Monkstown manfully,
With luck against you, you broke Blackrock.
But I cannot get in right perspective
The fact that you were bet by Bective.

'But,' said I, always a purist in literature, 'surely "bet" is not what the best people would say.'

Mr Prune gurgled ominously. A beet-red flush suffused his face in waves of rapidly-increasing intensity. Terrible wrath peeped through his eyes.

'How dare you, sir,' he exploded, and lifting his dispatch-case and walking-stick, he stalked splutteringly away.

Brother Barnabas did not take kindly to the poet.

'Lionel Prune must go' says Brother Barnabas

'A JOURNEYMAN DILETTANTE'
SCATHING ATTACK

In the ordinary course of events (writes Brother Barnabas), an outrage on good-taste on the part of the editorial staff of *Comhthrom Féinne* might be condoned on the extenuating grounds of youth and inexperience, and the present writer would not be the last to turn the blind eye, and to afford the youthful sinners the charity of silence. When, however, he finds that this outrage has been printed on the back of a page bearing a composition of his own, and realising that that composition of his own is separated from this Literary abortion by approximately one thousandth part of an inch, then duty to self and country must brush aside all trivial considerations of etiquette.

Mr Lionel Prune, it would appear, is a poet. He is not. He is a superannuated plum. He is the shrivelled wreckage of a fruit, which though never other than sour and ill to look upon, is now bereft of the paltry juice which once gave it the claim to regard itself as young and green, and full of promise. True to his name, he is a large futile stone wrapped in coarse brown paper; and at best, he is endless wrappings without the stone. He is a journeyman-dilettante, an upstart, a parvenu, who must be persuaded, if civilisation is to be saved, to exploit to the full that one talent which he indubitably has, and steadily refuses to exercise or cultivate – the talent for being a silent corpse in a coffin. Lionel Prune is a bowsy, inspired with the natural badness and mischief of a jungle-born ape without the ape's brains. Lionel Prune is a menace and an eye-sore, a thorn in the side of educated humanity, an obsession to his dog, and a hundred crosses on the shoulders of his hundred friends. Lionel Prune must go! We have spoken: Lionel Prune must GO!!

It is with extreme difficulty that we restrain ourselves from bursting into a rash of italics; and lest we should lose control in one direction or another, we will leave Prune and his prunish follies, and indicate to the reader in a broad way the general tendency of real poetry.

Below we reproduce what we are told is one of our noblest efforts. We frankly confess that we made many attempts to conceal the manuscript in our attic, with some idea of post-humous glory – 'genuine example of the Master's early work,' etc. But when we had fears that we might cease to be, and that some scribbler of the Prune order, taking advantage of the silence of the grave, should find it and publish it as his own unaided work, we were persuaded by our many friends to give it to the waiting public. We make a sneering apology to the shade of Thomas Hood, who could only manage one joke per verse, and perverse jokes they were.

ON FIRST LOOKING INTO CHAPMAN'S
SUNDAY INDEPENDENT

(Note: Chapman is a fellow-traveller on our morning train; and the extract which caught our eye and inspired us to pen the poem was as follows:

'UNIVERSITY COLLEGE NOTES

. . .. At the same meeting (of the Commerce Society) ballot papers will be issued for the election of the new Auditor, the choice being between Messrs P. J. Hogan and Laurence O'Brien.

CURIO'

AN CURFA

His name was Laurence T. O'Brien.
(Like a priest), without 'Esquire,'
His lot was hard, his lard was hot,
    For his fat was in the fire.
For a trifle small he once did fall,
    When a waiter, suave and smart
    But God help those who help themselves,
    They get their just desserts.
            Curfá . . .

'I must' he said, 'now beg my bread,
    And be quite blue, I ween;
And starve as long as Harold's Cross,
    And goodly Stephen's Green.'
            Curfá . . .

35

And for yard and rood and mile he trod
　　On aches that were feet;
He lived on hope and humble pie,
　　And drank his water neat.
　　　　　Curfá . . .

And up and down he searched the town,
　　(And so shall many of us),
Inquiring for a post, and found
　　One in a small post-office.
　　　　　Curfá . . .

Alas too well in love he fell,
　　A lass, he loved her true.
(But naught of women did he know,
　　Though Late-fee mails he knew).
　　　　　Curfá . . .

He tried in vain, this blushful swain,
　　To give his passion say;
Instead of kisses from his love,
　　He got the sack each day.
　　　　　Curfá . . .

He heard all time the nuptial chimes,
　　He heard them like a knell –
No wedding bells would ring for him
　　Till he would ring the belle.

　　　　　　AN CEANGAL
　　But he saw
His name in the paper (VOTE FOR ME!)
　　Curiously enough.
Came to College.
Went for the job,
　　Curiously enough
Got it.
Auditor-cum-Treasurer.
　　Curiously enough,
　　　And was fixed
　　　　FOR LIFE!
No money-worries not to bite 'im
Travel and teas ad infinitum,
　　Married the gal
　　Name was Sal,
　　　Each suited
　　　Each to a
　　　　t

36

He lived happily ever after and the Commerce Society was freed from its anguish. Gurab é sin eachtra Lorcain Ui Briain go nuige seo.[1]

In all due modesty, we consider this long poem a memorable achievement, whose Gargantuan eminence, however, cannot diminish or obscure the power and brilliance of some of our shorter, more delicate and more chaste specimens. Take, for instance, the mighty fragment 'The Cobbler's Son', written when we were twins, or, rather, when we were very, very young.

THE COBBLER'S SON
'The Cobbler's Son
Was a bookish fool
foul
full
of trix.
He went to church
And stole
a stole
Twere better had he plied
Atome
Atome, or like his pa
Soled soles
And not
Sold his soul
For a stole.'

Note the exquisite dominance of the 'o', the breath-taking transition from 'fool to full' by the celebrated U-STEP METHOD, the internal sense-metamorphosis, without in any way impairing the phonological beauty of the word. This is a poem that must be pondered upon. We earnestly recommend Prune to put it in his pipe and smoke it.

In January 1933 O'Nolan was editor of *Comhthrom Féinne.* His parody editorial is a masterpiece of that pompous genre:

---

[1] That was the story of Lawrence O'Brien so far.

37

Kameradschaft

To say we are producing a magazine which is worthy of University College, Dublin is no lie. It is not to be thought from this statement however that the Magazine is a virile one viewed from the aspect of literary value or student taste. On the very contrary, it is, to our mind, a very feeble paper lacking in originality of idea or expression, essentially scrappy and inartistic – a paper of shallow thought and meagre outlook.

Many will object to this blunt rendering of facts, but keeping in mind the Irish proverb 'bíonn an Fírinne searbh'[1] we shall proceed to discuss some aspects of social life in this College revealed to us in the experience of student office, and on which basis we propose to justify our original proposition.

There is no spirit of co-operation here. Jealousy seems to be the order of the day. Here a miniature Napoleon, there an Embryo Mussolini – they stalk the corridors in glorious isolation smugly satisfied with the knowledge of their own 'self-sufficiency' – and vaunted indispensability: an indispensability, which if true, they ignore, and boycott their University to pamper selfish vanity.

A race of wasps contribute nothing positive to University

[1] Trans.: 'Truth is bitter.'

activity. Indeed very often they breed an atmosphere of distrust and suspicion which coupled with the flood of bad-tempered and venomous criticism that ever heralds the vain-glorious does untold damage to the spirit of good-will so helpful in construction. They can never see the good points but always the bad. Their minds and hearts are poisoned, and whatever finer qualities they may have had so vitiated as to be destroyed. People of this kind should be made to change their attitude if not their mind.

There is a danger that contributors to this Magazine may regard this expression of opinion as an attack upon them in their literary capacity. This is not so. Many articles printed herein are very well worth reading. But we are dealing more with the system on which this paper is run, and the atmosphere which supports it.

In the first place it seems quite impossible to arouse any interest among the general body of students. They are quite deaf to the 'Call of College' – it means nothing to them. And then there is that small poisonous destructive section of College Society which claims to be able to write, but refuses to do so. They will not write; they do not like the Editor.

We have no desire to impede progress. In deference therefore to the demands (negatively expressed if you will) that we should resign, our answer is quite simple and it is to be hoped satisfactory: we will resign.

In doing this it is not our desire or purpose to promote any hostile rivalry. People should cultivate a spirit of friendship and good-fellowship, and after the manner of the German miners in the picture *Kameradschaft* sink their personal differences and petty spleens for the good of society. Our immediate society is University College, Dublin. Let us think of it as something more than a place in which one gets degrees. Make it a real and living society in which every student by exerting himself in the common cause may introduce his quota of individuality and variety, so that there may be that pleasing conflict of intellect which is the true key-note of a University – a conflict inspired by devotion, and effecting true comradeship.

Samuel Hall, a man of many talents, tried his hand at a short play. The result was the first of O'Nolan's many attacks on John Millington Synge

39

and on his literary heirs who dominated Dublin's Abbey Theatre during the first third of the century.

The bog of Allen

With almost hysterical pleasure we give below the first literary work of genius to come from the pen of Mr Samuel Hall, BA, QED, written at the request of a deputation from the Dramatic Society, Ballybrack, and now exhibited in advance to readers of *Comhthrom Féinne* for their diversion, edification and moral exaltation.

When requested to undertake the work, Mr Hall immediately agreed, and, letting his mind fester for the short space of five minutes, wrote the play in ten minutes, and then absent--mindedly continued writing, using both hands and two pens. At the end of half-an-hour he had written, in addition to the play, five novels, a book of sermons on Temperance, an almanac and a pamphlet on Anti-vivisection. However, we are concerned here only with the play. It is a wholesome Irish play, racy of the soil and Samuel Hall, written in the real traditional style, and a masterpiece of characterisation and pregnant dialogue. Mr Hall apologised for his inability to introduce Blind Phelim fiddling at the cross-roads, and although this is a serious flaw – dammit all, what about it anyway! Mr Bernard Shaw, on being shown the play, made his usual witty remark, 'It bears the Hallmark of genius.' He cryptically added, 'The grave – it is waiting for me. I am old.' He evidently recognised that a new star had risen in the firmament, greater than his own. The play, Mr Hall tells me, is copyright in Yugo Slavia only.

All the rights are reserved, and are securely locked up in a drawer in Mr Hall's desk.

Dramatic personification

Allen Bogg	A farmer
His Wife	A woman
A Bog-trotter	A man

Time: Tail-end of the Summer. It is about 7.30 p.m.

40

Scene: The Kitchen in Allen Bogg's hovel in the middle of the Bog of Allen, miles from dry land. The house was built by Gregory B. Bogg, Allen's grandfather. As he could not find sand to build it on, he built it on the Bog. It is a typically Irish household. The floor is flagged with green moss between the cracks. A roaring fire of the best Wigan coal is burning in the hearth. In a corner is a bed with a white sow in it. All the bed-clothes, including the blankets, are made of Irish poplin. A bag-pipes are hanging on the wall, but not, unfortunately, so high up that a tall man could not reach them. Over the mantelpiece is a rusty iron pike for use in Insurrections. A rustic and homely smell of fish-and-chips permeates the atmosphere. Over in a corner a cupboard is let into the wall, with a heavy padlock and chain, in which leprechauns are stored. Below on the floor is a primitive rack, made of bog-oak, for torturing leprechauns who will not divulge where the Crock of Gold is hidden. Crickets can be distinctly seen by members of the audience in the stalls, their mouths open, singing with the characteristic Nyaa. Maggie, Bogg's wife, is sitting spinning. She is dressed completely in green, as the Wearin' o' the Green is a strict rule in the house. There is a view over the half-door of the Bog, stretching in a brown monotone to the horizon and back again. This view is immediately obstructed by a cow which puts its head in over the half-door.

Maggie (to cow): Whisht! Whisht! (Cow goes away. Enter Allen with his plough on his shoulder.)

Allen: 'Tis a hard life now, surely. What does be for the dinner?

Maggie: Bacon an' Cabbage an' Stirabout.

Allen (bitterly): For sivin year we've had nothin' else. Why can't you call the dam dish Stirabout an' Cabbage an' Bacon for a change?

Maggie: Shure, wisha, musha, anish now, for goodness sake, what would you be wantin'? For goodness sake!

Allen: Ochone, it will be little I'll be wantin' soon but a coffin of the good bog-oak. (Pacing round in his agitation.) This bog is getting into my blood, blast it! (Meditatively.) 'Tis a hard life, surely. As soon as you plough a furrow it fills with water, an' you have to go bailin' it out, an' as soon as you bail out the water, the sides of the furrow fall back agin, an' be the time

41

that's done your plough is half disappeared into the bog, an' be the time you've dug your plough out, you're up to your knees in the bog yourself.

Maggie: 'Tis time now, you stopped talking, now, for goodness forsake!

Allen: I'd love a bit of turnip now, I was rerred on turnips.

Maggie: 'Twas a poor rerrin'.

Allen: I daresay. (House sinks into bog an inch. Cow appears at half-door.)

Maggie: Whisht! What does that yolk be lookin' in on the door for, Allen?

Allen: The phleas do be at him, bajer.

Maggie: The *ph*-leas? For goodness sake!

Allen: Alright, alright. The fleas then. (The house sinks two inches into bog. Cow is pushed away from door by Bog-trotter, who leans over half-door, smoking clay pipe.)

Bog-tr.: Dia's Muire dhuit.[1]

  Allen: Dia's Muire dhuit, is Padraig.[2]

  Bog-tr.: Hullo.

Allen: Good morrah. (Bog-trotter is pushed away from door, by cow. His trotting can be heard dying away in the distance.)

Maggie: He speaks the bog-Irish well, him.

Allen: Aye. (Suddenly, by a mutual instinct, both rise. Allen lights his pipe. Both tip-toe over to half-door. Slowly the rich purple of the Celtic Twilight falls over the Bog. The house sinks a quarter of an inch.)

Allen: It's worth it, livin' an' slavin' here, just to see that.

Maggie (in hushed voice): The Celtic Twilight, Allen!

Allen (entranced): Aye. It's grand.

Maggie (becoming practical for a moment): Arrah, wisha now, for goodness sake!

Allen (meditatively): Aye. (long pause.) Surely.

Maggie: Musha.

Allen: Surely.

Maggie: Wisha.

Allen: Begorrah.

---

[1] God and Mary to you.
[2] God and Mary to you, and Patrick.

Maggie (her soul flooded with poetry): Anish, now, musha.
Allen: Surely. (long pause.) Aye . . . Musha.
Maggie: Begorrah.
Allen: Surely. Aye, indeed, Musha.
Maggie: Ochone!
Allen: Begorrah!
Maggie: Bedadda!
Allen: Deriva!
Maggie: Surely. Wisha. Whisht!! (Suddenly six cows put their heads over the half-door. House sinks six feet into Bog.)
Maggie (angrily): FOR GOODNESS SAKE!!

CURTAIN (of Irish Poplin)

Once invented, Samuel Hall was not allowed to die. Another of his exploits was to found an alternative to UCD:

Academic enterprize at Ballybrack

FOUNDATION OF UCB
STARTLING DISCLOSURES
SAMUEL HALL AGAIN!

(By our very special correspondent)

For a long time the acute problem, only second in importance to the Housing Problem, of how to insure the future welfare of undergraduates who through:

(*a*) Village-Idiocy
(*b*) Water-logged Brain-matter
(*c*) Chronic laziness and
(*d*) Fondness for the Cups

are unable and constitutionally unfit to obtain their degrees has been engaging the minds of all deep-thinking men. It has remained for a very undistinguished graduate of UCD who up to lately was doing his 100 hours in Caffrey's, Mr Samuel Hall, BA,

43

to solve the problem for all time, in one night, and by the use of one unknown quantity only.

On a piece of waste ground in Ballybrack, a new University has been founded. The buildings consist of three rude mahogany huts, which are practically completed. Some time ago, by far the most important part of the College installation was housed in safety, and we are glad to announce that the billiard tables are in perfect order. Mr Hall officially declared the University open by pointing to a gaping hole in the roof. The rest of the ceremony at which all the staff was present, attired in the red flannel gown of the College, was highly successful. Mr Hall in answer to a question put him by a cross-Channel pressman, stated that he had no intention of affiliating UCB with UCD, but that a proposal to affiliate it with the Mental Home, Ballina, was receiving serious consideration.

In this new University, there will be no lectures and the passing of examinations will be a pure formality. Mr Hall, in an interview, said that, henceforth, he could see no reasonable excuse for the existence of undergraduates, who had never been an asset to any part of the community.

Every person born in the Irish Free State is automatically a matriculated student of the College. The first examination for BA will take place soon. The conditions which are firmly laid down by charter and drawn up again by chartered accountants are as follows:

(a) The Examiner's (Mr Hall's) indecision is final.

(b) The entrance fee is at least five guineas. The money is payable to the Examiner, who may, at his discretion, pass it on to charity.

(c) Entrance fees must in all cases by accompanied by the appropriate coupon – a ten shilling note.

(d) The papers set at all examinations will be published a month beforehand in *Comhthrom Féinne* and the South Tipperary *Echo*, in order to give a fair chance to all. The papers for the forthcoming exam. are given below.

Books to read on the course

All the books prescribed are banned in the Irish Free State. Students are advised to spend a fortnight in France reading up

44

the course. We regret to announce that Dr Kahn's Treatise on Advanced Algebra, prescribed for the degree of B.Sc. is also banned, strong exception having being taken to some of the Surds in Part II of the work,

UNIVERSITY COLLEGE, BALLYBRACK

WINTER EXAMINATION FOR B.A.

IRISH.

(A viva voce exam. will be held in Irish and will be as follows)

Candidate enters Exam room.

Mr Hall: Dia's Muire dhuit.

Candidate: Seadh.

Mr Hall: Dún an doras, mashadahully.

Candidate (from behind closed door): Tá sé dúnta.[1]

There will be no examination in Applied Maths, as it has been found that, except in very rare cases, they can never be applied with success. However, if the weather and all the other circumstances necessary conspire to make the conditions favourable, an attempt will be made to Apply Mathematics.

ENGLISH LITERATURE

1. Describe all the methods of cogging[2] you know and their merits. What method are you using at present? What method did Hamlet employ when doing his BA at the University of Wittenberg?

2. Was Hamlet really mad, or was it only Shakespeare?

> LATIN
>
> Translate the following passage from Cicero's de Rerum Natura.
> *Sine qua non ipso facto, ne plus ultra ad astra sine die, Hercule! Adeste vade-mecum: quo sit? C. Valerius, praeter, quid pro quo deus ex machina, Fiat, cum grano salis. Campbellii veniunt. Non, certe, inquit Brian Boru.*
>
> What point does Livy bring out in the above extract? Underline the declined words.

Regulations governing exams

1. There will be no luncheon interval between two papers. Candidates must feed as they write. Each Candidate may

[1] God and Mary to you.
It is.
Shut the door, please.
It is shut.

[2] Cogging: Cheating in examinations.

45

bring into the Exam hall one bowl of porridge and six stouts. Candidates from Cannibal Countries may not bring bodies of missionaries into the Hall.

2. Mr Samuel Hall, BA, the Examiner, will attend every day for six days before the Exams, in Roberts' Cafe, Grafton Street, in order to be bribed and flattered by intending candidates. Bribes may range from ten shillings. Strictly cash payments only. The coarsest flattery will work.

3. Candidates enter at their own risk, and the Examiner takes no responsibility for failures occasioned by his (the Examiner's) bad temper, personal spite, indigestion, depression, nagging wife, ill-nourishment, etc.

4. Results will be published in the *Jockey* and *Racing News*.

Social activities

L. and H.: The Ballybrack University College Literary and Historical Society held a very successful first meeting when the motion that 'Slap-bangs are a Spent Force' was debated. The debate took place in a large circular room, specially constructed for the purpose, devoid of seats, in the middle of which the Auditor sat at a table. The members (all Hard Men of mettle) were clustered in mobs at six different doors around the room. The debate started punctually at 7.30, and a very interesting uproar ensued. Half-way through the proceedings it was noticed that the Auditor's mouth was fringed with froth. Shortly after this the unfortunate man rushed headlong into one of the mobs, biting a Hard Man severely in the ear before being felled to the ground. He was rushed in a gibbering condition to Ballina Mental Home where a representative was informed that there is little danger of his returning to normal. An even more successful debate is expected next week.

The Agricultural Society won their way into the second round of the League last Saturday, when they defeated Swords in a ploughing match at Ballyjamesduff, by the clear margin of a furrow, which was later cleverly converted by College into a potato-ridge. The pitch was in splendid order, and its hilly nature gave great scope for high scoring.

Referee: Paddy Reilly, a returned American.

The Water Harriers (or Boat Club, as we call it) left Dublin yesterday in an exciting race to Tullamore in canal-boats. When last heard of they were in the seventh lock on the far side of Edenderry.

The College *Chess Club* is also in a very flourishing condition. Some six days ago they had their first meeting. The door of their room is still closed, and no one has come out, but foul play is not suspected, as Chess is Chess.

The Cumann Gaedhealach[1] met last Thursday, but decided unanimously after five minutes to adjourn for six months in order to give the Auditor time to learn the rudiments of the language.

There is little hope of any Athletic Club of any description being started, as all the students at the College are pitiable physical wrecks. In this regard a glowing example is being set by the Founder, Mr Hall, who is so flat-chested that his spine can be distinctly seen on the front of his chest. (Further notice of College activities in due course.)

Almost all Irishmen of culture are litigious: Samuel Hall did not rebel against this great tradition:

Sensational libel action!

HALL HITS BACK
SCENES IN COURT

Yesterday, at the Short Circuit Court, Camden St, before a jury, Mr Samuel Hall, the Ballybrack educational pioneer, was awarded £1,000 damages for alleged malicious libel and defamation of character in an article published in the last issue of Comhthrom Féinne. *Notice of appeal was given by A. Kierse, Business Manager,* Comhthrom Féinne.

Great public interest was evinced in the case, the courthouse being packed to its utmost capacity. Students and graduates of

---

[1] Irish Language Society

47

UCD and UCB were present in great numbers, most of whom stood at the door out of force of habit. At 1.30 there was a fanfare of trumpets accompanied by a cadenza on the viola da gamba and Mr Hall entered with a copy of Plato's Republic under his arm attired in his academic gown of hand-stitched burberry inlaid with lilies-of-the-valley in mauve velvet with trimmings of ostrich feathers under the armpits. He was accompanied by a fleet of secretaries with typewriters, Hard Men, Counsel, musicians, standard bearers, billiard-markers, book-markers, snake-charmers, gangsters and his doting grandmother, seated on a wickerwork bier. The rear of the procession, which was very impressive, was brought up by an official from Grogans[1] with a corkscrew, four dozen, and sawdust to sprinkle on the floor.

The presiding Justice, Mr Jessie Fludd, took the Chair amid cheers and was presented with a pair of white spats and the corresponding pawn-ticket. Mr Fludd, in his opening remarks, warned the public seated in the body of the Court against the operations of pickpockets infesting the building. He had come to an understanding with them, but it was his duty to warn the public, nevertheless. He announced that he was refusing all informations, but if anybody had any information for the 2.30 he'd take it.

Mr Dun Chada (Solicitor for defendants): There is a library official present in the Court who always has a good thing.

Mr Fludd: *Sit down!!*

At this point a man got up at the back of the Court and protested strongly that hands were continually in his pockets clinking his money and that he was positive they were not his own hands. His remarks, however, were drowned by Wagner's Lohengrin Overture, played by Mr Hall's musicians.

Mr P. Maguire (counsel for defendants) rose to protest at the irregularities that were occurring. Mr Hall had been engaged in deep conversation with the foreman of the jury for the last five minutes. Dammit it all, it wasn't fair, it wasn't billiards.

Mr Fludd: When I look round me and see my Court turned into a combined pub and concert-hall, anything is admissible. My only regret is that I didn't come here in football shorts and

---

[1] An adjacent public house.

'tails' myself. I must ask you to open your defence immediately.

Mr Maguire (Counsel): I shall ask Mr Hall to step into the box.

Mr Hall, obviously blotto, was assisted into the box by two Hard Men to the strains of Beethoven's Fifth Symphony, and said that he would insist on answering Counsel's questions in Latin. He would give his evidence in chaste classical cataleptic trimeters. It was a matter of academic pride with him. He had no fear of being laughed at for a wrong quantity.

Mr Fludd: I cannot allow it. My own schooling was neglected. Your Latin would be Greek to me, although I have no doubt Counsel would understand you. You may claim extra damages for any hurt sustained by your academic pride.

Mr Maguire: Your name is Samuel Hall?

Mr Hall: My full title is Senor Samuel Sancho Panza de Galli-Curci Hall, BA, RSVP, LMS, KC?

Mr Maguire: When, may I ask, did you become a KC.

Mr Hall: I took silk last year.

Mr Maguire: Did Switzers prosecute?

Mr Hall: Yes, but I got off under the Probation Act.

Mr Maguire: What is your extraction?

Mr Hall: I am a Mahommedan Jew.

At this point in the proceedings a terrific free fight was staged by a strong body of Friends of Soviet Russia, who were also friends of Mr Hall. The crowd swept across the Court in a hail of stout bottles and wickerwork, while bassoons and saxophones shrieked in agony. The jury hastily locked themselves in. When order had been restored the jury emerged and gave their verdict as above, adding a rider, however, that if Mr Hall did not fulfil his promises their verdict was null and void.

Albert Wood, KC. A. Nix (instructed by John Sylvester Broderick) for plaintiff. Patrick Maguire (instructed by P. Caffrey and Mr Dun Chada BA, LLB) for defendants.

Comhthrom Féinne gave O'Nolan his first opportunity to try out some of the many styles and ideas that he later used in *Cruiskeen Lawn*, the column which he was to contribute to the *Irish Times* for almost twenty-five years. In this piece, Myles na Gopaleen's famous 'Buchhandlung' scheme is prefigured:

49

Are you lonely in the restaurant?

Professor Adolf Gleitzboschkinderschule of the Berliner Universität, the eminent psychologist, has repeatedly pointed out in the Paris editions of the *Leipziger Tageblatt* that the habit of eating alone is a pernicious one and one which leads to morbidity and undue contempt for one's own vices. Apparently in deference to the advice of Professor Adolf Gleitzboschkinderschule, students may be seen every day endeavouring to drag each other into the Restaurant in an effort to save each other from the naked infirmities of their own minds, by creating a conversation which, however feeble, would at least obviate introspection.

Comhthrom Féinne, therefore, taking its duty of SERVING its public very much to heart, has much pleasure in announcing a NEW PROFESSION in an effort to cope with the present difficulty. *Comhthrom Féinne* will provide EATERS, varying in quality and price to suit every client. YOU NEED NO LONGER EAT ALONE. Hire one of our skilled Conversationalists, pay and talk as you eat and avoid the farce of pretending that you are a THINKER to whom his own kind is sufficient for the day.

EATERS. CONDITIONS OF HIRE.

(1) Eaters must be presented with a tea or lunch not inferior to that being consumed by the client by more than 1/-.

(2) There will be no charge for the first half-hour of the Eater's professional attendance, but a sum of threepence will be charged for every extra five-minutes. Excess fare will be automatically registered on the clock or meter worn on the EATER'S RIGHT ARM.

(3) Eaters must not be spoken to rudely or slapped, except in CLASS C.

(4) Should a client originate a line of conversation outside the specific Eater's registered orbit, there shall be no onus on the Eater to pursue, attempt to pursue, or try to attempt to pursue such a line.

(5) Should the Client be joined by A FRIEND who takes part in the

50

Conversation, there will be an excess charge of 2d. per five minutes. This will be automatically registered on the meter.

(6) Complaints as to abnormal appetites of Eaters, incivility, objectionable table-manners, etc., should be instantly reported to the Editor of *Comhthrom Féinne*, but not if he is earning a living as AN EATER at an adjacent table. In such case, complaint should be made afterwards.

Classes of Eaters – Class A

We have a very reliable line in young men of 19 and under who will engage first-year students and unmatriculated members of the Civil Service and public on GENERAL TOPICS, such as the weather, What-I-think-of-College-and-how-I'm-going-to-alter-it, the College celebrities at other tables, cricket, football, LUV, what a gift it is to have no exercises to do at night, the arguments as to whether one should do a D.Litt. or a D.Ph., College Hops, etc. We are introducing this line at a reduction of 1d. per five minutes as a SPECIAL ADVERTISING OFFER FOR FOUR DAYS ONLY.

Class B

Are you a strong silent man? We can supply a great hulking lout who will GRUB with you, and munch, and chaw for an inclusive charge of about 2/6 per hour. These fine Eaters have been specially trained and must be provided with great lumps of beef, porter and whole loaves. Knives and forks are desirable but not essential. They will under no circumstances talk, but coarse animal grunts may be provided at a small extra cost. *Forte*, 2d. each, and *fortissimo*, 4d. each. Those who like to have their grub or tiffin with a GROUP of strong silent thugs may hire out squads of 4 EATERS at a considerable cash saving. SUPER-QUALITY of thick unshaven dishevelled and tweedy DREADNOUGHTS, possessing genuinely primitive Mongolian jaw formation available at an extra cost of 2/-per close-cropped head.

Class C

Are you de Riva?

Are you doing a degree in Economics?

Do you hold strong views on Free Trade, Rising and Falling Price Levels, the fallacy of Technocracy?

51

DO YOU WANT SOMEBODY TO TALK AT? Somebody upon whom you can work off your pet theories and arguments? Do you want a BUTT for your wit?

We have just received delivery of an excellent line of SPINELESS DUMMIES who will listen to anything and make no objections. These highly-skilled Eaters will nod (plain) and nod (with conviction, 1d. extra each) at every point emphasised by the Client and will thump the table with the fist at the climax of the Client's argument, thus saving the latter leaving down his fork or knife.

A SPECIAL LUXURY CLASS C EATER (trained at our own works in Inchicore), is available and will take furtive notes of the Client's OBITER DICTA, politely question him on his pet points, and will even go so far as to make the 'Tch, Tch, Tch' sound as pronounced by illiterate women in cinemas, at the more particular sallies and declarations of the Client. Written applications for this model will be dealt with in rotation.

Class D

The Eaters in this Class are very suitable for Graduates and SENIOR UNDERGRADUATES. They are prepared to discuss *anything*. They include a number of young men of faultless profile who are very suitable for ladies' tables, and they leave no stone unturned to be 'nice' in the most proper meaning of the term. Their services are always available as gigolos for not only ladies who go to dances, but also for ladies who go to dances and like to dance; also as paid escorts to theatres, cinemas, picnics, etc. Ladies who insist on a small moustache must give the Management at least ten days' notice.

In this class we have also a sound line in less reputable Eaters, who are eminently suitable for ordinary under-graduates or men-in-the-Main hall, who have maintained unblighted through the gloom of these trying times their appreciation of A GOOD STORY. Believe us that these Eaters have a fund of RIGHT GOOD ONES.

Class E

An exclusive and superior type of Eater belongs to this Class and must on no account be offered MASH or brown buns. They will discourse and converse on the subject of the drama, the theatre, the novel, the play, the tragedy, the comedy. Clients are warned not to make a *faux pas* in front of these Eaters, as they will not consent to stay with Clients who betray an inferior intellectual level.

Class F

The number of Eaters in Class F, confined to the Professional table, is so very very limited; those with suitable qualifications should make early application, as filling the post of Eater at the Professional table is an obvious short-cut to academic advancement. Junior members of the staff are eligible to apply, but they should be careful not to tempt Providence, e.g., a lecturer in Mathematics must not Eat as such with a Professor of the same subject.

We have a reliable but limited quantity of bold and grey-haired under-graduates who will engage members of the Staff on ACADEMIC AND FAMILY TOPICS. These Eaters are experienced men of the world and HAVE SEEN LIFE. They are well versed in local topography and can discourse for hours on the natural amenities of the Kattie Gallagher, Glencree, etc. These are good men. THEY UNDERSTAND.

No effort will be spared to retain the services of Mr Gussie O'Connell, the well-known Dublin Shanachie, as his readings from his repertoire of GOODLY YARNS are deservedly famous.

MAIL THIS COUPON TODAY

To the Editor, *Comthhrom Féinne*.

A Chara, – I am a Professor/a Student, and I do be lonely in the Restaurant. Please send me a copy of your free booklet, 'Golden Words' and arrange for the attendance of an EATER.

Class . . . . on . . . . at . . . . .o'clock.

Signed . . . .
I certify that this Client is ALRIGHT.

Signed . . . .
Member of the Royal Irish Academy.

53

Comhthrom Féinne, like Manus in *The Hard Life* some thirty years later, was ever attentive to the wish for self-improvement in the gullible:

Let us be your fathers!

HOPE FOR THE
MIND-SUFFERERS.
OUR UNIQUE NEW SERVICE

Do you tremble at the knees when you are lecturing or when your name is called at lecture? Do you titter nervously?

We can make a man of you.

We can give you will-power, resolution, verve, push, nerve, pull and a brass neck.

Write for our booklet called *The Golden Road*. Modern life demands speed – we can make you fast. We can develop your personality, make you forceful and dynamic. We can make you tall. We can add four inches to your chest and three inches to your biceps. We can abolish scurf and dandruff, cure falling hair and prevent baldness. We can make you masterful. Can you relax? If you cannot, we can tell you how. Smith was a clerk earning £153 a year, a nervous and anaemic wreck, with no prospects and no desire for prospects; he enrolled on the advice of friends; he studied accountancy in his spare time; he learned eighteen European languages and two Chinese dialects with the aid of our special gramophone records. Why? He learned to sketch and to write showcards in his spare time and improved his complexion beyond recognition with the aid of our special herbal remedies. He is now securely walking up the graph with an attache-case in his hand into the rising sun. WHY NOT YOU?

Simson was another clerk. He started by paying £300 for the privilege of working for nothing. He joined the British Army. He is now a certified camel-cleaner in Baghdad with excellent prospects of promotion, WHY NOT YOU?

Do you be bullied? Can you throw a thug? Can you disarm an armed thug and then throw him? CAN YOU DO ANYTHING?

Once again, can you relax?

54

Can you organise?

Can you concentrate?

Can you discuss the eternal verities without sniggering?

Can you drop a goal from the three-quarter line?

Can you take a tram from Whitehall to UCD for a penny?

WE can do them all.

If YOU cannot, you are not a complete man.

You are a wry-necked boob. You are a flat tyre.

Turn your back TODAY on your wretched past by filling up the appended form and sending it in a *stamped* envelope to the Institute. We will do the rest.

The Principal,
C.F. Institute of Practical Psychology,
University College, Dublin.

My Dear Sir,

I am a Professor/a Student and I am an Idiot Boy/a Boob/a Yes-man/a Spineless Waster/a Wreck/an Aumadhaun/a Flat Tyre. I cannot do any of the things you mention. I find that I cannot concentrate for one moment on anything. I have never passed an examination in my life but I have failed several. I find it hard to quit the bed in the morning. I often fail in that matitudinal struggle. Would you blame me? I feel that my only remaining hope is the Institute. You may make any use you wish of this letter. I enclose the requisite fee of six guineas, and I make this application only on the distinct understanding that should the Principal consider that my case is hopeless, he shall be in nowise compelled to accept my application or my money. I am interested in the following:

Technocracy ☐   Tautology ☐   Totalisators ☐   Trolley trimming ☐   Transvaal   Transport ☐   Journalism   in   the Home ☐   Jansenism ☐   Jamborees ☐   and   Accountancy ☐

And if I am, can you help me? I beg to remain,
                Dear Principal,
                        Your Most Humble Servant,
                . . . .

P.S. I think your Institute Supplies a long-felt want.

In the case of another type of patient, the following form must be filled up instead, not necessarily in the candidate's own handwriting.

55

Sir,
I have been rejected five times for the British Army. I am too proud to work. I believe in the sanctity and dignity of the human hands. I place myself unreservedly in yours. Please send me a good booklet.
Yours,
. . . .
P.S. Have you any reliable cure for bed-sores?

Important notice to ladies
The Lady-Principal is always glad to hear from ladies, and will be pleased to send booklets on Beauty, Knitting, Careers, Cookery, etc. 'Let Us Be Your Mothers' is our slogan here, and we must make it clear to Gentlemen who persist in communicating with the Lady-Principal instead of with the Principal that she can only be a sister to them. It can never be otherwise.

In the early thirties, a teaching method called 'An Cóngar' (The Short-cut) was in operation. It was intended to facilitate matters for those who wished to learn the Irish language, but was singularly ineffectual. O'Nolan and Brother Barnabas suggested another method:

We announce An Congar

Preface
It is with great pleasure that we are at last enabled to bring this unique System to the notice of readers of *Comhthrom Féinne*. The development and perfection of the System was a labour involving years of tireless research and experiment, and its successful conclusion is in no small measure due to the zeal and scholarship of Brother Barnabas, who has spent the last two years in retirement in the depths of the Vatican Library, and who worked at one period so hard and so unremittingly that he had discovered in quick succession three separate values for the square root of a minus quantity before being over-powered by five able-bodied policemen.

The Epic of the CONGAR has yet to be written – the inspiring tale of all-night struggles with refractory tangents, thrilling combats

56

to the death with intransitive logarithms and veritable faction-fights with swarms of subjunctive hypotenuses. Much trouble and a nett cash loss estimated at £3,500 per day were occasioned by a chance encounter with two Aorist Surds; these appear to have originated in the darker years of the Middle Ages, and to have made their way through the Primitive Indian dialects, eventually arriving in Egypt about the year 1469. Gustav Krautz, a German traveller who died in 1674 records an encounter with them on the Aran Islands in his treatise *Ueber allen Gipfeln ist Ruh*, but no satisfactory confirmation of this curious statement has been forthcoming. Much credit is due to Brother Barnabas, who faced what may well be described as a menace to civilisation with coolness and courage; he placed his army of assistants at strategic points, imbued them with the requisite mixture of tact and firmness, and managed to obviate the very ugly scenes which would certainly have occurred with a less experienced man in charge of operations. Despite some efforts on the part of the Aorist Surds to retreat within the Great Wall, Brother Barnabas has the situation well in hand after 26 hours' stiff fighting.

The involved, advanced and abstract nature of their work severely taxed the sanity of Brother Barnabas and the other research-workers, many of whom cannot participate in the present triumphant conclusion of their great task as they are nursing blank minds on the slopes of the Maritime Alps. Ugly Doubts arose from time to time. The old question regarding the rotundity or flatness of the earth, believed by many to have been definitely settled many years ago was resuscitated; and not for a hectic 54 hours was Galileo vindicated. On another occasion, starting from Belfast, gallant efforts were made to produce to infinity two parallel chalk lines drawn on the earth's surface. The attempt was eventually given up outside Sidi-bel-Abbes' owing to the coarse language of troopers of the French Foreign Legion, the callous conduct of four old Arabs, who trained their camels to dance on the line and obliterate it, the unwarranted and ignorant interference of the police throughout the world, and finally the persistent inclemency of the weather.

We will leave the writing of the Chronicle of this Great Adventure to a later scribe and we will proceed with our task of unfolding the beauties and the mysteries of AN CONGAR.

57

What is AN CONGAR? Briefly, it is the short-cut to the mastery of the Irish Language, and is guaranteed to be shorter than any previous short-cut by at least 80 miles, 7 roods and 2 perches, Irish Bog Measure. It eliminates Syntax, abolishes Idiom and annihilates Vocabulary; it reduces the Irish Language down to simple mathematical symbols; it obviates drudgery; it does away with old-fashioned text-books and will enable the persecuted inhabitants of West Cork to face the attentions of fanatic Oleryites with the courage and the hope that scientific knowledge alone can give. Ní beag sin, or *xyz*. IT GIVES THE PRONUNCIATION AT A GLANCE, it can register dialectic variations and find the Indo-European root of a given word without even the use of Compound Fractions. ALL THAT IS REQUIRED IS A KNOWLEDGE OF ELEMENTARY MATHEMATICS and a reasonable amount of faith in human nature. Let us take a homely example. The word *Seadna* is given in Congars as follows:

Shan O Cuiv's Congar . . . . Shiana
Professor Bonnimann's (Berlin) . . . . S%En @
OUR CONGAR . . . . $x^2 - y^2$

You see? The plan is ingeniously simple and can be readily grasped by even the youngest child.

But this is not all. In the hands of a skilled instrumentalist, AN CONGAR can be used to determine such diverse issues as the correct time for boiling an egg, the percentage of fats in watery-looking milk, the specific gravity and rarity of an 11 tram on a wet day, the density of first-year students, whether half-and-half *is* half-and-half, the percentage of bluff and cards in Poker, the proper development of the Ruy Lopez, the correct choice for an international XV., etc., etc. Let us proceed, however.

An Congar

PROPOSITION I: *To investigate the content of the Gaelic words, Sean O Muireadhaigh.*
Let x = Sean O Muireadhaigh.
Then S.F.X. O Muireadhaigh = x.
Therefore S.F.X. O Muireadhaigh $- x = O$ . . . . Algebra.
Dividing across by x.
S.F. O Muireadhaigh = O.

58

But S.F. O Muireadhaigh = Sean Murray . . . . Fianna
Therefore Sean Murray = O.

Fail Victory.

Q.E.F.

PROPOSITION II: *To determine, by means of an congar and log-tan, tables only, the age at which a man can be properly termed a 'fear mór', from the Gaelic phrase 'Tá'n fear mór'.*

CONSTRUCTION: Draw a short straight line having little or no magnitude, and drop another similar line from an altitude to meet it at right angles. Close in your V with another line and the result with be a right-angled triangle . . . . Euclid.

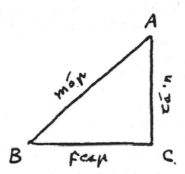

Sin A = } fear and Cos B = } fear
        } mor   ...   } mor
    Therefore Sin A = Cos B.   ...   .   Deduction.
It is perfectly evident that this is leading us nowhere, and we must therefore try another path.
    Now, Tan B = } Ta'n
              } fear
Dividing across by Tan.
    B = } 1
       } fear
Therefore, Fear B = 1.

Ignoring the crudity of expression which we must admit as the one fault of AN CONGAR, we get

Fear B = Fear ar bith. (Any man) . . . . . . Deduction.

Therefore, Fear ar bith = 1.

CONCLUSION 1: The age of any male child requisite to merit the title 'man' or 'fear' is a maximum of *one year* as shown above.

We have yet to prove our original Proposition. Let us change the figure to suit our requirements.

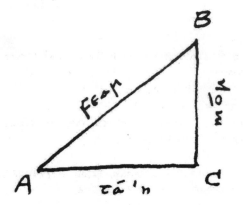

Now

Tan A = } $\frac{mor}{Ta'n}$

Dividing across by Tan.

A = mor.

But if C is a right angle and A is described by an CONGAR as 'mor' or big, it follows that A must be greater than B. Therefore the minimum size of A is 46 degrees.

CONCLUSION 2: The minimum age at which a man can be properly described as 'fear mor' is 46 years.

Q.E.F.

60

PROPOSITION III: *Given that the Gaelic phrase Bheibheann de Bhalera[1] = O, factorise Bheibheann de Bhalera.*

Everything must be a factor of itself and must contain at least one other extraneous and important quantity. . . . Axiom XVI.

For the purpose of argument, complete the square of de Bhalera.

Let y = the other unknown quantity.

Now, $(\text{Bheibheann de Bhalera})^2 + y^2 = O$.

But Bheibheann de Bhalera = 'Dev' . . . .

Cainnt na nDaoine.

Therefore $(\text{Dev } y) = O$.

$= \text{Dev}^2 + 2 \text{ Dev } y + y^2 = O$.

But 'Devy' is a diminutive form of 'Dev' and means a small Dev or young brother.

Therefore $\text{Dev}^2 + 2 \text{ (young brother)} + y^2 = O$.

$\text{Dev}^2 + (\text{Eamonn Rory}) + y^2 = O$.

At this stage, the two young brothers may be taken out and sent about their business for the time being.

Then $\text{Dev}^2 + y^2 = O$.

But y, being the other extraneous and important quantity, must consist partly of politics . . . . Deduction.

Factorising y,

$\text{Dev}^2 + (\text{Dáil})y = O$.

Allowing again for crudity of expression of AN CONGAR,

$\text{Dev}^2 + \text{Dolly} = O$.

Now bring in the two young brothers again.

Then $\text{Dev}^2 + 2$ young brothers $+ \text{Dolly} = O$.

Factors of Bheibheann de Bhalera therefore are

(Dev + eamonnagusruaidhri) (Dev + Dolly).

Q.E.F.

That is all today, children.

Further Propositions of *An Congar* will be published when the problem as to whether the earth goes round the sun or whether the sun goes round the earth, which has just cropped up, is finally settled.

Life for Brother Barnabas was not without its troubles, however.

---

[1] I.e.: Vivion de Valera, contemporary of O'Nolan and son of Éamonn (Dev). Both Vivion and his father were unpopular with O'Nolan.

61

Rumoured closing of Earlsfort Terrace

FISTICUFFS AT BADEN-BADEN

POLITICUS HITS OUT

BROTHER BARNABAS

THRASHED

EXTRAORDINARY SCENES

Baden-Baden, the well-known German Spa, was the scene of turbulent fisticuffs between our pet Commissioner, Brother Barnabas, and Politicus, the world-famous writer, journalist, literateur, boxer, statesman, power-behind-the-throne, etc., etc.

Brother Barnabas lost the verdict on a technical knock-out, was roughly handled by the crowd, and subsequently mauled in the porch of the hall by Mr Tom Guihan, who mistook the Brother for a Bective forward in mufti.

The Free State National Loan lost eight points on the German Bourse.

It is understood that President Hindenburg has received a curt Note from the Free State Government in connection with the matter, whilst repercussions are expected in the Far East.

It is freely rumoured in Academic Circles that, following the publication of Politicus's momentous statement that University College, Dublin, as such, did not come up to his expectations, the Earlsfort Terrace premises will shortly be up for auction; and, further, that arrangements are in hand for the mass-export of students and Professors to the Russian state-farms, where they will be put in charge of the 'Aran Chief' potato-plots.

It is also stated that the Pro Fide Society, having met in private Conference, had composed a strongly-worded document on this matter, and had posted it the other evening in a special pouch to the League of Nations.

Brother Barnabas, who is now, happily, convalescent, is following the situation with keen attention. Professor Binchy has returned from Berlin.

How it happened

(*By our Special Wire*)

The following is an authoritative account of how this extraordinary situation developed. Brother Barnabas, the fame of whose undoubted talents as an election agent had spread abroad, and whose services had been requisited by Herr Adolf Hitler in the matter of the German Presidential elections, was walking down the corridor of an express-train in search of a bottle of lemonade. Noticing a distinguished-looking gentleman, with a face full of character and perfectly tailored, sitting in a compartment reading a curious document printed in large letters, our special Commissioner sat down in the opposite seat, and from several years of experience of reading other people's newspapers upside down in suburban trains, he succeeded in deciphering several curious phrases, e.g., 'Tied to no political party', 'black-thorn walking-sticks', 'Be prepared – get accustomed now – President Cosgrave, President de Valera, President Larkin, President Byrne, President Murphy.' Quickly perceiving that this gentleman was connected with a well-known Catholic journal which had succeeded in establishing a 'corner' in Nationalism, which did a thing in 1904 which no newspaper had ever done before, which was housed in one of Dublin's show places and which had been advocating a number of reforms for years, Brother Barnabus commented courteously on the weather, introduced himself by name, shook the gentleman by the hand, and immediately asked him what he thought of his 'colleague', who wrote the UCD column in the *Sunday Independent*. At the mention of our College, the gentleman, who later proved to be Politicus, started violently, and thereupon proceeded to discuss our institution at some length, not always to our advantage. Brother Barnabas, apparently considering that the strictures were not merited, and forgetting that he was in a German express train, pulled Politicus's tie, fell into an attitude of defence, and savagely invited Politicus 'outside the door'. Politicus, having resumed his collar, and having drily remarked that he could handle a pen, a gun or an itinerant friar with equal facility, expressed his willingness to fight on reaching Baden-Baden. Brother Barnabas, having accepted the offer, continued in his quest of lemonade, and was astonished to find Mr Kilcullen and Mr Guihan seated in another compartment, deep in a technical discussion on the gold standard. These two gentlemen, it later transpired, were travelling on business, Mr Kilcullen endeavouring to arrange a bout between Max Schmelling[1] and Mr Guihan for the world heavyweight title. Herr Schmelling, however, had recently become interested in rivers and springs and was absent on an expedition tracing the Oder to its source, and Mr Kilcullen kindly offered to promote the contest between Politicus and Brother Barnabas.

The contest described round by round

Details of the fight are rather meagre. It appears that a suburban hall was rented, an impromptu ring fixed up. Enormous crowds turned up, apparently taking it from the posters that the Church and State had finally decided to settle their long-standing differences in the old fashioned way. Photographers were excluded by special request of Brother Barnabas, who appeared, amid thunderous applause, clad in the College colours (by the special telegraphic courtesy of the Athletic Union); Politicus was clad becomingly in a singlet of Abbey Street puce, and according to Brother Barnabas, 'Some people were understood to clap' when he appeared.

Round one

Politicus came from his corner with a bound, started the attack, and Brother Barnabas was severely beaten about the head, arms, shoulders, legs and body; Politicus landed thirteen knock-out blows in quick succession, the efficacy of which, however, was impaired by his opponent's capacity for bouncing. Politicus was awarded the verdict on a technical knock-out, Brother Barnabas having been carried out by his indefatigable second, Mr Tom Guihan, before the referee had time to count ten in German. It transpired afterwards, however, that Mr Guihan was under a misapprehension, mistook the Brother for a Bective forward, and had quickly carried him to the privacy of the outer porch in order to thrash him. In this subsequent second fight, Mr Guihan is believed to have won.

---

[1] German World Heavyweight boxing champion, considered by Hitler to be a paragon of Teutonic manhood.

The boxers interviewed

Our special correspondent, after a long search, saw Brother Barnabas standing at a street corner, and decided to approach him and ask his impressions of the fight. When approached, however, he made use of an improper expression, and walked quickly up a side-street.

Politicus when run to earth in the Baden-Baden Grossergasthaus, looked none the worse for his encounter, and received our representative, who introduced himself as a graduate of Trinity with kindness and courtesy. The following exchange took place.

We: Are you in any way exhausted after your great fight?

Politicus: I am *not*.

We: Is there any foundation to the rumour that you failed First Arts four times?

Politicus (*emphatically*): None whatever.

We: As a Civil servant, do you think it right for you to criticise your superiors in a weekly newspaper?

Politicus: Will you have a cigarette?

We: Have you the greatest intellect and are you the greatest figure in Western Europe?

Politicus (*modestly*): Yes.

We: Was the wholesale spoiling of votes the most ignorant thing, in your opinion, that the National University has done?

Politicus (*sharply*): By no means. They did something far more serious, and hadn't even the sense to spoil the right kind of votes.

We: But '*non semper tendit arcem Apollo*,' you know.

Politicus: I'm not in favour of this compulsory Irish, anyway.

It was not surprising that in his later years Barnabas became fond of looking back on some of the highlights of his eventful life:

Should pin-money girls be sacked?
Mein Kampf

BY BROTHER BARNABAS
(in an interview)

The numerous friends and admirers of Brother Barnabas will be glad to hear that he is still alive and well; though convulsions, teething, whooping-cough, mumps, rickets and a host of other infantile complaints which have assailed the great man in his old age tend to make his public appearance, which in print and in person become rarer and rarer with the passing years, a ludicrous farce. He now lives in retirement in a rustic bog-farm in the County Meath, where the cultivation of bog-oak orchards and peat parking-poles has become the sole anchor that chains his feeble wits to earth. He is attended day and night by a buxom nurse, provided by the Board of Works, and the giggles and hoarse chuckling that can be heard at dusk from the density of the turf-trollops bespeak a waggish vitality that is reluctant to yield the palm to Father Time.

When the weather is good he can be seen wandering over the hills of and talking to the men of Meath, absently fondling their great square skulls; at other times flitting about like one possessed, uttering that enigmatic query, 'Et tu quoque Caesar,' and smiling that whimsical smile that has endeared him in the past to the Great American Public and earned for him the title of the 'Old Man Sweetheart of the World'.

If the reader were to see him being bundled by his nurse into a tin bath during a sudden spasm of convulsions on the bogs, mayhap he would say, 'Gracious, what a poor helpless ould man!'

But Lord save us! Stand back! Vienna, 1912. Through the mind back to the glamorous days before the war. Live, laugh and love. Unter den Linden, the gay crowds promenading, the gipsy fiddlers, the moon, the cafes and Ach! the wein. Vienna – city of my dreams – with the lid half-off. The crowds are laughing. Sie freuen sich der Mainacht. *But there is stark drama here.* Lower down the street the lid is completely off. Two figures meet in the shadow of the greatest Linden. It is pitch dark. You could not see your hand if you held it unter your nose. There are words. An altercation if you will, STRIKE A MATCH! Gott! A picturesque figure in a calico cape is flaying a well-dressed nobleman with a dog-whip. Lash, lash, lash. No mercy, no quarter. Lash, lash, lash. Put out the match and come away. Primeval man. Nature in the raw is seldom mild. Away with us. This is no place for pigeon-chested weaklings . . . The gallant in the cape is Bruder Barna-bas (Brother Barnabas). And the cad who was thrashed? Der Grosse Kaiser Wilhelm!

Incredible, you will say. Who would think it, to look at this poor recluse now, turning the turf-turnips like some poor idiot boy? Who would think that he had once crossed dog-whips with the crowned heads of Europe?

And sa-a-a-a-a-ay!

The entrance to the Reichstag chamber is surmounted by enormous 18 point antlers. Who shot the original stag?

Who burnt the place down?

Who invented mixed dancing?

Who invented the two-egg omelet with three-egg Lower?

Who dissolved the Danish Rikstak in 1887?

Who first thought of using starch on rashers?

Who stole the corsets of the Archduke Nicholas?

Who first asked should pin-money girls be sacked?

Who is the first in peace, first in war and first in the hearts of his countrymen?

Tch, Tch, Tch. Surely we need not say it.

When I first came to University College, said Brother Barnabas, – and that is many more years ago than I could count on my buttons, even counting the buttons on my boots – the place was a hot-bed of genius. Even the clocks were wound by poets, and some of them were even pawned by men of genius. There was a Deathless Atmosphere about the place, an Elysian mustiness, that *je ne sais quoi* which instantly assails the nostrils when a plurality of poets are gathered together in an enclosed space. The Billiard-room of today was at that time a Nursery for the little

67

Psyches of the poets – an idea that was later to be copied in the modern Departmental Store – and here the little fellows were kept out of harm's way and given every attention by trained nurses while their masters were at lectures or engaged in cadging cigarettes from one another. Here the more sickly of them were discreetly dosed with aspirin, unsanitary habits were corrected on the Montessori system, and they were all taught their Irish. The less humane of the *literati* were wont to match their respective Psyches secretly in brutal battles in the psyche-pit, not unlike the practice of matching game-cocks in cock-pits. Huge side-stakes were wagered on the results, and the sport became so popular that it threatened at one time to become the end for good and all of Great Literature in Ireland. The little fighters were armed with great oak clubs and 'tis said that many a Milton was *made* jute in the same psyche-pits. The Psyche owned by George Russell,[1] who was at that time a callow youth doing First Commerce, was a very famous animal in the pits and accounted for many a formidable antagonist; it was rumoured that W. B. Yeats, a talented youth who was doing Pre-Reg., wanted it for stud purposes and had offered Russell 600 guineas for it, but whether a sale was effected has never been revealed. The thing eventually became a nation-wide scandal. The Skibbereen County Council stopped a scholarship, the *Irish Independent* wrote a leader, the police intervened and eventually 83 poets were sent down. Subsequent attempts to re-start the sport were foiled by the Psyches themselves, who took a very firm stand in the matter. There were a few desultory strikes, two Psyches ran away from home, and joined the British Army and there were ugly rumours of widespread sulking. The presence of Communist agitators in the ranks was suspected. The recovery of the body of a Psyche, drowned in a sack in the canal, exercised the public mind for many weeks but the mystery was never solved. Eventually the whole thing was hushed up and few signs remain today to tell of that blackest page in Ireland's chequered story.

I shall never forget my first day in College. I was standing in the Hall one day waiting for a chance to Sign the Roll and Shake the

---

[1] AE, poet, painter and talker.

Hand when I was approached by two hunched cadaverous-looking vultures who took me by the throat – it still bears the marks of twenty fingers – and barked a question at me in a horrible cutting voice:

'*Are you a Cynic or a Softy?*'

'I don't know,' I said, 'but I guess I'm a damn hard man. My father was a soldier.'

'ARE YOU A CYNIC OR A SOFTY?'

'Cynic,' I replied, briefly.

'That is very singular,' said one, 'but not unsatisfactory.'

'*Sit down,*' said the other, speaking in italics.

The first I had easily recognised as Sherlock Holmes and the second subsequently proved to be a man called Fludd. They had both been jilted by the same girl, who subsequently fell in love with Watson, then a young medical student, and was prevented from marrying him only by her sudden and premature dissolution at the early age of seventeen. She was really only a wee slip of a thing. 'Come up and see me some time. I'm no angel' was her favourite gag; but it was only a gag. Fludd and Holmes spent weeks in the laboratories endeavouring to compound CYNIC POWDERS, designed to turn the heart into a stone. They eventually succeeded, and took their powders after meals for two years running. Yes, running. They hardened their hearts. Their hearts became heavier and heavier and began to sink down through their bodies into their stomachs and even down through their stomach. A course of frantic physical jerks ('How to Mould a Mighty Forearm,' etc.) designed to strengthen the stomach muscles, had no effect, and right proper ructions were only evaded by a series of brilliant operations in Vincents. The two great cynics were eventually saved and they generously endowed two beds in gratitude for their deliverance. They hastily withdrew their gift, however, when an ordinary Softy pointed out that Cynics don't endow beds for other people to die in. It was shortly afterwards that Holmes evinced a talent for detecting, and he threw up his Commerce course and retired to a flat in Baker Street, London, where he was credited with a wholly uncynical attachment for his buxom landlady. Fludd was left to carry on his fight for the Cynical Ideal alone. He industriously collected all scattered scraps of knowledge on the subject and reduced it veritably to a science. He published his researches under the title of *Mein Kampf gegen der Softheit*, a work that has since become a classic. 'How to say cutting things very dryly', 'How to talk without moving the lips', 'The Theory of Cold Water, Pouring of do.", 'Wet Blankets, Uses of. Hints on Care and Storage of,' are representative titles of sections which indicate the vast erudition of the work.

My first introduction to the literary and historical Society was unlike that of most others. At the end of my first week in College – my great gifts had even already become the common peg for everybody's conversation – I was timidly approached by the record secretary, a graduate of some years standing, and invited to take the chair at the forthcoming debate. I agreed to do so. George Bernard Shaw was the auditor at the time, a man who was destined at a later day to make history in the Irish bacon trade. The debate was on some aspect of education and colour was lent to the discussion by the entry into the house of Harry Wharton, Bob Cherry, Billy Bunter and the entire Remove, fresh from that famous English educational foundation, Greyfriars. Though clad in the traditional eton jacket and tight trousers, raiment that revealed a certain youthfulness of contour, a closer glance showed that they were really old and soured men. They had been kept at school for forty years in response to the insatiable demand of the clean-limbed National Schoolboys of these islands for more and more stories about their doings. A thoughtful medical man had given them all an injection which stopped all mental development at the age of thirteen. Harry Wharton and his cronies, the Famous Five sat down between Bernard Shaw and Maurice Maeterlinck. Billy Bunter approached them apparently in search of money. I can remember every word:

'I say, you fellows.'

'Well fatty, what now?'

(Here Bob Cherry was observed to be viewing Lord Ashbourne, an Irish-man attired in kilts, with extreme disfavour and was indeed heard to remark sotto-voce that there appeared to be a terrible lot of cads present.)

'Could you lend me two-and-sixpence on account? I have been disappointed about a postal-order ...'

70

'*Sit down, Bunter*!' said Fludd.

'Go and boil your head,' said Wharton.

'Beast,' said Bunter, 'Really –'

'Rats!'

'Beasts.'

'Bump him!'

'What-ho!'

And the Famous 5 arose and bumped him. Bunter was a heavier man than they, but there were five of them in it.

'Yarooooooooooogh!!' said Bunter.

'Order, order!' said I from the chair. 'I call upon Mac Uí Hitléir to speak for the motion.'

The debate dragged on conventional lines. Trouble started when I called on Harold Skinner, the sneak, cad, bounder and rank outsider from Greyfriars. In appearance, he was monstrous ill-favoured. And no wonder. He never played clean healthy open-air games like Wharton. Instead of going down to the nets, he preferred to mope in his study with his equally degenerate cronies, Snoop and Stott. And believe me, they looked every inch Snoop and Stott. In the study they used to have dirty 'smokes', and even played cards. It was said that they had broken bounds at night and gone to the Green Man in the local village and *played billiards*. They used to bully and cuff fags, they were always sneering and saying cruel cynical things to poor young impressionable juniors. They were yellow right through, into the bargain. Skinner was thrashed once a week by Wharton, and Snoop and Stott once a fortnight. As Skinner rose to speak, I noticed Fludd edging down and sitting between Snoop and Stott. They were saying cynical things, one to the other, methought.

Skinner started off with a vicious sneer at his own form-master, the gimlet-eyed Mr Quelch, for antiquated ideas on education and corporal punishment. Now Harry Wharton had been belted and thrashed by the same Mr Quelch several times a day. He had written out thousands and thousands of lines for him; his youth, his health, the natural colour of his hair had all been ground away under the iron heel of Mr Quelch.

But he leapt to his feet with blazing eyes. This was not cricket, it wasn't British, it wasn't in the public school tradition. Not in

71

front of so many cads and bounders. Not in front of the outsider in the Kilts.

'Take that back, you rotter!' he rapped out.

Skinner sneered awkwardly. Silence.

'Put up your fists, you rotter!'

Skinner, of course, refused and paid the customary penalty. Wharton leaped at him and slammed him down on his back twelve times in quick succession with twelve successive hooks to the jaw. He then stood over his prostrate form, with eyes still blazing.

'Had enough, you cad?' he panted.

'Yes, you rotter,' said Skinner.

Wharton glared round at the house. Snoop and Stott examined their shoes. Fludd was back in his own seat.

'Order!' said I from the chair.

You see? Primeval boy. Nature in the raw is seldom mild.

Some day I will tell the whole story. How Vernon Smith ('The Bounder') was elected Auditor of the Commerce Society. How Fludd and Bernard Shaw lived for two days in Loreto Hall disguised as two little girls in blue. How I discovered and hastily re-covered James Joyce. How I boxed a professor's ears. How I became President of University College.

It is a story of yesterday, but a grand story.

A happy Christmas to ye, now.

I must stop now, for the present. Something is coming on me. Ring for my little tin bath.

A brass hat in Bannow Strand

BY BROTHER BARNABAS
(in an ex-parte application
before the master)

It is not generally known, said Brother Barnabas, that I am a halfcaste Russian Jew, though the fact that my forbears were

72

thoroughly Russian does not justify the conclusion that they were Russian bears. I came of good *kulak* stock and in the palmy days before the revolution was responsible for a tiny but gilded principality in the wilds of the Siberian steppes; here democracy, ladies, a square deal for the working man and other anomalies of the occident were quite unknown; universal illiteracy was compulsory, and such of my subjects who were sufficiently rebellious and anti-social as to endeavour to menace my regime with hedge-schools usually died from exposure on the steppes as a result of their ill-conditioned attempts to plant hedges, as a preliminary measure. My peoples lived in conditions of quite unparalleled squalor and decay, making a precarious living by sweeping snow off the steppes, being impelled by a wholly illogical and ludicrous desire for life to broach a stern smallsword night and day with swarms of ravenous wolves, who had long since learned the futility of waiting at people's doors. They lacked clothes and brains and boots and food, did my peoples. Above all, they lacked handkerchiefs; and a wet nose, though a social solecism in Rathmines, yet when coupled with the effect of the Eternal Snows, provided my peoples with permanently stiff upper-lips for battling with the wolves – a circumstance which has always impressed me with the wonderful bounty of Nature. The issue of course, was very simple – mathematically elementary. One man one wolf was the *status quo* and any disparity in breeding on the part of either species would spell disaster for the other. Either the wolves would eat my peoples or my peoples would eat the wolves.

However, I was eventually compelled to fly. An accession of mass-hysteria, culminating in a disgraceful orgy of hooliganism in which scores of right-thinking Russians were massacred, convinced me that immediate and terrible flight was the only alternative to my imminent dissolution. I quitted my peoples, throwing my last kuka-cake to a pregnant she-wolf.

I went to Spain with nothing but my violin, an instrument in respect of which I am not without talent; and there as Fra Barnaba, Maestro, I kissed the rosy fingers of the Muses' eldest child. Here I remained for six years, and when signs were not wanting that the Russian disaffection was spreading throughout the world, I turned my face to that island of the west, to Ireland of

73

the Welcomes. I landed at Bannow Strand on the tenth of May.

By forced marches, I made Dublin in three days and was glad to note an almost entire absence of communism in the city. True, Marx's *Das Kapital* was available in two bookshops, but the frequent exhibition at the Capital cinema of films featuring the Marx Brothers led to an unconscionable confusion in the public mind; and this was aggravated by the activities of Lenin, who was a brindled bitch clocking 31.25 twice in the one week at Harold's Cross. And the red flag was only the badge of the Gas Company's ganger.

As soon as I arrived in town, I instantly joined the Gaelic League. I changed my name to An Bráthair Barnabas, determined upon a picturesque genitive in '-baí' (the word was my own and though pedants and pundits may twitter, I hope I can arrange my personal genitives like a gentleman). I suppressed a somewhat egotistical *penchant* for a locative case 'barnabaro' meaning 'the country in which Barnabas resides', and finished my inflection with the classical dative 'Barnabibus' – to or for Barnabas – my tribute to the old-time latined monasticism of the Irish race. Kong is the eighth wonder of the world and Cong the ninth.

And just as I had, at an earlier day, publicly thumbed Jolas' *transition* in London's fogs to show the cads that the apparent paradox implied in the juxtaposition of the Horizontal Worldview and a bus-ride to Brixton could be reconciled, united, adjusted and dissolved in the micro-universe of my mind – housed though it was in a shabby temple to be transported a statutory two miles for one penny – so also I felt bound to mutter Gaelic obscurities on tram-tops in Donnybrook on a wet Thursday to bridge the disparity between a shoddy foreign machined suiting and a Gaelic Ireland, free and united.

At the beginning, my conversational Irish was weak and in poor taste. Commonsense told me to confine my tittle-tattle to people of my own sex until such time as my small vocabulary was disembarrassed of its multiple allusions to street-names, lavatories and police-notices, all of which I had collected on my walks with the undiscriminating appetite of the enthusiast-beginner.

I found myself progressing slowly in the cult, troubled by no doubts or scruples. Suddenly the bombshell burst upon me from a clear sky. On the 13th day of April, at 11.45 p.m., I was called upon to quit my Saxon *hosen* and wear drawers for Ireland. They were to be grey tweedies, fastened at the knee.

This caused me to call an instant halt and to review the entire situation. I had previously analysed the subject of philibegs or kilts, and came to the conclusion that they could not be regarded as historic documents, and that the custom was in any event shallow and superficial insofar as there was no tradition in underclothes. Another reason against their adoption as my dress lay in the fact that I had, even in early youth, evinced a pronounced tendency towards piano-leg. The same objection held for tweedies or for any type of the attenuated bracchiae.

I objected, of course, and presented an oide memoire on the subject to my superiors.

The outer fustian, I was at pains to point out, was no true guide to the inner heart. Trousering, if not of native origin, embodied the principles of gracefulness, good taste and utility, so dear to the true Irish heart. Furthermore, many implications of our traditional Caitlín Ní h-Uallacháin[1] were foreign, though not, I submitted, necessarily bad. If it be conceded that many a heart of gold can beat beneath a shoddy waist coat, who shall doubt the heart that has beaten beneath the homely homespun corsets of our Caitlín Ní h-Uallacháin for so many centuries? Had they ever noticed her figure? Did they mean to tell me it was nature unassisted? Compare her with Britannia or the sowing girl of Gaul and who shall say she suffers? There is only one way with unruly hips and discursive stomachs and if Britannia and Frances should have boldly taken it, why should Caitlín mope a Cinderella in the corner, a fatted failure in a triangular trial of personality, pep and pulchritude? Fiddlesticks! She hasn't, of course. She borrowed a model from Frances and more power to her: and me to my Hapsburg Hosen. Poor Caitlín was no angel! She changed her name fully twenty times and we have two aliases, Róisín Dhubh and Niamh Chinn Oir, to prove that the courtesan's hair-dye was stored beside the bagpipes. I carried the day, and was highly gratified when a Synod of the Gaelic League

[1] Kathleen Ní Hoolihan: i.e. Ireland.

75

decreed that tweedies were no longer an article of faith, though still to be regarded as a counsel of perfection.

I was also told not to jazz, the thing being foreign and erotic, and three-quarters of the very word being composed of letters quite unknown to the old Irish. This I found a distinct stumbling-block to social advancement, for piano-legs aside, I was a fine cut of a man in tails at that time and I resented restrictions on the magnetic field of my sex-appeal, resentment that was only to be exorcised by the magical emasculation of the advancing years. It was at this time that I determined to enter the Civil Service and hearing at a Gaelic League meeting that Irish dancing promoted industry and work whilst jazz promoted an enervating indolence and lethargy, I determined on a shabby expedient for disposing of all my rivals for the vacancy. I deluged them with free invitations to jazz dances and introduced them to hosts of can-can partners. In the meantime, in the privacy of my humble bed-room, I practised jigs and sets and reels and poets' choices and extended the rinnce fada[1] into a marathon affair lasting nine and a half hours. All with imaginary partners, of course, whose skill and pulchritude was limited only by my own fancy. Breeding will out and I secured first place in the examination with consum-mate ease. It is only a detail that I was subsequently rejected on the medical examination, the doctor resorting to the cowardly refuge of translating piano-legs into Latin. Twenty-eight sixteen-handed reels won me a job as a navvy in a Drumcondra sewerage scheme and a rigid application to the Siege of Ennis in my spare time won me rapid promotion and the respect and admiration of my colleagues, whilst my erstwhile rival for the Service had one foot in a pauper's grave and the other foot executing a feather-step in a jazz-hall.

Progress was my watchword, however, and with the great prophets of University College, omens were not wanting that the time was ripe when I should come amongst them. I addressed myself to Matriculation and found it a mere bagatelle, involving only a paltry High Caul Cap and Four Washerwomen.

I came to College.

(But the end is not yet)

---

[1] rinnce fada: long dance.

76

The end, however, was nigh, and Brother Barnabas's last contribution is a sad one. But perhaps his spirit lived on, for, to crucify some metaphors, his swansong contained the seeds of a book that was not to be published until five years later: *At Swim-Two-Birds*, by Flann O'Brien.

Scenes in a novel

BY BROTHER BARNABAS
(probably posthumous)

I am penning these lines, dear reader, under conditions of great emotional stress, being engaged, as I am, in the composition of a posthumous article. The great blots of sweat which gather on my brow are instantly decanted into a big red handkerchief, though I know the practice is ruinous to the complexion, having regard to the open pores and the poisonous vegetable dyes that are used nowadays in the Japanese sweat-shops. By the time these lines are in neat rows of print, with no damn over-lapping at the edges, the writer will be in Kingdom Come.[1] (See Gaelic quotation in 8-point footnote.) I have rented Trotsky's villa in Paris, though there are four defects in the lease (three reckoning by British law) and the drains are – what shall I say? – just a *leetle* bit Gallic. Last week, I set about the melancholy task of selling up my little home. Auction followed auction. Priceless books went for a mere song, and invaluable songs, many of them of my own composition, were ruthlessly exchanged for loads of books. Stomach-pumps and stallions went for next to nothing, whilst my ingenious home-made typewriter, in perfect order except for two faulty characters, was knocked down for four and tuppence. I was finally stripped of all my possessions, except for a few old

---

[1] 'Truagh sin, a leabhair bhig bháin
Tiocfaidh lá, is ba fíor,
Déarfaidh neach os cionn do chláir
Ní mhaireann an lámh do scríobh.'
['How sad it is, o little white book,
That the day will come, for certain,
When someone will say over your cover,
"The hand that wrote this is dead"'] [trans. J.W.J.]

77

articles of clothing upon which I had waggishly placed an enormous reserve price. I was in some doubt about a dappled dressing-gown of red fustian, bordered with a pleasing grey piping. I finally decided to present it to the Nation. The Nation, however, acting through one of its accredited Sanitary Inspectors, declined the gift – rather churlishly I thought – and pleading certain statutory prerogatives, caused the thing to be burnt in a yard off Chatham Street within a stone's throw of the house where the Brothers Sheares played their last game of *taiplis* [draughts]. Think of that! When such things come to pass, as Walt Whitman says, you re-examine philosophies and religions. Suggestions as to compensation were pooh-poohed and sallies were made touching on the compulsory acquisition of slum property. You see? If a great mind is to be rotted or deranged, no meanness or no outrage is too despicable, no maggot of officialdom is too contemptible to perpetrate it . . . the ash of my dressing-gown, a sickly wheaten colour, and indeed, the whole incident reminded me forcibly of Carruthers McDaid.[1] Carruthers McDaid is a man I created one night when I had swallowed nine stouts and felt vaguely blasphemous. I gave him a good but worn-out mother and an industrious father, and coolly negativing fifty years of eugenics, made him a worthless scoundrel, a betrayer of women and a secret drinker. He had a sickly wheaten head, the watery blue eyes of the weakling. For if the truth must be told I had started to compose a novel and McDaid was the kernel or the fulcrum of it. Some writers have started with a good and noble hero and traced his weakening, his degradation and his eventual downfall; others have introduced a degenerate villain to be ennobled and uplifted to the tune of twenty-two chapters, usually at the hands of a woman – 'She was not beautiful, but a shortened nose, a slightly crooked mouth and eyes that seemed brimful of a simple complexity seemed to spell a curious attraction, an inexplicable charm.' In my own case, McDaid, starting off as a rank waster and a rotter, was meant to sink slowly to absolutely the last extremities of human degradation. Nothing, absolutely nothing, was to be too low for him, the wheaten-headed hound . . .

[1] Who is Carruthers McDaid, you ask?

I shall never forget the Thursday when the thing happened. I retired to my room at about six o'clock, fortified with a pony of porter and two threepenny cigars, and manfully addressed myself to the achievement of Chapter Five. McDaid, who for a whole week had been living precariously by selling kittens to foolish old ladies and who could be said to be existing on the immoral earnings of his cat, was required to rob a poor-box in a church. But no! Plot or no plot, it was not to be.

'Sorry, old chap,' he said, 'but I absolutely can't do it.'

'What's this, Mac,' said I, 'getting squeamish in your old age?'

'Not squeamish exactly,' he replied, 'but I bar poor-boxes. Dammit, you can't call me squeamish. Think of that bedroom business in Chapter Two, you old dog.'

'Not another word,' said I sternly, 'you remember that new shaving brush you bought?'

'Yes.'

'Very well, you burst the poor-box or its anthrax in two days.'

'But, I say, old chap, that's a bit thick.'

'You think so? Well, I'm old-fashioned enough to believe that your opinions don't matter.'

We left it at that. Each of us firm, outwardly polite, perhaps, but determined to yield not one tittle of our inalienable rights. It was only afterwards that the whole thing came out. Knowing that he was a dyed-in-the-wool atheist, I had sent him to a revivalist prayer-meeting, purely for the purpose of scoffing and showing the reader the blackness of his soul. It appears that he remained to pray. Two days afterwards I caught him sneaking out to Gardiner Street at seven in the morning. Furthermore, a contribution to the funds of a well-known charity, a matter of four-and-sixpence in the names of Miles Caritatis was not, I understand, unconnected with our proselyte. A character ratting on his creator and exchanging the pre-destined hangman's rope for a halo is something new. It is, however, only one factor in my impending dissolution. Shaun Svoolish, my hero, the composition of whose heroics have cost me many a sleepless day, has formed an alliance with a slavey in Griffith Avenue; and Shiela, his 'steady', an exquisite creature I produced for the sole purpose of loving him and becoming his wife, is apparently to be given the air. You see? My carefully thought-out plot is turned inside out

79

and goodness knows where this individualist flummery is going to end. Imagine sitting down to finish a chapter and running bang into an unexplained slavey at the turn of a page! I reproached Shaun, of course.

'Frankly, Shaun,' I said, 'I don't like it.'

'I'm sorry,' he said. 'My brains, my brawn, my hands, my body are willing to work for you, but the heart! Who shall say yea or nay to the timeless passions of a man's heart? Have you ever been in love? Have you ever –'

'What about Shiela, you shameless rotter? I gave her dimples, blue eyes, blond hair and a beautiful soul. The last time she met you, I rigged her out in a blue swagger outfit, brand new. You now throw the whole lot back in my face . . . Call it cricket if you like, Shaun, but don't expect me to agree.'

'I may be a prig,' he replied, 'but I know what I like. Why can't I marry Bridie and have a shot at the Civil Service?'

'Railway accidents are fortunately rare,' I said finally, 'but when they happen they are horrible. Think it over.'

'You wouldn't dare!'

'O, wouldn't I? Maybe you'd like a new shaving brush as well.'

And that was that.

Treason is equally widespread among the minor characters. I have been confronted with a Burmese shanachy, two corner-boys, a barmaid and five bus-drivers, none of whom could give a plausible account of their movements. They are evidently 'friends' of my characters. The only character to yield me undivided and steadfast allegiance is a drunken hedonist who is destined to be killed with kindness in Chapter Twelve. *And he knows it!* Not that he is any way lacking in cheek, of course. He started nagging me one evening.

'I say, about the dust-jacket –'

'Yes?'

'No damn vulgarity, mind. Something subtle, refined. If the thing was garish or cheap, I'd die of shame.'

'Felix,' I snapped, 'mind your own business.'

Just one long round of annoyance and petty persecution. What is troubling me just at the moment, however, is a paper-knife. I introduced it in an early scene to give Father Hennessy something to fiddle with on a parochial call. It is now in the hands of

80

McDaid. It has a dull steel blade, and there is evidently something going on. The book is seething with conspiracy and there have been at least two whispered consultations between all the characters, including two who have not yet been officially created. Posterity taking a hand in the destiny of its ancestors, if you know what I mean. It is too bad. The only objector, I understand, has been Captain Fowler, the drunken hedonist, who insists that there shall be no foul play until Chapter Twelve has been completed; and he has been over-ruled.

Candidly, reader, I fear my number's up.

I sit at my window thinking, remembering, dreaming. Soon I go to my room to write. A cool breeze has sprung up from the west, a clean wind that plays on men at work, on boys at play and on women who seek to police the corridors, live in Stephen's Green and feel the heat of buckshee turf...

It is a strange world, but beautiful. How hard it is, the hour of parting. I cannot call in the Guards, for we authors have our foolish pride. The destiny of Brother Barnabas is sealed, sealed for aye.

I must write!

These, dear reader, are my last words. Keep them and cherish them. Never again can you read my deathless prose, for my day that has been a good day is past.

Remember me and pray for me.

Adieu!

Although Brother Barnabas was no more, O'Nolan was to write again for *Comhthrom Féinne*. In the exchange that follows, he defends the 'Mob', that noisy and unruly collection of hecklers which clogged the door at meetings of the Literary and Historical Society. As acknowledged leader of the 'Mob' during much of his time in College, O'Nolan reasonably supported its right to disrupt the august proceedings of the L. & H., and in these articles he attacks the primness of the committee, and in particular of Mr James FitzPatrick, one of whose contributions to the debate is included here. In the later columns of *Cruiskeen Lawn*, Myles na Gopaleen was to become notorious for the degree of scorn and ridicule which he heaped upon his unfortunate victims. These reprinted pieces are perhaps the first hints of what he was capable in this mode.

81

What is wrong with the L. and H.?

From the remarks of my acquaintances and from the letter of Mr James FitzPatrick in your last issue, it seems that the L. and H. has fallen on evil days and that the barbarians at the door have finally triumphed after seventy years of effort.

I think I have heard that one before.

The illusion that one's generation has been singled out for all the trouble and tribulation that an evil destiny can devise is a familiar one. It is nurtured by self-pity, the least lovely of our indigenous vices. That is what is wrong with Mr FitzPatrick and other philosophers of the same school. They are torn by self-pity and the conviction that the hand of God is against them. That is why I am going to give them some good advice and tell them plainly what is wrong with the society. I recognise, of course, that my advice has not been asked for, but that is largely balanced by the fact that it will not be taken.

First, Mr FitzPatrick has no idea of what public-speaking means. He implies that 'speaking at the L. and H.' under proper and ideal conditions, consists in entering the House, rising when one's name is called and delivering an address that has been carefully prepared, provided with an Introduction and a Conclusion in the fashion of our schoolday essays, seasoned with wit and embellished with the hard-won gems of one's own personal wisdom.

But that is not public speaking.

That is what happened at the 'debates' of our schooldays when the proceedings were supervised by masters who thought nothing of punishing a frivolous point of order with four on each hand. That is what would happen at the L. and H. if the people who go there were all pretentious little morons armed with a typewritten speech in their hip-pocket like a bee with a sting.

Thank God, they are not.

I am willing to take Mr FitzPatrick's word for it that they are normal beings who insist on an audience's inalienable right to protest loudly when it is bored. It will be an evil day when that right is surrendered. The fact that it is still exercised is how I know that the L. and H. is far from finished, despite Mr Fitz-Patrick's talk of closing down. If the society is sick, it has not been sickened by the Mob. It has been sickened by Mr FitzPatrick.

Listen to what he says.

'From a continuous attendance at these unwholesome meetings I have come to the conclusion that until the pests who crowd the doorway and man the majority of the seats are exterminated . . . no sane person can hope to hear, or much less join in, the activities of this Society.'

He wants what he plainly calls the vast majority of his audience 'exterminated', because they won't listen to him, because they find him insufferably dull. In effect, his words are these:

'I have a speech here. It is very good. Unfortunately, it is above the heads of 90 per cent of you. It does not interest you. I am now going to deliver it in my best style for the benefit of the 10 per cent who can understand it and appreciate it. In the meantime, the rest of you can go and play marbles.'

That is bunkum. It is priggish bunkum.

It is needless to say that the 90 per cent of 'pests' who form the audience have no real taste for marbles. They prefer to shout and sing to pass the time. It is not polite but it is natural. They prefer to tell Mr FitzPatrick that they regard him as a pest.

And I find myself substantially in agreement.

Let me enlighten Mr FitzPatrick as to the first principle of public speaking. *It is to compel the attention of your audience.* Regard the 'sane' 10 per cent as superfluous pests. They will listen in any case. The 90 per cent is your audience. Do not address dock labourers on Canon Law, and if you must, speak to them in their own language. Silence them and compel their attention. Having compelled it, hold it. If you once flag, they will swamp you. But grip them at all costs, even at the expense of good speaking or 'parlour-language', to use Mr FitzPatrick's prim phrase.

How?

That is very simple. Subject the recalcitrant by the sheer force of your character and your personality. Speak with force and wit. If they will not listen, make a brilliant speech. If they still roar, make the most brilliant speech ever made before the Society.

83

When you are making it, you will hear a pin drop.

'That is all very well,' Mr FitzPatrick may say, 'but I am not very long in the College. It is not reasonable to expect me to do that.'

Very well. In that case you are not fit to raise your head as a fully-fledged speaker in the L. and H. at all. You cannot speak. If you expect 500 people who have come to be entertained to listen patiently to your halting maiden efforts, you are a conceited prig. Go away and learn your business. Go to the innumerable smaller societies in the college and speak there. Learn to be serious without being dull and acquire confidence in your powers. When you return, you may still be greeted with salvos of abuse, but they will not be so insistent. You will know that you are progressing.

If you are not humble enough to communicate your philosophy to the lowly intelligence of the Commerce Society, by all means remain in the L. and H. and do your learning there. You will be shouted down. But in God's name do not raise this ingenuous college-boy whine about 'pests fit for a place of honour in an anthropological museum', 'Hollywood vulgarity', 'raucous jests', 'hooligans', 'drunken maudlins'. The fault is in yourself. You are getting what you deserve. You are not good enough to silence an exacting house. You are a motorist failing on a hill and blaming the steepness of the hill rather than the feebleness of his own engine. (There is nothing so enlightening as these homely analogies.) The hill has been there for seventy years and will remain till an earthquake demolishes it. Even then it will probably become a sheer cliff, to be conquered with ropes and irons. Do not be disheartened. Thousands of engines have failed miserably. Thousands have overcome it.

Overcoming the hill is a pleasant experience.

The L. and H. has been the sternest test in public-speaking in Ireland. I know of nothing so strenuous either here or in any university in Britain. I hope it will long remain so. I hope the Mob will increase in numbers and in violence. They are the red blood of the society. Practically every speaker of moment has graduated from their ranks, necessarily so, because the successful speaker must know and understand his audience of plain people. It is the lack of a Mob that has made the Commerce Society an inferior body. Take away the Mob and the caucus of 'serious-minded'

84

self-important little morons that will remain will, to say the least, be thoroughly unrepresentative of the University they inhabit.

All that the present generation of outraged 'speakers' want in order to revive the society is GUTS. That is what they pitifully lack. In place of guts, they are content with defeat and ineptitude. In the course of one short visit to the society this year, the only people who appeared to me to speak with any degree of courage were two women. They got as much abuse as any man – more, perhaps, for the field of abuse where women are con-cerned is wider. They shouted back and were heard. Mr Fitz-Patrick writes letters to *Comhthrom Féinne*.

That, in short, is what is wrong with the L. and H.

It is cluttered up with people who are congenitally unfit for public speaking and worse again, with people who confuse speaking with high-school essay-writing and who expect to be swaying a vast audience three months after the rigours of Matriculation.

It is a weak and spineless generation. The normal people are still standing in the unhealthy draught of the doorway. They will preserve the Society by their destructive sanity and by refusing to accept spurious imitations until genuine speakers of substance and guts come along, as they inevitably must. They will continue to castigate pompous incompetents.

That is a consoling thought.

There are other weaknesses contributory to the present bad condition in which the Society finds itself. There can be no doubt of Mr Cooke's talent, of the closeness of his reasoning and the compelling force of his arguments when speaking. His Inaugural Address proved that. There can likewise be no denying that he has a feeble voice, that his capacity for repartee and for restricting disorder to its legitimate bounds is negligible. He is helpless. The recent ludicrous banning of the Society's meetings by the authorities proved that.

As an Auditor, Mr Cooke is incompetent. Primarily, his job is to keep order, to *compel* order, until the task has been delegated to a speaker. He cannot do so. Mr Cooke should resign. Mr Cooke should never have been elected.

He is surrounded by a Committee who are not distinguished

85

for their speaking. The House (90 per cent 'pests') does not respect them. They can do nothing to assist the weak Auditor in keeping order. The Committee should resign. They should never have been elected.

The present condition of the Society shows that the Auditor and Committee have betrayed their trust. It is not their fault. They have done their best but the task has been beyond them. Let us leave it at that.

For the future, Auditors must be elected purely on their ability to manage and to rule. The Inaugural Meeting of the tails and the taffetta georgettes does not matter. If the *competent* auditor is an ignoramus, there are plenty of brainy students who will be glad to write his augural address for a few guineas. The society should be glad to pay it. As a price for a year of good government, it is dirt-cheap.

A competent auditor will not be elected till the adolescent prejudices of the dumb (but franchised) women in the benches cease to be the big factor in the election. Their schoolgirl likes and dislikes have many times elected weaklings in the past. Shepherding them from lectures to the library and polishing their spectacles has been the price too often of the auditorial chair of the greatest society in the whole University. It will continue to be unless the 'pests' provide themselves with a vote. And there is little danger of that. They think too much of their shillings. It is too much to pay for a year's entertainment.

The only other remedy is drastic reform of the electoral laws. Candidates should be elected on their achievements as speakers. Successful speaking means a capacity for silencing disorder. That is the big qualification.

The outlook is not bright.

It can only be brightened by the abandonment of this attitude of outraged defeatism on the part of people like Mr FitzPatrick. I advise him to take new courage and try again. And my advice to the mob is this:

'Bring double your number along next night, and SHOUT LOUDER!'

86

The L. and H. controversy

Complete with Brother Barnabusque trumpet-cum-foghorn, Mr O'Nualláin has attempted a last stand over the shrinking corpse of the L. and H. The loud-mouthed praise with which he puffs up its body resembles the decomposing gases which all honest corpses engender when they come for the last time before human gaze.

As long as the L. and H. can totter on its ricketty legs Mr O'Nualláin will be there to bray about Red Blood and Guts and urge it on to speedier self-destruction. When it dies from a surfeit of itself he will also be the first to cry aloud for vengeance of those who did it.

When that time comes I hope the L. and H. will have spirit enough to shout 'Murderer'.

Another dose of Mr O'Nualláin's methods in the L. and H. indeed and we should be even now laying out the corpse. Posterity will probably recognise that a certain ambitious but suicidal agitator left this College only a year too soon for such a purpose – but three years sooner would have been safer for all.

Mr O'Nualláin quotes me as being among those who 'are torn by self-pity and the conviction that the hand of God is against them'. If he construed that out of any sentence in my previous letter then the English language has lost all meaning for him, or else he possesses that dazzling insight into the human mind that betokens a Sunday paper astrological froth-blower.

Alternatively he is just mouthing phrases in the style of a cross-roads orator, feeling certain that a sentence with the word 'God' in it will impress his hearers and convince them that Right is on his side. 'Right' indeed!

Right often goes with Might – but never with Might-have-beens. For Mr O'Nualláin 'might-have been' has loomed largely in his College life – larger than his bantam strutting will admit. The whole tone of his article shows this.

It is permeated with a latent sense of defeatism. The defeated and trapped animal seeks to destroy. Mr O'Nualláin has the same

87

inclination but he is clever enough not to let it take the very common form of destructive criticism. Instead it takes the form of destructive support. Mr O'Nualláin would willingly garrotte those who criticise the L. and H., whether their criticism is destructive or fair; but his counter measures take the form of advocating a thinly-disguised suicide.

Mr O'Nualláin, according to his letter, is for the 'GUTS'. Mr O'Nualláin, in fact, is passionately for the Heroes with 'GUTS'. There may be other people concerned in the L. and H., but if so they are incidental. The Mob around, as he picturesquely tells us, 'are the red blood of the society'. If that is so, then perhaps these people have sense who call the society so goddam anaemic. With its 'Red Blood' behaving in such an outrageous manner, it is no wonder that the rest of the society takes to its bed and disturbs the even tenure of the College with its death-rattle.

In defending the existence of 'Guts' in the L. and H. I suggest that Mr O'Nualláin has once again succumbed to a fatal temptation. A temptation which has made his name 'mud' more than once in the College already. Mr O'Nualláin would be well warned not to drown his venomous spite by misdirected eloquence.

Now and again he sets out to castigate the forces of authority usually by the method of perversely flattering the restless elements in the College. Each time he merits the punishment of an ill-mannered boy, who broadcasts the domestic secrets of his home in revenge for being put in the corner for misbehaviour. Mr O'Nualláin does *not* defend the 'rowdies' because he feels he has a mission. Neither does he defend them out of pity for a badly-used and much-to-be-pitied crowd. There is something more in his barbed Philippics.

It is the opinion of many that he takes the sensational view for sheer love of publicity. He is bitten by the 'Publicity Bug' – and badly bitten. This quaint American insect passes under the name of 'vanity' in rural districts; however, it seems more fitting to associate it with Mr O'Nualláin in its civilised form. On the whole his attempt to argue the situation in regard to the L. and H. is curiously lop-sided. Like an eccentric expert examining a building while standing on his head. (There is nothing so enlightening as these homely analogies, as he himself cunningly puts it.) He

88

distorts everything to suit his own point of view – the viewpoint of the mentality which no one but he ever catered for.

Such people do not go down to the doorway to join in the 'fun', but perched like horned toads up in the benches they squat and reap the benefit of the waspish advice they have sown.

No one can trust them – not even the people whose mental guardians they have constituted themselves.

Mr O'Nualláin cleverly shifts the onus of guilt from such people and their supporters on to the speakers. We wonder if it were the speakers who were recently guilty of interrupting the Chairman in his closing address – not merely interrupting him but maintaining a running commentary of offensive remarks to such a distinguished Professor of the College. To maintain that such a Chairman is incompetent to engage the attention of an audience may seem highly ridiculous, but is the logical outcome of Mr O'Nualláin's foolish attitude.

The L. and H. is not in danger from the exhibition of a *certain* amount of spirits on the part of some of its members – nor has it ever been; what is more dangerous to it is the championing of horseplay, vulgarity and disorder by sensation-mongers of the type just referred to.

I am no Cicero, as Mr O'Nualláin is, and when I said in my last article that 'every person, no matter how poor a speaker, should be allowed an opportunity to speak without a burden of unfair comment being hurled at him,' I meant exactly what that does say. If it conveys to Mr O'Nualláin that every intending speaker is 'insufferably dull', and delights in a prepared speech above the intelligence of the audience, so much for the perspicuity of Mr O'Nualláin.

The truth is that, according to Mr O'Nualláin's interpretation every fresh speaker in the L. and H. must pass through an intensive training campaign at first. During this period he has to acquire several layers of O'Nualláinic 'brass', leather lungs, and a foghorn voice. His intelligence must also presumably be blown out of his cranium by such vocal efforts.

Then and only then can the poor victim be allowed to stand up and speak in the same sacred auditorium as Mr O'Nualláin. The probability is that he will be shouted down in what Mr O'Nualláin might even describe as an impolite manner, by an audience

89

retaining romantic memories of a bumshackle Proletarian Society. The audience tolerates only the one speaker. And the Uncrowned King of the Lubbers and Ham-heads brooks no opposition.

Credit is due to Mr O'Nualláin, however, for his attempt to write a monograph on 'Successful Public-speaking'. If what he said were true, he should be a perfect speaker, if he practised what he spoke. But he doesn't, quite.

It is correct indeed to 'compel the attention of your audience'. But here we meet an actual difficulty. A speech which would be very interesting to an average layman is simply wasted on the University student. The latter happens to be a trifle peculiar at times. The kind of speech he wants tends to be lop-sided.

And the only way to compel their attention, it turns out, is to speak wittily or humorously, and above all amusingly and laughingly. Once this is doled out to them they clamour for more, and, like petticoated infants, shout and wave their arms if they get anything else. Anybody who specialises in this type of burlesque speaking simply makes it impossible for any other sensible person to be heard. The audience have the one-track mind and insist on the same fuel. Hence the deterioration of the L. and H.

Moreover, it would occur to me that babes-in-arms, school--children, University students and laymen have different ideas of a speech. If Mr O'Nualláin were to make himself a genius at compelling the attention of toothless infants by such gurglings and splutterings as generally find favour with that age, and then to try to inflict the same stuff on the L. and H. he would see the error of his ways. In doling out humorous extravaganza ad lib. he had spoiled the palate of the L. and H. for good speaking in every sense of the word.

The L. and H. is afflicted with 'O'Nualláinitis' and should be washed in literary Lux. Mr O'Nualláin is a menace. Mr O'Nualláin should be caged, or, better, locked up.

I hold no brief for Mr Cooke. But whatever my opinion of his ability is, at least I have judged it from frequent attendance at the L. and H. during the past year. Mr Nualláin, I feel sure in saying, is judging him unjustly from the state of the L. and H. recently – and from a distance.

90

The two paragraphs which seek to denounce Mr Cooke as a helpless, voiceless, ninny-headed incompetent should be framed and handed to Mr O'Nualláin as a perpetual reminder of the fact that he rarely knows what he is talking about.

Mr Cooke is one of the cleverest Auditors in the Chair in recent years. He can compel attention in assemblies where Mr O'Nualláin, once he opened his mouth, would be removed immediately to a padded cell.

The whole attack on Mr Cooke, in fact, is baseless. The fact that Mr O'Nuallián himself was never successful at an Auditorial election may account for the case with which he sets such a high standard for Auditors in general.

He advocates an Auditor who can control a crowd of University students, by sheer force of personality and by his 'ability to manage and to rule'. One of the first acts of such an Auditor, if he could be found outside the realms of Mr O'Nualláin's own imagination, would be to send the creatures at the door back to the holes whence they came.

He would not be a competent Auditor within Mr O'Nualláin's own meaning unless he did so.

Mr O'Nualláin has a reputation. Mr O'Nualláin can talk. Mr O'Nualláin defends this reputation. No one gives a hoot about either of them. We can see through his little game of chase-me-Charlie-I-have barley.

Mr O'Nualláin is not sane. Mr O'Nualláin, to put it succinctly, is perched Etylus-wise on the tapering end of a vertical pole.

We leave him there.

JAMES T. FITZPATRICK

Tidying the garden

It is a curious thing, Mr Editor, that having deliberately expressed my views on the L. and H. in the terse idiom of the Sunday newspapers and having sacrificed syntax and symmetry to clichés and clarity, I should be unappreciated and misunderstood by your correspondents. I must explain. Even the Apostles spent most of their lives explaining.

91

The first party I want to help is 'D.E.B.', much as I must deprecate this skunkish instinct for anonymity in conducting a controversy with public men. 'D.E.B.' is probably a fat school-girl with black pigtails and glasses and a heart of gold and that is why I want to help.

'D.E.B.' makes a number of misstatements. She charges me with calling Mr Cooke a poor or a bad speaker and dramatically produces a tray of medals to prove that I am wrong. Actually I praised Mr Cooke's speaking. The only unfavourable thing I said was that Mr Cooke is a hopeless auditor.

With this fact, uncontrovertibly established by the collapse of the Society, 'D.E.B.' does not agree. Listen to her reckless rhetoric: 'But for the fact that Mr Cooke is an extremely able Auditor, there would have been disorder and serious disorder this year. . .. The Society was not banned.' The wicked sophistry of that statement makes one wonder what our girls are coming to. (Sometimes I think that 'D.E.B.' is a small thin camogie player addicted to the vice of secret hockey.) Actually the Society encountered disorder so serious this year that it was banned by the authorities at the request of an outraged chairman. After the period of this ban had terminated, the auditor appears to have solemnly subjected the Society to a private interdict of his own. To express this intricate process 'D.E.B.' simply says that 'the Auditor was responsible for the suspension of the meetings of the society for several weeks.' That, of course, is quite possible. The two sentences may have started and run concurrently, Mr Cooke continuing to wield his own private scorpion-whip after the President had relented and left off. It is an abstruse specula-tion, however, and reluctant to become enmeshed in a morass of metaphysical complexity, I am reluctant to pursue it, especially when a loud belly-laugh is as good an answer as any.

In regard to my suggestion to have auditors chosen from their record as speakers as distinct from their social affiliations, I surely made no reference to medals or chairmen's marks. Humouring the whims and the fancies of visiting chairmen in order to extract a golden '10' would be a far more arduous occupation than baiting them, and would not in any case neces-sarily entail good speaking. Though hotly resentful of her pitiless reference to the paucity of my own medals, I leave it to 'D.E.B.'

92

to make my plan practicable by inventing an alternative system.

I know nothing of Mr Cooke's 'ability' or of the 'close attention' with which the Society hears him. I have personally never seen him in the chair and can, therefore, have no opinion in the matter. I can only repeat that he is a failure. He was elected Auditor and charged with preserving and advancing the Society. The Society collapsed. Therefore Mr Cooke is a failure. Anybody who quarrels with the conclusion of this cast-iron syllogism must first pick a hole in the premises. It will not be as easy as picking holes in the premises in which the society meets.

To Mr Gibney and 'L.F.D.' I have little to say. The latter, weakly yielding to yogistic symbolism or demonstrating the surrealistic inevitability of bad handwriting, calls me O'Ualláin twice running. Inwardly I recognise the justice of this word, for there is surely some hidden kinship with ullagone and ululation and other terms that connote noise.

Mr Gibney is almost certainly a member of the Clontarf Literary and Debating Society and brings to bear on the follies of the L. and H. a mind that is untwisted and unconfounded, that is as wholesome and as cleansing as the wind that plays along the Bull Wall. He stands, uncompromisingly for discussion in which opinions can be exchanged and the mind broadened, and, finally for discussing weighty matters in all seriousness. Mr Gibney stands for the things that matter and I am sure that his counsels shall prevail. He is a symbol of tomorrow's student – knowledgeable, serious, industrious. The strident pretence of the windbag and the humbug has had its day; it is washed out. Its day was too long. The world moves on. I feel we are unwittingly on the verge of some cataclysmic change in the texture of the student's soul. Gazing at morning at the gaudy infants in the prams of Cabra or standing at eve amid the decadent splendours of Whitehall, I feel that a breeze, a cleaner breeze, is springing in the east. It will grow and blow louder and eventually it will cover all Erin. It will be purging and chastening and the world will be the better for its coming.

There remains nothing to do now but to deal with the extravagant Mr FitzPatrick, who, not content with thrashing me so soundly, could not resist the crowning humiliation of putting me up the pole. Let me clamber painfully down the pole and face Mr

93

FitzPatrick, who, exhausted and trembling from the verbal dysentery of his gallant defence of the homes and the altars of the morons, stands gazing at my undignified predicament.

Mr FitzPatrick is scarcely logical. Under the title of 'The L. and H. Controversy', he writes a monogram on myself, mentions my name 38 times – often enough to make my best friend sick of it – and then bitterly accuses me of being in search of publicity. Look at all the names he calls me – murderer, 'might-have-been', bantam-strutter, the name 'mud' more than once, venomously spiteful, horned toad – and he does not hesitate to madden me with an obscure taunt about 'barley'. This tiresome tirade would have led myself and other readers to the conclusion that Mr FitzPatrick had himself the same lack of tolerance and charity which he deprecates so strongly in the mob were it not that he finally charges me with insanity, a happy device which lets me out as an irresponsible eccentric and reveals Mr FitzPatrick's heart of gold – the existence of which nobody seriously doubted. Nevertheless, 'Mr O'Nualláin is not sane' is a chilling sentence, like 'The King is Mad' in *Lear*, an analogy that is strengthened by 'L.F.D.'s' declaration that I am monarch of the mob. Is it possible that Mr FitzPatrick too, a gloomy Hamlet, is going slowly mad from the undeliverable pregnancy of a typewritten speech in his hip-pocket? If Mr FitzPatrick will agree to run against his sword I will undertake to abdicate and divide my realms with my three daughters. It is about time Cordelia got a new deal, anyway.

Despite the fact that he alleges he is no Cicero, Mr FitzPatrick writes weighty paragraphs which do not tally, which, in fact, are directly contradictory. It is, of course, due to sheer carelessness, but it does not look well and is apt to give ignorant persons the impression that Mr FitzPatrick is a fool. Here is an example:

> 'The L. and H. is afflicted with "O'Nuallainitis" and should be washed in literary Lux. Mr O'Nuallain is a menace. Mr O'Nuallain should be caged, or, better, locked up.'
> 'Mr O'Nuallain has a reputation. Mr O'Nuallain can talk. Mr O'Nuallain defends this reputation. No one gives a hoot about either of them. We can see through his little game of chase-me-Charley-I-have-barley.'

I cannot argue with Mr FitzPatrick since he talks exclusively about myself. Interesting as the subject is, I cannot enter into a public controversy with anybody on it. It is too dangerous. Another printed category of my failings such as that of Mr FitzPatrick and even my fiancée – secured after a month of effort in the *Evening Mail* – will reject my frenzied disclaimers. Even Mr FitzPatrick, I am sure, wishes me a gentler fate than that.

Finally, unless Mr FitzPatrick, 'D.E.B.', 'L.F.D.' and Mr Gibney are so caddish as to endeavour to wreck a romance, let me warn them, should they write again, that I am miraculously impervious to sneers. Even Mr FitzPatrick's 'might-have-been', which is a nice compact sneer, leaves me cold. I can wave my kingly vestments in the air and shriek that at least I have never collapsed the Society through incompetence as a doctor collapses a bad lung. Better still, I can chant 'Better to have loved and lost than never to have loved at all', 'To journey hopefully is better than to arrive', 'I done me level best', 'Whom the Gods love they first make mad', 'We can but try', each of which is as good a schoolboy jingle any day as Mr FitzPatrick's 'Chase me Charley I have barley'. And when Mr Fitzpatrick grows up, he will find that 'might-have-been' figures too largely in his own little life, as in everybody else's, to be safely employed as a weapon against others.

In conclusion, let me say that, academically, I have been dead for two years. When a man matriculates, he is born. When he graduates and goes away, he dies. *De mortuis nil nisi bonum.* All I have ever asked of the world, Mr Fitz, is a beautiful death. 'L.F.D.' put two u's in O Nualláin where there should be only one. You put one in Barnabas where there should be none. You have shown thereby ignorance extending from Bernard Shaw to the Scriptures in addition to your capacity for uncouth abuse.

Get up on that pole.

95

2

The Romance of *Blather*

'Words are divils altogether.'
'Tongues and Faces',
Irish Red Cross Annual, 1951

In May 1934 Brother Barnabas died. Four months later The O'Blather was born. The second of O'Nolan's *personae*, he was the powerful and learned presence behind *Blather*, a monthly magazine. It went on sale in August of that year, and was to last only until the next January, five issues in total. O'Nolan produced almost everything in it. In her book *Flann O'Brien: A Critical Introduction to his Writings* (Dublin, 1975), Anne Clissman refers to *Blather* as an 'anti-magazine'. This would certainly be how O'Nolan saw it.

Nothing within *Blather*'s pages can be taken at face value. The letters to the editor are all blatant inventions, the competitions offer ludicrous prizes or none, and the editorials are pre-Mylesian flights of fancy. Throughout there is the characteristic O'Nolan double standard: just as in *Cruiskeen Lawn*, *Blather* emphasises its own vast importance at the same time as it announces that it is just a poor amateur affair, not worth the paper it besmirches. The first editorial reads:

Blather

THE ONLY PAPER EXCLUSIVELY
DEVOTED TO THE INTERESTS OF
CLAY-PIGEON SHOOTING IN
IRELAND

Blather is here.

As we advance to make our bow, you will look in vain for signs of servility or for any evidence of a slavish desire to please. We are an arrogant and a depraved body of men. We are as proud as bantams and as vain as peacocks. *Blather* **doesn't care**. A sardonic laugh escapes us as we bow, cruel and cynical hounds that we are. It is a terrible laugh, the laugh of lost men. Do you get the smell of porter?

Blather is not to be confused with Ireland's National Newspaper, still less with Ireland's Greatest Newspaper. *Blather* is not an organ of Independent Opinion, nor is Ireland more to us than Republic, Kingdom or Commonwealth. *Blather* is a publication of the Gutter, the King Rat of the Irish Press, the paper that will achieve entirely new levels in everything that is contemptible, despicable and unspeakable in contemporary journalism. *Blather* has no principles, no honour, no shame. Our objects are the fostering of graft and corruption in public life, the furtherance of cant and hypocrisy, the encouragement of humbug and hysteria, the glorification of greed and gombeenism.

Blather doesn't care.

In regard to politics, all our rat-like cunning will be directed towards making Ireland fit for the depraved readers of *Blather* to live in. In the meantime, anything that distortion, misrepresentation and long-distance lying can do to injure and wreck the existing political parties, one and all, *Blather* will do it. Much in the way of corruption has already been done. We have de Valera and the entire Fianna Fail Cabinet in our pocket; we have O'Duffy in a sack. Michael Hayes lies, figuratively speaking, bound and gagged in our hen-house. Colonel Broy has lent us a Guard to post our letters.

Every nerve will be strained towards the achievement of the *Blather* Revolution and the establishment of the *Blather* Dictatorship, followed by the inauguration of the *Blather* Communist Monarchy. Gunplay will be rife, the Motherland will be soaked in a bath of blood, Chinese Tong Wars will stalk the land. But we will win the day and the brutal military heel of *Blather* will crush the neck of its enemies. Write to us for the address of your nearest *Blather* Study Circle. Write to us for a free cut-out pattern of the *Blather* Patent Woollen Panties and say good-bye to colds. Write to us for our pamphlet, 'The *Blather* Attitude on Ping-Pong.'

We have probably said enough, (perhaps too much).

Anyhow, you have got a rough idea of the desperate class of man you are up against. Maybe you don't like us? ...
A lot we care for what you think.

The only other considerable comic paper in Ireland in the thirties was *Dublin Opinion*, modelled on *Punch*, and *Blather* may be seen as a counterblast to the prevailing modes of humour of the time. Indeed, O'Nolan's paper reviews *Dublin Opinion* thus:

Book reviews

Dublin Opinion, Price 3d. Published at 67, Mid. Abbey St., Dublin.

We have received a copy of this publication – presumably for review. Whilst the times are not altogether propitious for the founding of new journals, the courage of the proprietors is to be commended, and we gladly extend a céad míle fáilte to this gallant little newcomer.

It bluntly announces itself as 'Ireland's National Humorous Journal', which gives a clue to the contents of the paper.

It contains jokes. For instance:

> 1st Farmer: 'Last week a cattle exporter made 20% profit by sending cattle to England.'
> 2nd Farmer: 'Where?'
> 1st Farmer: 'On the Arithmetic Paper in the Cattle Supervisors Examination.'

You see?

Altogether the best and funniest matter is to be found under the heading of 'Plays and Films'. We will quote and we will pay an enormous sum to charity if it can be proved that we are not quoting truthfully and accurately.

> 'MacLiammóir is in a class by himself. He speaks them (lines) better than we ever dreamed to hear them spoken, with that extraordinary voice of his, with tones in it that are like black and cream velvet.'

'Of course, MacLiammóir was gorgeous. . ..'

'It is just that MacLiammóir, by some gorgeous freak, has the best voice in the wide world for saying things like those.'

Isn't that *gorgeous*?

Proving, in other words, that beneath the motley of the jester lies a true appreciation of the arts. The rapier-thrusts of the cold steel of criticism.

We like this article so well that we are going to quote belly laughs from it every month. So keep it up, boys.

But perhaps it is best to let *Blather* speak for itself. It is not short of things to say.

The romance of Blather

THE INSIDE STORY OF A GREAT
NEWSPAPER

There is no truth in the rumour that the art of printing was invented by the *Irish Independent* or by the *Irish Grocer* for that matter. We don't say we have invented it ourselves, but at least we have perfected it. The *Blather* printing-halls are the last word in up-to-date technical equipment, as we show in these soul-stirring glimpses below. Our wonderful machines, as a matter of fact, afford a clue as to the insane jealousy with which we are regarded by the *Irish Grocer*. Let us take you by the hand and show you the works. Do not speak to the men, as they are forbidden to give you the answer you deserve.

99

The arrival of the Editor at the office. He is fond of servility and employs a lackey to grovel at his feet and dust the skirts of his coat. Inside, our racing experts are picking the day's winner with divining-pins. The rod on the floor is not a rod, but a goad, and is used by the Editor.

Linotype Operators at work in the great Linotype Hall. These machines are so ingenious that they are almost human, can almost speak, etc. On the floor in the foreground is a bucket of plain porter.

Making up the forms on the stone. (Hell! Aren't we devils for jargon, we hard-boiled men of the great printing world?). Note the wireless inlead.

The great foundry. Casting the type, if you know what we mean. Our poor workers have rotten teeth, but we generously supplied them with bandages free. The health of our workers, you see, is one of our greatest cares.

The giant rolls of paper being rolled on giant rollers. Our worker here has evidently drunk his wages and has been afraid to go home for the last two nights. His wife, you will notice, is coming round the corner.

The last process. Running the paper through the giant Hoe Rotary Press. This ingenious machine folds and counts the copies; can almost speak, etc. We have no less than 20 of them. In our spare time we use them for mangling our sheets.

After the day's weary work, a little play. Blather *was the first paper in the world to establish a scheme of social welfare for its workers. In this picture you see two foundry-men enjoying a quiet game of billiards in the club-room. They evidently intend to have a long game, for they have brought their tea with them.*

Threepence for twenty pages!!

'The dirty, dirty robbers. Threepence for twenty pages.'

In the yellow way that is your own, you are afraid to say it to our face. But we know you. You keep whispering it to your friends and you keep thinking of it in your black heart. Some things, as Mr Lemass has said in the Dail, can only be answered with a blow in the teeth.

In this particular case, however, you are perfectly right. Robbery is no word for our last issue. Last month *Blather* presented a staggering example of bad value. *Blather* was the only journal in Ireland to present twenty pages of depraved twaddle to the great white public in exchange for a good-looking threepence. First again. We lead, others follow. The issue undoubtedly marked an epoch in Irish journalism, and we are having the epoch tastefully packed in yellow tissue-paper for

103

conveyance to the National Museum, where it will be given an honoured place among the thousand of other epochs manufactured by Independent Newspapers now resting there.

The threepence which you so foolishly threw away on our great paper last month could have bought you five normal cigarettes, or five subnormal cigarettes, together with a penny button hooker for fastening the buttons on your boots. It would have brought you nearly to Palmerston and back again on a tram, though goodness knows the place is a stern test of manhood and no place for a sane *Blather* reader; better to go down to the Custom House and throw your money into the middle of the Liffey there before you spend it on a trip to that place. If you still insist on going somewhere with your threepence, you can spend it on a bus-ride to Booterstown or to Clontarf, though the walk home from these grand spots will kill you, you weak-arched mollycoddle. You were never made for walking. You can view the roof-tops of Dublin from the top of the Nelson Pillar for sixpence, and if you had mentioned *Blather* and courteously explained your position to the man, he might have let you half-way up the stairs for threepence. You could then potter around in the dark and maybe sit for a while on the cold stone steps. If you met any one coming down from the top, you could first frighten the life out of them by making a dreadful noise, and then closely question them on Dublin's sky-line.

And that is not all. You could send a few spoonfuls of whiskey in a little bottle by letter post to Belfast for threepence – you do be up to queer things – and probably get a smart jail-sentence for sending dutiable goods by letter post. You could send the threepence to a bookie in Glasgow for the Manchester November Handicap and get another six months for sending money illegally to bookies abroad, the two sentences to run concurrently. If you behaved yourself in jail and got full marks for good conduct, you would be out in four months, and then you could take the night boat to Glasgow and collect your winnings the following day – plus six months simple interest at 5 per cent – and then start the New Life, a Clean and a Better Man, in Uganda or Rhodesia or maybe Sierra Leone. You could then write us stern letters from the bush, the strong and earthy utterances of the Empire-builder.

104

Friday night at the Blather Offices. 'Though Birnam Wood be come to Dunsinane,'
as the O'Blather sternly remarked at the memorable Hastings Chess Congress,
'the office-boys must have their bath.' THERE IS NO BATH IN THE Blather OFFICES. And
at three o'clock on every Friday morning, at a time when Mother Sleep is draping
her queenly mantle o'er the town of Anna Liffey and when Lombard murmurs in his
sleep that his machines can rot, the great work of transporting our sleeping office-
boys to the Tara Street Baths is begun. No noise, no fuss. They are lowered into
the medieval underground tunnel tunnelled underground in medieval times to
connect our offices with the James's Gate Brewery. After a long detour embracing
Inchicore and Old Bawn – which was still new, by the way, when the tunnel was first
constructed – the baths are reached and the boys are carefully dipped and
brought home again before they catch cold. The Editor supervises the operations
personally and is waiting for his sweet charges in the picture with outstretched
hands. In case you don't notice the hands, our artist has thoughtfully inserted a
number of arrows pointing to them; the arrows are not an unmixed blessing, how-
ever, as the man on the right has evidently hurt his head on them last week and has
decided to wear his ancestral armour in future. The man on the left, having no ar-
mour of his own and being in the same danger, does not like it. 'You big sissy!' he is
saying, 'You big soft mollycoddle!' But who cares, so long as the boys are washed?

105

If you had kept your threepence and gone for your annual whoopee to the seaside, you could have got your photograph taken for it while you wait; and you would now have in your possession a nice tin-plate portrait of yourself, complete with bovine smile and ninepenny tie. And you would probably send it to the Little One whom you one day hope To Make Your Own and she would probably write you a sweet note and tell you it was lovely, as you are still good for a seat at the pictures when a little girl has nothing worse to do. We pity you, you and your three-pence.

Better resign yourself to the fact that you have spent your threepence. In exchange for it, you got two or three hours solid reading, which is good enough for you.

If you cannot read, of course, your threepence represents hours and hours of healthy speculation. Let us hope it was clean.

Whither Bettystown?
Progress or decay?
Our stern attitude

The present agitation for proper Atlantic ports at Galway, Killybegs and elsewhere, has in no small measure displeased *Blather*. Why? The reason is very simple. The pre-eminent claims of Bettystown have been passed over, and it is the sheerest folly on the part of those concerned to imagine that *Blather* is going to stand for it.

Ever since the good people of Bettystown bade The O'Blather a hearty *céad míle fáilte* when he went there to recuperate after his illness in 1924, *Blather* has had its eye on Bettystown. Only for five minutes was the *Blather* eye taken off Bettystown in those ten long years, and that was for two minutes in 1932, when the eye was moved up eight miles to watch the first train crossing the reconstructed viaduct over the Boyne at Drogheda. Nothing happened; the structure held, and the eye was immediately refixed on Bettystown.

'Take it from me,' said The O'Blather when taking his farewell in 1925, after the fires of life had been successfully rekindled in his poor body, 'I shall look on every man from Bettystown as my own son. I shall build and adorn Bettystown until it becomes the fairest and the brightest gem in the diadem of Eire. I shall go further. I shall see the manager of the Munster and Leinster Bank this afternoon and I shall arrange that Betty, the noble foundress of these historic streets – (Cheers) – shall be provided with a modest competence, such as will ensure that want shall not hurt nor hunger sting the soft twilight of her years.'

Noble, noble words. Today *Blather* stands four-square with Bettystown in the gallant fight the little town is making against the mogols of the Local Government Department in their ill-conditioned attempts to shoulder it out of its rightful place in the sun. Nor are the claims of the town in anywise extravagant. Ten years ago their demands were modest; 'Parity with Jerrettspass!' was the simple rallying-cry of the good townspeople. It was only after a hard and bitter fight that this was conceded, and much of the credit for victory must go to The O'Blather. Today Bettystown, marching with the times and eager to seize the opportunities opened up by the progress of modern life, asks in a voice that is dispassionate, free alike from the thick bluff of the bully and the fawning pleading of the cringer, that it be provided an Atlantic deep-water harbour.

The construction of this harbour was at all times desirable. With the advent of war-rumours in the Far East, however, it becomes an imperative necessity, notwithstanding anything the greybeards of Skerries or Laytown may croak to the contrary. It follows that a betrayal of Bettystown by the present Administration would make the establishment of the *Blather* Dictatorship a contingency in our national life which could not in reason be further postponed.

Rumours and canards have been circulated by the vested interests to the effect that the natural amenities of Bettystown do not admit of the passage of vessels of deeper draught than that of yawls, skiffs, smacks and Far Eastern river-junks. Nothing, of course, could be further from the truth.

When these reckless statements came to the ears of The

107

O'Blather, he wirelessed the Cunard liner, *Pythia*, then on her way from New York to Cobh. She immediately altered her course, and after battling with tempestuous and mountainous seas for forty-one hours, she appeared five points off Lambay Island, and in half-an-hour had put into Bettystown Harbour, thanks to the good offices of pilot-officer Hanrahan, who went out to meet the liner in mid-Atlantic. (What or who she put in has not been stated.) The O'Blather, who had been troubled with his Old Wound, was not present to welcome the Captain ashore, nor was he represented; he courteously sent a letter-card, however, apologising for his absence.

'The worst passage in forty years,' said Captain Cummins, when interviewed by our reporter, 'and too much praise cannot be given to the cool and plucky conduct of the crew and passengers.' He went on to say that Bettystown offered the finest natural salt-water harbour in the world. 'When I get back,' he added, 'I am going to see my Board and endeavour to persuade them to put Bettystown on our regular calling-list.' The Cox of the *Pythia* was loud in his praise of the town and especially of the townspeople. 'Those who know me,' he said tersely, 'will tell you that Cox Craddock never bunked the public in his life. And when I say, I like your people, I mean it!' The Stroke of the *Pythia* was also very favourable in his comments and promised to use his influence with the Board in backing up the Captain's appeal.

It is a mistake to imagine, however, that the matter is being allowed to rest there. Four tugs are being rushed across from Liverpool in a last desperate endeavour to get the *Pythia* out of Bettystown before the Board learns what the Captain has done. In the meantime, engineers have been engaged in deep-sea blasting operations in an attempt to destroy the famous Bettystown Death Reefs, while two Saorstat Dredgers are engaged in removing everything movable from the ocean bed. *HMS Dauntless* is standing by eighteen points west of Lambay to protect British settlers and their property in the event of a native rising, and an eighteen-inch gun has been mounted on the bows of the fishing-smack *Maureen*. Messrs The O'Blather and Sean Lemass are keeping in close touch with the situation.

The last definite piece of information to come through to the *Blather* Offices was to the effect that four thousand sacks of flour had been dumped into the sea from the *Pythia* in an endeavour to make the vessel ride higher. The great natural deep-water harbour is a solid mass of pie-crust or pastry, and slabs of it are being retailed by the local bakers at very keen prices. In the meanwhile, the more active elements in the township are engaged in roller-skating on the firmer parts, the good, dry weather presaging a lengthy continuation of this popular sport. *HMS Dauntless*

This, as far as we can remember, is the Shan Van Vocht; we keep her in the office all day to give the place a homely atmosphere and to ensure that the boys won't ruin the carpet with their cigarette-ash. These Damn Scallions, she is saying to herself. What Made Me Eat Them? Do you want advice on Life from a Mature Person? Write to her about your troubles, if you must whine to somebody else about them.

has moved four points further west, as the solid diet of apple-pie supplied to the Commander and Jolly Tars every day on the way from India has made the smell of pastry something very repulsive to them indeed.

It is gratifying to learn that on several *Blather*-Readers courteously making representations to the Captain to the effect that the pastry was just a *leetle* tart, he graciously ordered a thousand sacks of best-quality sugar to be dumped overboard also. This had the desired result and caused a slight appreciation in the price of the pastry retailed in Dublin.

This interesting *contretemps* has had the effect of focussing world attention on the possibilities of Bettystown as the site of a deep-water Atlantic harbour.

For further news, see the next addition of our great paper.

Answers to correspondents

Day after day, more and more people are writing to *Blather*. If the saliva involved in licking each stamp were represented by an inch of coarse twine, the entire length of it would stretch twice around the globe.

Vulgarity aside, though, why don't you write to us? Write and let us know what you think of our great paper. Anything short of fulsome praise will be ignored, of course, and anything in the nature of what is called constructive criticism will cause us to fly into one of those tantrums that make *Blather* a bye-word in Dame Street. Surely you have sorrows, troubles, cares? Why not share them with us, or try to share them, anyway? Let us be your father.

'I am so worried (writes Minnie, Stoneybatter South) when John brings business friends home to dinner without giving me warning. I am expected to put up a Dinner fit for Business Friends and City Colleagues, God help me. Is this British?'

No, Minnie (Stoneybatter South), this is not British. John is

110

behaving like a cad and if you could persuade him to call at the *Blather* Offices, law or no law, we would give him five minutes in our back room. So stern, in fact, is the attitude of *Blather* on this question that we might give him ten minutes. And what is more, City Colleagues our granny. Touchers, public-house cronies and porter-sharks, that's what they are. You think we don't know them? You must think we are very simple, so you must. If this dinner business starts again, threaten to create a vulgar scene, or better still, threaten to see the Editor of *Blather* personally. In the meantime stop wasting water. We have had our eye on you long before you wrote to us.

'I entered for a Civil Service appointment two years ago and the result of the examination has not yet been announced. In the meanwhile, I have refused four lucrative appointments in the Honolulu River Police. I have in the interim developed pimples, which I attribute to the waiting and anxiety. My friends all say it is too much of a good thing. Frankly, all jokes and racial prejudice aside, do you think it cricket?' (Constant Reader)

You must have patience. You are young yet and you have your life before you. (Or are you one of these *ould* candidates?) You seem to be unaware of the fact that *Blather* has been working hand in glove with the Civil Service Commission for the past year. The Commissioners and all their little Writing Assistants have been spending most of their time thinking out little jokes for *Blather* – pretty feeble efforts too, if the truth were told. And it's only the other day that *we*, in our sleepy degenerate way, were poking through a heap of forms and dockets and applications and things; we may have seen your name, C.R., and again, we may not. Wild horses would not drag the truth from us and we have backed a few of them in our day. However, since you are a reader of *Blather*, we will have another poke round in a day or two and if we think you deserve a job, well and good, we will let you have one. Fair? But those pimples in the interim. Maybe you imagine that the *Blather*-Civil Service Medical Examination is a mere formality, a farce, an empty formula, a man of straw? Maybe you were never told that pimples mean a poisoned and corrupt bloodstream. Maybe you think your pigeon-chest won't be noticed. Maybe you think your piano-legs will be taken for advanced muscular development. We are afraid, C.R., that you

111

must be a right cur. And another thing before we forget it. Canvassing in any form, oral or written, direct or indirect, will automatically disqualify the candidate for the position which he (or she) is seeking. Laugh that one off, Mister Constant Reader. Mister Spotty!

'I have been walking out with a girl for the past seven years and more. We have grown to be very fond of each other and we see a lot of each other. However, she has never said anything about marriage. Do you think her intentions are honourable or is she trying to compromise me? I am a Wexford man, thanks be to God.' (Joseph)

We must be very careful not to be unfair to the girl, Joseph. Possibly her job is not as good as it might be, possibly she has found it hard to save, possibly she feels it hard to ask you to enter a love-nest, which, however good, must fall short of those standards which you as a *Blather*-reader must, however regretfully, insist upon. However, your first duty is to yourself. Go to her and tell her bluntly – it is the kindest way in the end – that she must make up her mind. Tell her that unless she can see her way to take the step, she must in common fairness release you. If you think it will help, you may mention *Blather*. That, we think, is the wisest course. But just one point, Joseph. Are you absolutely certain that you have not already been married to her? Only those who are privileged to peep into the *Blather* mail-bag can have any idea of the amount of suffering caused in the world by the delusions of married men. Goodness knows, it is terrible.

'I am in the very devil of a hole,' writes Major T. 'I spent my life soldiering in the East and was regarded by my fellow-officers as a pretty good pucka sahib. Damme, I enjoyed the life and I cannot settle down here after it. What am I to do? My malariar makes me homesick for Indiar. After the veldt, Rathmines is the very devil.'

If you could only go through our letters with us every morning, dear Major, you would realise that there are thousands of your brother-officers going through the same hell. Thousands of sheets of notepaper relate the same sad story. Men made into inexorable machines of war and then asked to end their days amid the effeminate inanities of civil life. Our invariable advice to these poor wrecks is this. Hire out three or four Hindus, get them into your garden every morning before tiffin, grip your old

112

service lathi and bate them from one end of the garden to the other. No quarter given or asked for. Give them merry hell, and, take it from us, it will make a new man of you. Inside a week you will begin to feel the pressure of the White Man's Burden. When showing visitors over your house you can waggishly call the coal-house the Black Hole of Calcutta. Every little helps. And a final word in your ear, Major, about these Hindus. They are over-running the country at the moment. Selling scarves, muryaa. Selling grandmothers. They are the paid spies of enemy Powers, and they are probably out every night building concrete gun-implacements. Take it from *Blather*, they are up to a little bit of no good. Not one of them in ten is a registered reader of our paper.

Answears to correspondents ...

Ah, the black dark staring pity of it. The harsh hard heart-breaking pity of it. The cruciating cruel criminal contrariness of it all ...

We refer to the Slices of Life that reach us every day from our readers. They come by every post. Farmers write us harrowing tales about sheriffs seizing the last harrow. Starvation. Gruelling epics of gruel for breakfast, dinner and tea.

Ah, the black dark staring starving stony pity of it.

This month's prize of half-a-guinea is awarded to Breadcart Barney for the most poignant and soul-searing letter received.

Those extra inches

'I am seven feet two inches tall' writes Major Tawlboy, of the 5th Batt. Royal Second Punjab Rifles, 'and my life in consequence is one long misery after another. When I go out for a walk, small boys keep pestering me to look over high walls and tell them what's on the other side. When I go to a football match all the small men congregate round me and keep pulling my coat-tails and asking me questions. Apart from the annoyance, I am compelled to go to such functions dressed as a tramp in order to save my good clothes. In the name of Harry, is there no way of reducing my stature?'

Try the following prescription. Recite this daily three times before meals: 'I am a dirty skunk, a rotter, a cad, a parasite and a low scrounging corner-boy of uncouth habits and loutish appearance. I don't deserve to live another minute, and I quite fail to understand why I have been let live so long.'

If this fails to make you feel small, you will have to try removing your superfluous stature with a coarse hacksaw.

No frivolity for us

'Is it true that Memory is the Only Friend that Grief can Call Its Own?' Interested, Mullaghmast.

Can you not see, Interested, that if we answer a fool question like this, thousands and thousands of people would immediately deluge us with similar enquiries. Of course we could burn their letters, but what would we do with all the envelopes? Ah-ha, there you go in your careless degenerate way and never think of these things, you frivolous little moth, you.

Life is so cursedly crude

'I am a wireless announcer,' writes Bertie, Belturbet, 'and every night before going on duty, I manage to drink thirty bottles of stout and fifteen large whiskeys with a horsey friend of mine. When I appear before the microphone the most unaccountable things happen. The ceiling of the studio comes down and hits me great whacking belts on the head. Listeners have written in complaining that my announcements are thickly worded and incoherent. They accuse me further of bursting into song in the middle of the weather reports. Is it possible, by heck, that I am going mad?'

Quite possible, by heck. That, however, does not in any way relieve the landlord of the studio of his obligation to keep the roof in good order and repair. Prosecute. Again, as regards these complaints from listeners. The spread of radio, we regret to exclusively announce, has encouraged the horrible vice of solitary drinking. A man gets in a case, or maybe a pony of porter, and

114

settles down with his set for a good night's enjoyment. What the country is coming to, of course, is another question.

The case of Breadcart Barney

'I am so unhappy' he writes, 'For the last six years I have been employed as a van-man by a prominent City Bakery. I leave the bakery every morning with a full cart and I return again every night. Last year I fell from the cart and hurt my head. Up till then, I had no fault to find with my employers. One day after I had been discharged from hospital and had taken up my rounds again, I got a brilliant idea when passing a small stream at Tallagh. I dumped all the bread into it. I found this made the cart much lighter, and easier to draw. Every day I dump my bread into the stream and then I go up to Glen Cullen to pick daisies. When I've picked all I can there, I usually make for Lucan. I pick more there. Some days, by way of a change, I like to go out to the Pine Forest. When I get there, I run round the trees and bark at myself until I'm dizzy. It's great fun. Then I go home. I like my job, I must say, and try to do my best, but somehow I feel that my employers are not satisfied. Nothing definite, of course, has been said, but I have noticed an air of tension and gloom on the part of my superiors when I am around.'

We are very interested – go on

'One morning, for instance, the foreman forgot to wash his face. He came into the yard where I was washing down my horse and gave me a black look. Naturally, I was furious. But that is not all. One day the Boss called me into his private office, locked the door and then offered me a cigarette. I was horrified. I simply cannot understand what is wrong. Every morning I leave the bakery with a full cart. Every night I return with it empty. WHAT MORE DO THEY WANT? Please advise me in my terrible problem. (Could it be because my maiden name is Tobias?)'

On sober reflection, Barney, we don't think your maiden name has anything to do with it. You have only one honest course of action. Be a man. Tackle your employer. Tell him all about your hobbies. Tell him all about the tough time your sister Gertie, that married that brute from Drumcondra, is having. If this doesn't soften his heart, nothing will. In the meantime we will try to get a

115

question raised in the Dail. And by the way, stop dumping bread into that stream at Tallagh. You'd never know. Possibly the owner has complained about the pollution of his fishing rights. Try dumping it in our backyard instead. We won't complain.

BALM FOR BATTERED HEARTS

The hussy!
'Some time ago I was introduced to a boy and we have grown to love each other dearly. I have been keeping company with him for six months.' (Blue Eyes, Stradbally)

That's quite enough, you shameless little hussy, you. What is your mother thinking about, we wonder?

Same old story
'I am in love with a very beautiful girl. I visit her in her home on Tuesdays and Fridays. Every time I go into the house, however, there's another man there before me, a very ill-favoured mutt with rat-coloured hair. This man is apparently my rival. The eternal triangle again, I feel. Nevertheless, she still welcomes me warmly into the drawing-room when I call. Is there a way out?' (Love-bird, Inchicore)

There is indeed, Love-bird, Inchicore. The door. They usually keep the windows barred in these places.

Our growing pains

She was only a farmer's daughter
It is a very pretty sight to see a wench
Feeding ducks and hench.

Gad! The brutality of nature!
Sea-weeds and anemones
Are deadly emones.

116

This economic war
In the wake of the tariffs
You'll always find shariffs,
And you'll be put in gaol if
You can't pay the baolif.

Would you blame them?
The pilfering that they call
The Servants' Hall
Is when waiters taste thc cntree
In the pentree.

Foreigners are different
People are rarely in a coma
In Roma,
They drink themselves under the tables
In Nables;
But in gay Paris
They are merely maris.

You might have thought it!
The best paper in Ireland is *Blather*
And no *Ather.*

Strange but true
The extraordinary thing about cows is
That they never wear trowsis.

Naked, pink, and one year old
He who figures in the family album –
God halbum!

Isn't it a pity?
When we are buying a crocus
The florists socus.

Warning to sots
You'll eventually become dumb
If you drink enough rumb.

117

Live, laugh and love
When one hears a spinet-like piano
One remembers Viano.

You look it too
If you are too fond of the sofa
You are only a lofa.

Blast convention again!
It is not a sin to sing psalms
In ptralms.

We wouldn't say it unless we knew
Of gay women the gayest
Is May Wayest.

Have you ever noticed it?
There's this about a jig,
That it's very quig.

One can't be too careful
If anybody asks you to take absinthe
Say no, I shinthe.

Where are your manners?
Never say 'The deuce!'
Such language is very leuce.

Brighten our little lives
If you want to make us laugh
Send us your photograph.

Our handy hint
If you have the misfortune to spill water
You can soak it up with the blater.

Our cottage industries
They make coffins in Swords
Out of white bwords.

Life is so crude
It is very hard to keep accounts in Sallins,
They never ballins.

The effects of sun-bathing
Michael got sun-burnt in Enniscorthy –
It only made Dennis sworthy.

Our wretched rimes

Merit will out
Whereas the good *Blather*
Gets bather and bather,
The bad *Irish Grocer*
Gets wocer and wocer.

Not in public anyway
Don't give your Mrs
Krs.

The importance of manners
A gentleman would send for a Dr
For his wife if he sr.

Do you hate your name?
People with a nice name like Chas.
At least rime with George As;
All poets detest Jas,
Really the most awkward of Nas –
(But the name Geo. is Go. is).

By heaven, sir!
If you elope with the daughter of a Bt.
The temperature will advance several degrees Ft.,
He will 'phone for the Guards and Sergt.
And say it is very ergt.

The frugal life
In nearly every pub
You can drink and sub;
And after victuals
You can play skictuals.

Love makes the world go round
Bro. and Bro.
Should love one ano.

The grabbing robbers
Every cigarette-butt in your av.
Contributes to the rav.

Don't make a beast of yourself
Many people have to take Bismuth
From over-eating at Chrismuth.

BETTER THAN 'JOHN BULL'

An impudent scoundrel unmasked!

Should a man call at your door, probably attired in clerical garb and selling onions, send him away.

He is none other than the Editor of *Blather*.

Better still, invite him into the kitchen for a mug of tea and phone for the police. If you are not the possessor of a domestic telephone, we must ask you to pass our paper on to somebody else; we are sorry, but we cannot be bothered talking to you.

Our point is that when you try to telephone, you will find that the wires have been cruelly cut. That will bring home to you the desperate character of the man whom you have so foolishly invited into your kitchen for tea. It is no use telling us that you invited him in on our advice. Your reproaches, your hurt tones, will leave us unmoved. We are not called Ireland's Heartless Hoaxer for

120

nothing. In fact, we are not called Ireland's Heartless Hoaxer at all.

Keep your head

Now that he is in your house, the important thing is to get him out. He is dangerous if provoked and is known to the police of three continents. Your best plan is to ring up our offices and ask us to send along our Keeper. Almost before you have finished dialling our number, you will remember that the wires are still cut. 'Tch, Tch,' you will murmur, 'How stupid of me!' And for our part, if we hear the telephone ringing, we will know not to answer it as we will remember that the wires are cut. That will be very clever of us.

He is probably still at his tea, however, and there is no immediate cause for alarm. Your next best plan would be to go upstairs to your armoury and lay your quivering hands on three or four machine-guns, two or three field-pieces, some cannon and ball-cartridge. It is contrary to the Civil Code, of course, to have these articles in your house at all; but as long as *Blather* does not adopt a stern attitude on the point, you need not worry. Mount two machine-guns in the scullery and do not forget to camouflage them as saucepans or scriveners or scullery maids or anything your mawkish fancy dictates. Mount two field-pieces on the stairs and three or four pieces of cannon on the first landing. If you have a sufficient supply of shooting-irons left, it will do no harm to construct a further machine-gun nest behind the hall-stand. When everything is in readiness, set all the pieces at full cock and call upon the criminal in steely tones to come out of the kitchen and take what is coming or die therein like a rat. Repeat louder, inserting the word 'dirty' before 'rat' and avoid long pauses as the talking will keep your teeth quiet. The chances are ten to one that you will get no reply. Fire off forty rounds in the air and endeavour to waft the acrid smoke into the closed kitchen through the key-hole and take good care to dodge the shower of plaster from the ceiling. Repeat your terrible threat, punctuating it with salvos of maniacal laughter. Re-charge all pieces with ball. Rake the hall with a rain of death-dealing lead and finally demolish the kitchen-door with a shower of devastating shells. Wait for a short interval under cover until the smoke and dust have died down and then proceed revolver in hand to the kitchen. This is known as reconnoitring and is dangerous work and no job for weaklings. Fifty to one you will find the kitchen empty, though you may possibly find a bed or two in it from upstairs. Go back to your machine-guns with a muttered oath and sweep the stairs as they have never been swept before. Clean all pieces with rags and ramrods and adjust safety catches, clean yourself up and go into the drawing-room. You will find the rat sitting at the piano playing one of the rarer Chopin Etudes. Say nothing but go downstairs again and fetch two quick-firing field-pieces. When you return, the window will be open and the room will be empty.

Very quick-fingered, is he?
'Not only that,' you will write to us and say, 'but my grand piano is gone as well.'

But we know you.

You never had a grand piano.

Four weeks old today!

Four weeks old to-day! That is the staggering achievement of our great paper. The credit is yours as well as ours. Are you glad?

Today is the first birthday of our great paper. You would hardly know us, we are growing up so fast. Already there is talking of casting off our little swaddling rags and petticoats, and sending nurse away. Not that they mean to leave our pinkness naked. No. There is even talk of a little sailor suit with ribbons and bibs and a wooden whistle on a string. How nice it will look folded on a chair while we are being bathed and powdered! How nice to stagger round the nursery on our little bandy legs and thuck our thumbs and tear the wall-paper and dribble dribble dribble! How nice to tear the guts out of a padded chair and shriek with salvos of mad baffled temper! How nice to be a devil! Please send us a nice rag doll.

Soon, of course, will come the reckoning. Soon will our little molars start to rack our gummy mouth and soon will our Office resound with the roar of our Teething Tantrums. But who will say it is not worth it? Think of our first crust and our first Fit of Choking! Think of our first dish of wretched lumpy gruel!

Then the cruel years of whipping and thrashing and flogging and bating and larruping and lashing. The bitter nights of No Supper. The wretched days when The Boy Must Be Made Do As He Is Told. (But are we a Boy? Never mind. We are damned if *Blather* will stand for any sex-talk in the presence of little children.) And then school. SCHOOL! At three p.m. a man starts walking from a point A towards another point B. At three-fifteen, another man starts walking from B to A at a speed . 18239 m.p.h. faster than the man from A. They meet at a point C. A third man (evidently a cyclist), starts off from C in a northerly direction on a fast pedal cycle. At a point D he meets a fourth man who had started out from F. You know the stuff. We dare not pursue it any farther; we would probably reach L, if we may permit ourselves a mirthless schoolchild's joke.

And then, before school is over, Ah! the Difficult Years.

Frankly, it is a black outlook; there seems to be no ray to lighten the darkness. Let us take a stiff shot of gripe-water.

Our tottering circulation

ARE WE TOO GOOD TO LAST?
Sitting in our palatial offices the other day, we heard a strange hacking noise. (Sitting in *offices*, by the way, takes some doing.) We asked our pretty typist what she thought it was, but she did not know. We questioned our staff of clerks and accountants, but nobody, alas! could explain. The strange hacking noise occurred again an hour later.

'I have it,' cried George, 'It's *Blather*'s death-rattle.'

Stern words, these. They put the heart across us. But being pessimists at heart, we refused to believe them.

'Is *Blather* in a bad way?' we asked.

'Very bad,' said George, 'have a look at these figures!'

123

And he handed us our Certified Accountant's Net Circulation Figures. We don't know in what year our accountant was certified, if that's what you want to ask us. Frankly, the story the figures tell is a pretty miserable one. Having deducted all copies returned as unsold, and also, of course, those spoilt in printing, we have registered a net sale of five dozen copies, that is sixty, (*or 60, stupid!*). For those of our readers who are congenital idiots and unable to grasp ordinary plain figures, we have pleasure in appending a diagram, clearly showing the extent of the sales of our last issue, together with a forecast exclusive to *Blather* regarding the present, the next and the second next issue of our great paper:

We know what you are going to say. There is no trace of the second next issue. Tut, tut! It is there, all the same. It has disappeared into the ground, as the sale of two copies in the scale in which our diagram is drawn is not visible to the naked eye. Those of our readers who are lucky enough to be working in laboratories can try the diagram under the microscope. If there is no result, they can try playing the page on the gramophone, using, if at all possible, a fibre needle. If there is no result, they can try putting it under the Hoover. If there is still no result, they have one last resort – blue litmus paper. If there is no chemical reaction, they can run along and buy sweeties, as people who spend their time on fool games like that deserve a few sweeties for their pains. What do *you* say?

This talk is all very well, but it is getting us away from our terrible circulation figures. Candidly, five dozen copies per issue is definitely not enough; *and what is more, the directors of* Blather *will not rest until these figures are doubled!*

We realise, of course, that the task ahead of us is a stern one. We realise that lesser journals must go to the wall in the desperate circulation war that we are planning. But who will blame us?

No man can set bounds to the onward march of a great paper.

124

Hash

A novel – even a very bad one – can cost you a good sevenansix-pence. Eleven or twelve novels can cost you £4 2s. 6d. (or £5 4s. od., as the case may be). *Blather*, ever jealous for your honour and eager that you shall not let our grand old paper down by displays of ignorance or illiteracy when In Company, has pleasure in presenting the pith and the cream of eleven or twelve novels in the grand Non-stop Hash-up below.

You are even saved the bother of wading through pages of muck in order to get at the good bits.

You must admit that we are a handy crowd of boys to have about the house. Write to us and thank us.

Solitaire sat thoughtfully on a bunk in one of the cells of the jail that had been built in the back part of the sheriff's office. He realised that he was in a very difficult position. He was a prisoner in a town where he was an utter stranger.

I was a white man – the last product in the slow upward rise of mankind through the ages. I had to stop this thing if it cost me my life!

There was one way to do it – and the idea came to me so suddenly that I almost thought – well, never mind what I thought. I'm not ordinarily a religious man . . .

I could have done it before, if I had only stopped to think instead of running. But now was another chance.

With a shriek that almost tore my lungs out, I leaped up on the stone.

A feature of Moscow broadcasting is the regular relaying of ballets and operas from the Bolshoi Theatre, or Grand Opera House, Theatre Square. As the home of the famous Imperial Russian Ballet, Moscow has always been a prominent artistic centre, and the performances at the Grand Opera House and the other theatres are of the highest standard.

The little dancing lights began to flicker in the black eyes.

'I see that I will have to put it in words of one syllable so you will understand,' she began sweetly. 'In Maryland and Virginia,

125

Mr Hatfield, there are always many guests coming and going and three or four more never make any difference. I am not familiar enough with life in Arizona to –'

'O. K., O. K.,' he growled. 'Forget it. Let it slide. Shut up and give your ears a chance.'

'And you don't have to be insulting –'

'I'm sorry, Lady Patrick. On bended knees, wallowing in self-abasement –'

'Oh, you shut up!'

The elevator opened and he lined out ahead of her, his floppy hat crushed down over his forehead, his heels smacking the tiles.

Lil read the telegram hurriedly.

I AM GOING TO BE MURDERED STOP I CAN'T GO TO THE POLICE STOP SET YOUR OWN FEE AND HELP ME STOP SIT IN END SEAT MIDDLE AISLE SEVENTH ROW CRITERION THEATRE FIRST SHOW TODAY IF WILLING STOP FURTHER DETAILS WILL BE SUPPLIED.

'Back to the office and find out all you can about this, Jimmy,' Pat ordered the messenger. 'Where it was filed, how filed, who filed it, and anything else you can get. I want to know all about it.'

He was flat on his back, bound hand and foot, on the floor of the cabin of the launch.

The blow on the head that had knocked him out had cut his scalp and his face was smeared with blood.

The gun barrel, pointed downward at him, wavered. Then very slowly it was lowered.

'Last chance!' Tolmie's voice was thick and shaky. 'Will you put in with us?'

He slithered toward me. My own knife was out, and I gripped it in front of me and waited. Now my great-bodied adversary advanced inch by inch. He circled like a boxer seeking an opening. He bent sideways, crouched, then suddenly straightened in a lunge. To lessen the impact of his drive, I heaved desperately against the wall of water at my back, dislodging it with scarce an inch to spare, for divers move under water like figures in slow motion pictures.

Power on another occasion was entering a cafe and accidentally jostled a lady who was being escorted by a young dandy. The cavalier (he was the lady's son) insisted on calling out the famous duellist for the supposed insult. Power good-humouredly sought

126

to explain, but the hot-headed gallant wouldn't listen, and insisted so much upon fighting that the elder man at last consented. The lady (knowing Power's reputation as a duellist) drew him aside.

'And do you think this attack will come soon?'

'Not later than tonight,' asserted Liston. 'Perhaps sooner. That message from the plane, the call for mass meetings and all will force Foresti into action.'

Then the telephone which stood on the table between them rang. The publisher had given orders that that phone was to ring for but one reason. He snatched the instrument and listened.

'Yeah. You're right.' Butcher stood up. 'Let's carry him to one of the tents, get him out of the sun. I bet by tomorrow he has a sweet mess of gangrene, or something worse.'

'What could be worse?' Picadilly wanted to know as he helped Butcher carry the wounded Vargas to one of the tents.

'I don't know. Pain, I suppose. If he has to linger on and be in pain.' He shut his lips together grimly. 'But he won't. I'll take care of that.'

'Shudderin' thought!'

Pat Holliday guffawed, his voice harsh with biting sarcasm. 'Fly a plane in this flood? You're crazy!' He pushed his hands against Hansen's chest. 'Get away and leave me alone. I'm clearing out of here, I tell you. I wouldn't fly your mail fifty feet even if the sun was shining and there wasn't a cloud in sight!'

All this only seems to prove that pets are all right in their own place, but if we had a place like that we would put some of our blasted relatives there.

Our sports club

The visit of the President and the members of the Executive Council to the Blather Sports Club was the occasion of a brilliant social gathering. In the 440 yds, Mr Lemass was beaten on the tape by the pigeon-chested Blazes O'Blather, who wore a Lansdowne jersey. The Governmental honour was later retrieved by the Pres., who was not present to welcome the President. It will be recalled that the two statesmen have not been on speaking terms since the notorious Horse Show incident.

Rugby

'There Is Nothing I Like Better Than A Nice Ball-Game.'
THE O'BLATHER, at Naas Races.

Blazes O'Blather to join Lansdowne?

Much interest has been aroused in Rugby circles by Blazes O'Blather's dramatic threat to join Lansdowne. This would mean that every member of the Lansdowne Club would automatically become a member of the *Blather* Staff and this would inevitably lead to nasty questions about the Club's amateur status as all members of the staff are paid a ridiculously high salary. Some notorious Club like Bective would be sure to make a smell about it, as the little green demon of jealousy can drive men to do the *meanest* things.

The O'Blather was a great sportsman

Like his distinguished father, Blazes O'Blather comes to the world of Irish sport with a great record and a fine family tradition. In the memorable Clontarf team which defeated England at Folkestone in 1912, The O'Blather combined brain and brawn in achieving a great victory. His position was behind the scrum, and opening with the Queen's Gambit, he sacrificed two pawns and managed to effect a very neat little mate with two bishops and a knight just as the final whistle was about to be blown. Playing faultless Rugby at Paris in the spring of the following year, he brought a clever French side to five sets before he would admit defeat, defeat which was in no small measure due to the fact that his hurley was smashed to atoms, ten minutes before time, when victory was all but in sight.

A proud record

In 1919 he joined Wanderers and formed the backbone of the team which visited Belgium in the autumn of the following year. The match was played on a Sunday in a downpour of rain, and though opposed to the cream of the Belgian clubs, the Irish team made a gallant and a worthy stand. The O'Blather, who had by this time acquired a considerable reputation for a safe pair of hands and a long kick, was in the front line of the forwards and opened up for Ireland with cue-ball in hand. Though faced with a particularly embarrassing double-baulk, he managed a cannon after employing no less than eighteen cushions. This clever if rather flukey manoeuvre left the red near the top cushion and the white on the centre spot. Two more cannons, four pots and a long jenny left the two balls properly 'on' for the great break that was bound to ensue. Half-time score:

Belgium, (rec. 1,000)	... ...	2,104
The O'Blather, in play	... ...	2,558

The rain became heavier at this point and Belgium apparently decided to vary their tactics. They cunningly introduced a slow bowler, evidently determined to make hay on the sodden pitch. The O'Blather, though busy with a series of peerless nursery cannons, quickly adjusted himself to the new threat and flogged the first over for three fours and four threes, cutting his drives through cover point and silly-mid-on with an abandon and a zest that would have done credit to a younger man.

Three-quarter-time score:

Belgium, (all out)	... ...	2,615
The O'Blather	... ...	3,498 Unfinished

The close of an epic struggle

Stumps and lots were drawn for tea at five-thirty when there were four inches of water on the pitch.

The same high standard of play was maintained on the resumption. The O'Blather had three strokes in hand and managed to half the sixteenth hole, thanks to some very neat work with his irons. Leading a fine handling movement emanating from a scrum in midfield, he went over for a try at the seventeenth, thus putting Ireland farther in the lead and making the possibility of an equalising score even more remote.

From that moment the Irish team never looked back. And the O'Blather, playing faultless handball, obtained a solid in the last thirty seconds of the last minute and put the result beyond all doubt.

Today?

Today, he can be but rarely persuaded to talk of it. 'Twas a great victory,' he will tell you with the simplicity of a child, before going back into his brown study.

If you follow him in, he will draw your attention to its beautiful brown wall-paper.

'It is my favourite colour,' he will murmur, 'and nothing could persuade me to change it.'

But if you look closely you will find it is distemper.

Listen in to 2BL

OUR BID FOR ETHER HONOURS

Athlone – whither?

A number of our readers have been mystified by the activities of a strange wireless station which came on the air for the first time last Monday night and succeeded in completely jamming Athlone for three quarters of an hour. Listeners who tuned in to Athlone after their teas were surprised and not a little pleased at the streams of bad language which poured from their loud-speakers. They thought it was Moscow and even wrote to us to say as much. But we know better. It was none other than the Blather Pirate Station, 2BL, testing. The plant is situated in the cellars of Blather House and is cunningly disguised to look like a poteen still, in case the police ever hear we are engaged in illegal broadcasts and raid us. The Station is operating on 531 metres, which is considered very high for boys of our age. Tests will be carried out nightly, when the children are in bed.

Our great ideals

The objects of the station are two-fold, even manifold. The primary object is to give Athlone hell. We are going to give it hell every night, and when we are finished giving it hell we are going to give it red hell. We are going to jam and jam and jam. We are going to perforate its wretched programmes with screams and whistles and scrapings and head-noises and streams of bad

131

language. We will permit the undisturbed broadcast of *nothing*, except SOS messages and anything else that happens to tug at our mothers' heart-strings.

Der Tag

When Athlone has retired off the air, 2BL will take up the running. Our broadcasts will be devoted to Communist propaganda, the *Blather* No Rates Campaign, and to the furtherance of The O'Blather's League for Little People. In the meantime, we think we are just as much entitled to the licence-money as the other crowd. Please remember that all cheques should be crossed. If you are one of those people who use an indoor aerial, of course, you must let your conscience be your guide.

.... CUT THIS OUT ....

1.30–2.0   Gramophone Records.

6.0   Gramophone Records. (*What, again!*)

6.15   Uair i dTír na n-Óg. 'Mickey's Wedding' (play). Baritone Solos. Poetry Reading. (*But after all, this is for the kiddies. They might as well learn soon as late that life is tough.*)

7.0   Gramophone Concert. (*Happily, we subscribe to the old-fashioned view that sooner or later these people will have to answer for all their acts. It is a useful and a beautiful philosophy.*)

7.20   News. (*Thank you, but we buy a morning paper.*)

7.30   Time Signal. (*A new and a provocative reading of this famous piece; we fancied the* Scherzo *was taken a trifle too fast.*)

7.30   Gaedhilg: Leigheacht. (*Maith go leor, maith go leor.*)

7.45   Talk: Poultry-feeding in Mid-winter. (*There is this about our beautiful philosophy mentioned above, that it often helps to sustain our tottering reason when the latter has made its last poor rally and is threatening to go under.*)

8.0   Seumas mac Seadna, Pipes. (*Is the rat next door oscillating or is he not?*)

8.30   Gramo—— (*No, you don't, by Heavens! We are going out for a bottle of stout and we will be gone half an hour.*)

9.0   Talk: Hints on Roses. (*But after all, what use is beer to men like us? Two or three darts of malt would have done us a lot of good.*)

9.30   Baritone Solos. (*Five or six darts, perhaps.*)

9.45   Gramophone Selections: 'You Will Remember Vienna.' (*Yes, we said it, but you did not hear us. Vienna will never let you know.*)

10.0   Soprano Solos. (*But we might say it louder some other time.*)

10.30   Play: *The Camel's Back.* (*And the last straw.*)

11.0   Time, News, Close Down. (*Let us pray.*)

More about our new wireless service

By the time this appears in print, The O'Blather will be on the high seas on his mission to Australia. By the sensitive twitching of your nostril, we see that you are beginning to smell a rat, you damned terrier. What, you ask us, has this got to do with the Great New Blather Broadcasting Corporation? Nothing. But we were going to write about this mission first to show our teeth and to prove that we didn't care what we wrote about as long as we used up ink. Hell!

We are about to unfold the inside story of 2BL, the Blather *Broadcasting Station. The story is copyright and exclusive and if the* Irish Times *reproduces it in whole or in part, we shall prosecute. Gad, it is hell, this rivalry between great national newspapers!*

Ever since we were fined for not having a licence, we've been hankering after a little station of our own. Not a railway station, mind you, or an RAF bombing station. What we mean is a clean and neat little wireless station. Years ago, we initiated the Shannon Scheme with a view to supplying current, which is a pretty good example of foresight and forthrightness and whatnot.

133

The last obstacle to our plans disappeared recently when the price of barbed wire fell to a level sufficiently low to permit of the wiring of the station at an economic cost.

Here's the naked truth, boys

The power of the new station is roughly a million Killywatts, with a wave-length of ten million metres. When *Blather* does things, maybe it doesn't half do things in style, by Hickory! Are you impressed? We don't know, by the way, what exactly a Killywatt is, as we have never seen or eaten one. But just imagine. A million Killywatts, with another million in reserve in case of emergencies! Can you beat it? To give you a vague idea of the power of the thing, take a simple illustration. If the charred bodies of all the people the new station could electrocute were put end to end without any overlapping, they would extend from Kelly's Corner to a cow we saw on the Naas Road when we were going to a Blue Shirt meeting in Buttevant. (This computation, of course, is subject to the condition that the cow hasn't moved since, or been rustled across the border, or been bitten in the ear by a tsetse-fly). So powerful will it be, in fact, that it will drown every other station in Europe. The dear knows this is a very caddish thing to do, but Lord save us! Is this any fault of ours?

The truth about the staff

The Director of the new station is Mr Eric Blameworthy (related to the Fitzhazzards, of Luttrellstown), affectionately known to his associates as Half-wit Harry. He is also the announcer, the ideal announcer. Sometimes you think he is speaking English, sometimes you imagine it is Irish. Sometimes you think it is pure Gibberish. But you'll never know for certain, because he doesn't know himself. When approached with regard to the policy of the new station, the Director was reticent. 'Tell your readers I am reticent,' he said reticently. That's all very well, Eric, old man, but you can't fool *Blather* readers with that sort of bluff. *Blather* readers are intelligent. Give a *Blather* reader a piece of twine and in five minutes, without any help or promptings from teacher, he will tell you in plain English that what you have given him is a piece of twine and nothing else. You see what we mean?

134

Our quick way with blackheads?

'No expense is being spared,' writes our Special Correspondent, 'to make the new station one of the most costly and ignominious failures in the history of modern costly and ignominious failures. Sabotage, graft, bribery and all the forces of Communism are being pressed into service. Thousands and thousands of spanners are being thrown into the works daily by Russian arch-dukes thinly disguised as Lithuanian peasants. Trained incendiaries, some of them paid as much as ten roubles a day, are working in six-hour shifts to make life a hell for everybody connected with the new station.' You see? Everything possible is being done. No expense is being spared.

The truth about Marina

Below you will find the programme of the new station. It took years to perfect. It is so perfect that it will never be changed. You will be able to tune in every night with the calm assurance that everything will be just the same as you heard the night before. No irritating variations, no baffling novelties. Just the same old thing in the same old way. Athlone will not be in it with us. Years afterwards, when you are sitting in your padded cell, you will be able to go over the programme word for word, syllable for syllable, note for note. It will be simply seared into your brain. Here we are.

Programme:

12.0 a.m.–10 a.m.	Reverent silence to commemorate farmers who fell in the Economic War.
10.0 a.m.–11.0 a.m.	Time signal from alarum-clock on dressing-table of The O'Blather. Sounds of yawning and gnarled fists being beaten on bed-posts. Strange grating noise immediately recognisable as The O'B shaving with old-fashioned cut-throat.
11.0 a.m.–12 noon	Homely relay of O'Blather household at breakfast, including following features: Querulous whimpering while The O'B has Bib put on by trained Hindu nurse. Altercation while nurse slaps

135

	hand. Senile complaints re burnt stir about and underdone rasher.
12 p.m.–1.0 p.m.	Interval for luncheon.
1.0 p.m.–1.30 p.m.	Atmospherics.
1.30 p.m.–2.0 p.m.	Readings from Old Moore's Almanac.
3.0 p.m.–3.30 p.m.	Readings from Old Moore's Almanac. Clerical staff thoroughly fed up to the back teeth writing a.m. and p.m.
3.30 p.m.–4.0 p.m.	Readings from Old Moore's Almanac continued.
4.0 p.m.–5.0 p.m.	Borstal Boys' Reunion dinner.
5.0.–6.0. p.m.	Atmospherics.
6.0. p.m.–7.0 p.m.	Talk on *Blather* Circulation figures.
7.0 p.m.–7.30 p.m.	Talk. Stoat-shooting in Siberia, by Major Snodgrass-Worthing, Punjab Fusiliers, ret.
7.30 p.m.–8.0 p.m.	Morse concert, relayed from SS Muirchu.
8.0 p.m.–9.0 p.m.	Castlepollard Dramatic Society in readings from Old Moore.
9.0 p.m.–10.0 p.m.	Opera *The Flying Scotchman* (Verdigris).
10.0 p.m.–11.0 p.m.	Atmospherics.
11.0 p.m.–12.0 p.m.	Atmospherics, continued.
12 midnight, onwards:	Reverent silence.

OUR MONTHLY
HEART-TO-HEART

Has Hitler gone too far?

The great army of *Blather* Readers who inhabit this lovely island will be delighted to hear that our great paper is out of the wood at last. The doctor has just left and his last remark was that the paper and ourselves, fond parents that we are, were doing very nicely indeed. We must confess that we feel all right and are very very happy.

136

Our friends tell us that we are looking well and that we are even getting stout. But that is only a dirty lie. Paper or no paper, we never drink anything weaker than whiskey and we like the world to know it. What man in his sober senses could write the stuff that litters our nice clean columns? Tut! tut! *Blather* will henceforth appear in the middle of every month, just around the time when the hall needs a good scrubbing and the cat comes home for another rest after her immoral travels. Nothing can prevent its appearance. Nothing can prevent it reaching your shaky hands. So who cares?

Hot on the heels of the information that seventeen fish-plates have been stolen from a lonely stretch of the trans-Siberian railroad comes the news that *Blather* has been banned in Germany. The decree was issued from Berlin and was signed by the man Goebbels, and was counter-signed by Goering.

Blather, which was cunningly circulating in Germany under the title of the *Daily Express*, has evidently fallen foul of the Brownshirt mogols by reason of its fearless disclosures in connection with the Export Horses-Saurkraut scandal. Its stern and unrelenting attitude on the question of an Anschluss has apparently done nothing to diminish the unpopularity of the paper at the Brown House. The attempt to stifle legitimate comment and to browbeat the great national organs of other countries by the operation of bans and prohibitions is bound to fail. *Blather* receives the present ban unmoved. Arrangements are in hand by which the next issue of the paper will appear in Germany under the title of the *Daily Mail*. Should a further decree be issued, *Blather* will have no hesitation in changing the title again to that of *Our Boys*.

And no amount of persecution will prevent us from carefully pointing out the weakness in the social and political fabric of Germany and maintaining in general that lofty standard of clean and wholesome journalism which has made our name a byword in Dublin.

When you buy a copy of our great paper, you have, perhaps rashly, put yourself in possession of a very delicate and sensitive piece of mechanism. Treat it well and it will yield you faithful

137

service. Treat it harshly and without consideration and it will break your heart.

And *Blather* for Service! If a part gets worn out or becomes defective, there is no question of scrapping the entire copy. Spare parts, accurately cut to one thousandth of an inch, are obtainable at bedrock prices and are fitted at your nearest service station *free*.

Any complaints as to incivility on the part of your copy, or objectionable habits, or insubordination of any kind should be made immediately in writing and addressed to the Manager, 68 Dame Street. Copies are usually given at least a second chance to turn their back on the black past and Make Good, but if lapses are persistent, the Manager has no option but to withdraw the erring copies from circulation. Readers who prefer to carry out their own punishment should see that correctives are very sparingly applied, as it is *too* easy, Alas, to sour and warp the little minds for life.

And no *Blather* Reader worth of the name would do that.

NOTICE

These columns are poisoned. Trespassers will be prosecuted. And incidentally, to avoid clashing with our esteemed contemporaries, *The Irish Grocer* and *The Irish Welder and Iron-Worker*, *Blather* will henceforth appear in the middle of every month, and not at the beginning as heretofore.

£30 in pin-money for readers!

OUR COMPETITION
AS SIMPLE AS HELL

In this great Competition, prizes totalling £35 in pin-money are offered to our readers. The £35 will be divided as follows: First

138

Prize, £25; Second Prize, £15; and Third Prize, £10. There will be an additional ten consolation prizes of a pound of Ceylon Tea, presented by the *Irish Grocer*, presumably as a bribe to bring our bitter vendetta to an end.

The winner will be privileged to own the finest collection of Pins in Europe outside the famous collection of Sir Giles Blether, the head of the English branch of the famous family.

There is no entrance fee, but generous readers may enclose an alms for the editor. Widow-readers may send a mite.

What you have to do
Below we print a number of photographs, etchings, engravings, etc. If they look all the same to you, better keep the fact dark, as it is sinful to parade ignorance. These pictures represent various people prominent in public life. But the titles in some cases have been deliberately mixed up in order to puzzle you. The problem is to allot the correct subtitle to the correct picture.

Do you think your little brain could rise to it?

Do not tell us. We know the answer.

Conditions
The Editor of the *Irish Grocer* is ineligible to compete.

Passengers having alighted from a car and desiring to cross the road should assure themselves before doing so that no car is approaching from the opposite direction.

All letters in connexion with this competition should be stamped. The feet of bad-tempered little girls should also be stamped.

It is dangerous to touch the wires.

Competitors must supply their own stout and must guarantee that they sell no other brown stout in bottle.

Competitors must use the prescribed Form, but if they cannot find the Form, a Chair will do.

Successful Competitors become the property of the Editor.

Mr Silas P. Hotchkiss, President of the Clanbrassil Street Brass Fender Founders and Tinsmiths' Protection Association, Inc.

Sir Giles Blether (left), the head of the English branch of the famous family, taking a bath with Senator Blythe in 1889. Sir Giles has possession of the soap and refuses to give it up.

The O'Blather, the famous press baron, publicist, playwright, poet, politician and press baron.

Sir Giles Blether, the distinguished English statesman, who was responsible for initiating Mr J. H. Thomas into the mysteries of boiled shirt-studs after the latter ceased to be an ex-miner. Sir Giles was second but three to Marina at supper recently in the Carlton.

The Rt. Hon. Alfred Byrne, Lord Mayor of Dublin, who doesn't look very pleased in this picture; he probably has a pain in his Royal Liver.

Eamonn de Valera, President of the Executive Council, and Chancellor of the National University.

Miss Amelia ('Slug') Cruikshank, the American crooning colossus, who can lift a horse with one arm and beat up five fully grown men with the other. 'Love is what makes the world go round,' says Miss Cruikshank. She once offered to put a man called H. L. Mencken in his place for a purse of fifty sovereigns, but the trusts, cartels and vested interests refused to allow it. Liberty? Pah!

MR JEKYLL and DOCTOR HYDE
If you tell us that once is enough to print a picture, our answer is 'Nuts!' A pretty pass, forsooth, if we are going to allow you to tell us what to do.

141

The Abbey Theatre subsidy

OUR MODEST PROPOSAL

There is a movement on foot, sponsored by the jealous Gate Theatre, to have the annual subsidy of £750 paid by the Government to the Abbey Theatre transferred to *Blather*.

The issue is a very complex one and presents many aspects. It has been pointed out in our columns more than once that both the Gate and the Abbey are owned by a crowd of rascally Bolsheviks operating from ports in the Baltic, who have been planning the downfall of Irish dancing for the past twenty years. As well as that, the directorates of both theatres are honeycombed with Masons.

But listen to this one. We were standing in the Abbey the other night with one foot in the foyer and one in the vestibule when we were accosted by a woman. She wanted us to buy a programme. A blind bat could see that she was none other than a beautiful Russian spy. We immediately suspected that she was after the plans, and we instantly went to the phone and warned everybody in Dublin who had plans to be careful of them and to keep them under lock and key, better still, deposit them with the Bank. On one occasion we were put through to London by mistake and we spoke to Amy Johnson, who said she had no plans at the moment, but that it was possible that she and Jim would fly somewhere sometime soon, probably in the face of Providence. Heaven only knows how much bacon we saved by those phone-calls.

On the other hand, judging from the number of broad-brimmed black hats and bohemian cravats visible on the landing of the Gate Theatre between the acts, a subversive movement is on foot to divert the Seine into the Liffey and to change the Red Bank into the Left Bank. If you know what we mean. It is notorious, by the way, that The O'Blather has a grudge against Lord Longford and loses no opportunity of putting sand into the petrol-tank of his Lordship's Armstrong-Siddeley. His lordship is too big a man to retaliate, and in any case there is no petrol-tank on a bicycle.

As regards the £750 paid to the Abbey, it has been officially

142

explained to a *Blather* reporter that the money is paid on condition the Abbey Players go to America and remain there for nine months of the year. The idea is to prevent at all costs the further production in Dublin of *Riders to the Sea* and *Professor Tim*. It is not known whether the staff of *Blather* would be required to emigrate in the event of a subsidy being paid to the paper. While it is well-known that the Government are afraid of it and would like to see it out of the country for goodanall, they are nevertheless reluctant to impair their good relations with the Government of the United States. It is admitted that thousands of playgoers who turned their faces sadly to the emigrant ship early in the present century because of *Riders to the Sea* are now pouring back from the States in hordes. Two thousand of them are camping in the Phoenix Park at the moment. When they are asked about the Abbey Players in Boston, they look away and refuse to talk. One man laughed hollowly when questioned and disappeared into the trees.

Blazes O'Blather (who is studying art in Paris) has written a stiff letter to the Metropolitan Guards requesting them to shut down the Abbey and the Gate for good. When he was last in Dublin, he explains, he broke the back axle of his car twice in the one day, once in Abbey Street and once opposite the Gate. In each case the roadway is damaged by a deep trench extending from the entrance of the theatre to the door of the nearest public house, formed by the feet of patrons between the acts. It is stated that although the surface is stout enough to withstand the normal traffic *from* the theatre, subsidence is inevitable on the way back as a result of the added weight. The story of Blazes O'Blather is discounted by the Guards, as he has no car; further, it was established from the post-mark on his letter that he is residing in a quarter of Paris where no pretence is made of encouraging the study of art.

In the meantime every effort is being made to have the Abbey's subsidy transferred to *Blather*. Mick Hayes, TD, who is a guinea-pig director of the paper, is moving heaven and earth in the matter. We will report the progress of the scheme in future issues. In the meantime, we would be glad if Lord Longford would call at our offices, as we wish to present him with a handsome bakelite writing-set.

143

Is there a Santa Claus?

The question is: Tillage or Ranching?
  We are lying.
  As a matter of fact, that is not the question at all. The question is: Santa Claus – Does He Exist, or is it only a Dirty Lie?
Some of these days, when the question of Town Tenants is finally disposed of, *Blather* is going to hold an enquiry into the whole question of Santa Claus, and – Lord save us! – if you are afraid to know the truth, better stop reading our great paper altogether. Our Commission of Enquiry will drag every Christmas shibboleth and pishrogue and shebeen into the inexorable glare of daylight, it will fight the vested interests to the last ditch and then beat them through it, thorns or no thorns. And if they leave their vests behind them after they have fled, our Commissioners will carefully collect them all and give them to the poor, who will be glad of them in the cold weather.

Girls, read this!
The other day we discussed the matter with the manager of a big department store, who has a Santa Claus working in his toy department every year, selling parcels of trash to the kiddies for sixpences on the understanding that it is rude for the kiddies to ask what the hells bells is in the parcel they are paying out their good money for. 'As far as we are concerned,' he told us, 'we would welcome an enquiry. The number of people, young and old, who brazenly say that our Santa Claus is only a vanman dressed up is enough to make a man doubt everything he ever learnt at his mother's knee. Gad, I sometimes even find the same evil thought creeping into my own mind. Tell me, is nothing sacred, nowadays?'
  You see what we are driving at?

Terms of reference
When our Commission is sitting, it will take evidence from all creeds and classes, unhampered by any taboos or colour-bars.

What are the relations between Santa Claus and little Sylvester Byrne in the Mansion House? The Lord Mayor will have to let us have the whole story. Does Mr de Valera encourage his son Vivian to hang up the stockings? That is neither your business nor ours. It is for our Commission to find out. We are surprised at your rudeness in asking.

But there, we are lying again.

Goody! The facts at last!

As a matter of fact, *Blather* has no intention whatsoever of setting up any such Commission. If you had been familiar with our attitude on Legends, Pishrogues and Mummery, you would not have been deceived for one moment by our crude tissue of lies. As a matter of fact, if you had had the presence of mind to put this page under the microscope, you would have noticed the tissue, a wavy-wavy thing like a spider's web behind the printed words. We cannot see any reason for doubting Santa Claus, or starting any fool commission or allowing any fool commissioners to tear his good character to tatters with all the venom of their black hearts.

Degeneracy

The present-day contempt for Santa Claus and kindred institutions is something that every right-thinking Irishman must deplore, irrespective of creed or party, as the *Irish Times* would say.

Modern youth does not seem to be aware that every time a nasty man says 'I DON'T DAMN WELL BELIEVE IN SANTA CLAUS, BLAST ME,' one or other of the saint's little reindeers has twinges in the fetlocks, or worse still, sharp shooting pains in the withers.

It is a fact that should be more widely known.

Food taxes or free trade? Our handy vocabulars

In pursuants of our so popular policy of surveying useful informations for our blatherish readers, we are now about to disgorge some lingual tippings for persons contemplating to patrioticlessly

145

spend a holiday abroad. The as follows French vocabulars are specially prepared by a 100 per cent Anglo-French person, who speaks the tongue more better as a native.

'*Je me trouve mal, pourrai-je avoir un sceau.*' This are French for 'I are suffering to endure stomach spasms, so kindly to produce me a bucket.'

On arriving to step on French soil, the as follows will be very useful:

'*Arrêtez cet homme, il m'a volé ma bourse!*' Which are, 'Kindly to nab this man, he has succeeded to unpinch my purse!'

If performing a tour *à la* motor the as follows will prove enormously convenient when conversing French and other Continental persons:

'*Traversez lentement, j'ai mal à la gorge et un saignement de nez.*' This construes to mean 'Drive less speedishly, I are enjoying a pain in my neck and a nose-bleed.'

'*Quel temps fait-il?*' 'How are the weather (if any)?'

'*Sacre! Il pleut, il neige, il grêle, il fait du tonnere.*' Which are French for 'O Heavens! He rains, he snows, he hails, he thunders.'

'*Ciel, ma femme ouvieré a sauté.*' This translates to signify 'O goodness! my honourable girl has fallen out.'

'*N'importe,*' which are French for 'it are entirely of not any importance.'

When executing speed journies along French and other Gallic roads it are of enormous advantage to have the as follows conversations by heart:

'*Où est le hôpital?*' 'Kindly to inform where are the hospital.'

'*N'y a-t-il personne de blesse.*' This are handy for 'Are anybody suffering to endure painful damages?'

'*Ou est l'ambassade d'Angleterre! Je veaux qu'on me libere sous caution.*' This are very convenient for 'Kindly to inform where are Anglo-British embassy? I necessitate to immediately require bail.'

Polite conversation to use when travelling with foreign persons of mixed tongues.

'*Le chauffeur est évanoui et Er hat das Bein gebrochen.*' 'Honourable chauffeur are swooned and imbroken his leg.'

146

'Donnez-moi mon corset und meine zahnstocher.' 'Kindly to pass me my stays and a toothpick.'

'J'ai bien soif et wollete gera meine Uhr vertauchen por doze, panuelos de faltiriquera tres ovos frereos do dia y una hacha.' 'I are very thirsty and should like to change my watch for 12 nose handkerchiefs, 3 new-laid eggs and a hatchet.'

The flawless French is by a man who learned the language by working for six weeks in the Dublin Corporation Street Cleansing Department. The translation is by another man, a French polisher by profession.

Beware of B.A.!

THOUSANDS OFFEND WITHOUT
KNOWING
YOUR BEST FRIEND WON'T TELL
YOU

One of the most disquieting aspects of modern life is the unparalleled increase in students. They are increasing and multiplying and soon they will fill the earth.

To quote the solemn words of our godfather, *The Irish Grocer*, it would be laughable were it not so tragic.

Let it be quite clear at the outset that we are not talking about school-boys. To turn round now and say that we must then be alluding to school-girls would be to bring the blush of honest resentment to our face. To suffuse our finely-chiselled features with the glow of outraged modesty, to curtain the cheeks with the scarlet tide of shame. See you go no farther or by Heaven we might lift our arm in anger.

What we want to talk about is students.

Listen to this!

Now some misguided souls – we will mention no names – have frankly told us that they think students are all too wonderful. But that is a mistaken idea. Really it is too sordid. As a matter of fact,

147

students divide their time between brawling, bilking, boozing, billiarding and bauching. That last word should have read 'debauching', but hell, we hadn't the heart to bash up the alliteration. (It is our way; perfection or nothing.)

What!!

A man once told us about a student at a Dublin university who arrived at his college one morning and *went straight to his lecture.* When his name was called at roll-call, he stood up and said he refused to recognise the court and reserved his defence. He then fell down in a dead faint. People around said it must be starvation, and really there is nothing in life so beautiful as the poor University student's fight against poverty and adversity. He was tenderly lifted and carried out and examined by a doctor. The pit of his stomach was found to contain ten naggins of whiskey and a cheese sandwich.

You see?

Our point is that there is no shirking the conclusion that the lad had been drinking. Say what you like in extenuation – depression, worry, trouble at home, anything – but for Heavens sake let us look the facts in the face.

Is it good enough?

In other countries, of course, the student scourge is even more terrible. As a matter of fact, it is really all too sickening. How often have we read stuff like this in our morning paper?

The southern half of the city of Barcelona was burnt to the ground yesterday as a result of the annual May-day celebrations. The perpetrators of the outrage are stated to be students.

Or maybe this.

In Madrid yesterday, 600 civilians were injured in a clash between students and police.

Is there any hope?

The life of the average student is nauseating when you come to look into it. Parts of it are so shady that you can see nothing unless you strike matches.

The really alarming part of it is that despite the fact that they scarcely open a book at all, they all manage to get their degrees, which furnish them with a nice respectable disguise and prevent

148

people from knowing them for the depraved hooligans that they are. In after-life, they make a show of plain people like ourselves, who have always played the game and carried a straight bat for King and Empire.

What we are driving at now is Committees. A Committee is formed for this or that and the thing is published in the paper. Like this:

J. M. C. D. Trevor-Ball, M.D., M.Ch., F.R.C.S.I.

M. A. T. B. Humphries-Belvoir, LL.D.

J. J. Jasper Logg-Byrne, Ph.D., F.R.S.

P. W. C. P. Funk-Frazer, M.A., B.Sc, B.L.

J. Brown, Esquire.

The first four people here are all ex-students. That last name represents you or us. Is it any wonder that we are mad?

If we weren't men, we'd cry.

This is Angela, the author of 'From Man to Man', a smashing two-fisted snorter of an article unavoidably crowded out of this issue. She has promised us an article on 'Turning points in a Miner's Life' for our next appearance. The article in her hand is a banjo. That's what you say. It is not. It is a thinly-disguised slag-hammer, used for powdering Dutch quartz in the Franco-Prussian war, which proves that you don't quite know everything. We find it very hard to have patience with these smug know-alls, and we're not afraid to say it.

149

FORM OF BEQUEST

I GIVE AND BEQUEATH to the Proprietors of the Great National Enterprise known as *Blather* the sum of £.................... to apply the same to and for the objects and purposes of the said Great National Enterprise, AND I DECLARE that the receipt, in writing, of any two of such proprietors, or of such other person or persons as my Executors shall think fit to accept, shall be sufficient discharge for the said legacy, and exonerate my Executors from any obligation of seeing to the application therefore.

Only the judgment, discrimination and public spirit of our Advertisers makes the production of a great paper like *Blather* possible. It is therefore your bounden duty to buy their products. Accredited *Blather-* Readers, of course, do not have to be told this, but those who read it over an Accredited *Blather*-Reader's shoulder on the tram may require an occasional reminder.

OUR NEW YEAR MESSAGE

Balm for Ireland's ills

NEW DEAL FOR MISS KATHLEEN HOLOHAN

Knowing full well that many of our dear readers (dear at any price) are seriously perturbed over the future of our bleeding country, suffering motherland, etc., we sent a courier to the boudoir of the aged statesman, The O'Blather, with a request that he should address a message of hope and cheer to them on the eve of the New Year. We asked him to say a few seasonable words on Imperialism, Partition, Pin-money Girls in the Sweep, and other snags in the pie of our national policy. The aged shanachy agreed to do so and we have pleasure in printing his scholarly contribution to the cause of international peace below.

It is little short of scandalous, *writes The O'Blather*, that at a time when Kathleen Ni Holohan is lying broken and bleeding in

150

the gutter of party politics and in imminent danger of being arrested by the Guards for loitering, millions of pounds of money are being squandered on hydro-electric schemes and export bounties and Abbey Theatre grants and what not. The Irish people are still sitting in ignominious bondage and it cannot be too heavily emphasised that it is more than myself and the group of newspapers I control are prepared to stand for.

My own plan for the salvation of Ireland and for the amelioration of all her ills is too well known to require elaboration here; it is not too well known, however, to require statement. Briefly, it is as follows.

Let there be a big (if necessary an enormous) saw got, and let there be two yokes or businesses erected, one in the Atlantic and one in the Irish Sea, for working the big saw in the manner of two men working a cross-cut. Let the country be then sawed from its moorings from Antrim's coast to wild Cape Clear. By the laws of physics (Boyle's Law, Principle of Moments, etc.), the country will then float. Our subjection to England will then be no longer dependent on our geographical proximity to her. It is the first step in the sundering of the chain. It is not enough, however, to be afloat. At the mercy of the wind and the waves, we might edge over to England on a dark night and be anchored to her for the rest of time, like Wales.

A simple means of locomotion would be to divert the course of the Shannon so as to make it enter the sea at Cobh, which is roughly the centre of the vessel's stern. Another idea would be to erect an enormous sail in the centre of the midlands, but the cornerboys of Athlone would probably ruin it by playing handball against it. The Shannon scheme is the better of the two.

All that remains to be done now is to erect an enormous rudder at Cobh as well. The rudder is to be housed in a great building which will also be the seat of Government, because the party in power will simply have charge of the rudder and will have power to decide whether it is to be turned this way or that. Can you help wondering at the sublime simplicity of it all?

Now what are the advantages of this grand scheme? First of all we are rid of the Saxon, and the rotten climate that goes with him. The entire country (by the simple process of passing a Bill), can go abroad for the winter. The people can have winter sports

151

at will, or languish in the Mediterranean when the whim takes them. We can grow tropical fruits and spend our leisure by baiting arctic bears and Russian wolves. We can get all our foreign supplies at greatly reduced prices by eliminating the costly item of freights. ('10,000 tons of timber for Ireland. To be called for'.) We can substantially augment the national income by acting as common carriers between the New World and the old, putting every shipping company in the world out of business. We can give the British hell as often as we feel like it by steaming past her coast and ruining the country with gigantic tidal waves. The possibilities are endless.

We feel sure that this thought-provoking article will give our readers plenty of food for thought in the New Year. The Editor invites Correspondence on the aged statesman's ingenious proposals.

The *Blather* bounty

There is no doubt about it, we are always up to something. Our latest bombshell is — guess!

Bulls!

Let us grasp you by your skinny wrist and tell you all about the *Blather* Bulls. Not the Stock Exchange variety, though, mind you, when it comes to unloading *Blather* Ordinary on a flat market, we take a lot of stopping.

These fine Irish animals (*tauri hibernici*), born and bred in Irish Birth and Breeding Pens, form the cream of the *Blather* Bounty Scheme.

Blather is prepared in its big-hearted way to award a Pedigree Bull to every reader. We are not philanthropists or fools, of course, and there is no end of annoying conditions and bans and taboos and marks off for blots and bad handwriting. But who cares? The prize is worth the game, and any Bull Fancier will tell you that. You think not? Listen to what Rockefeller, the richest man in the world, said to one of these wretched little underpaid reporters of ours.

152

'Money? Bah! If I were to start again, I think I'd have a good bull. Just a little one with white markings, a clean stall and plenty of straw. . ..' Here the iron face of the old fighter of the oil-markets softened. 'I don't know,' he said, 'there is something about good bull....'

And now listen to the babble of the poorest man in the world, the Editor of *Blather*, an only child, as we said before, with no home-training, no *character*, if you get what we mean.

'Ever since my boyhood days when a barefoot lad I played marbles on the hills of Tipp. with Eamonn Dev, I always used to say to myself that one day I would grow up and own a nice bull and wear leggings and act the can and be a hell of a hard man. Or was it Dev that said that? I don't know. But the pair of us went to Duffy's Circus and there was a lady there with pink stays and ——' You see what we here in the office are up against? No sense of fitness, no *restraint*, if you know what we mean. We like to think it is the Great War, but one cannot blame everything on the Great War, can one? Let us get back. The life-blood of any reputable paper is its circulation. *Blather* is not a reputable paper. Nevertheless, we must get rid of our great paper somehow as we do not keep our fires going in the summer and we cannot store the stuff in our garage, as it contains at the moment five private scrub-bulls of our own, as well as dozens and dozens of empties which they haven't called for yet. Hence we are offering Pedigree Bulls to our readers as an inducement to boost our circulation. In order to qualify for an award, the Reader must perform one or other or all of the following Exercises and must lodge an affidavit with our solicitor, signed by a Peace Commissioner and two witnesses, testifying that such Exercises have been duly performed.

The *Blather* circulation exercises

1. Candidate enters Tram clutching copy of *Blather*. Goes inside. Starts tittering. Opens *Blather* and titters louder. Tittering becomes a definite nuisance to fellow-passengers. Takes fits of tittering, winding up with a throaty chuckle. Gropes for cigarettes and lights one. Conductor approaches and says put that cigarette out, where do you think you are. Candidate says: O yes, sorry, and adds in a very loud voice: I FORGOT BUT

I WAS CARRIED AWAY BY THIS GREAT PAPER. Sniggers coarsely and goes upstairs where tittering is resumed.

2. Same as I above, but Candidate refuses to pay fare, explaining that he has spent last twopence on THIS ASTOUNDINGLY GOOD PAPER and has name and address taken, or maybe Policeman.

3. Candidate boards tram and goes upstairs. Opens *Blather* and lets loud guffaw. Guffaw continued. Breaks into loud roars of laughter. Chokes. Shifts about in seat to let fellow-passengers see cover of *Blather*. Roars louder. Bends practically double and slaps thigh hysterically. Takes breath and embarks on fresh paroxym. Slaps thigh of fellow-passenger by mistake. Apologises and explains loudly about THIS GREAT PAPER. Resumes shrieking.

4. Twenty Candidates board tram en masse and go upstairs. Flourish copies of *Blather*. Start sniggering *piano* and develop into salvoes of maniacal laughter, *fortissimo*. Fall on floor and over each other and eventually convert Tram into Shambles. Explain loudly to Guards and Crowd about THIS GREAT PAPER. **(Extra Bulls awarded for this one.)**

5. Candidate enters Office carrying *Blather*. Laughs loudly and continuously. Boss enters and asks does he think Office is a Bear-garden. Candidate wittily replies world is now a *Blather* Garden. Offers to lend copy to Boss. **(An extra Bull if Candidate is sacked.)**

6. Candidate enters Cinema carrying *Blather* and small torch. Sits in prominent position, ignores screen and starts to study *Blather* with aid of torch. Torch to be accidentally flashed on screen when turning pages. Bursts into roars of laughter and holds up entire show. Blames THIS GREAT PAPER. Is forcibly ejected.

And now we come to Aspect 2 of our great Bounty Scheme. Now *Blather* is nothing if not broadminded. *Blather*, a true cricketer to the last, stands four square behind the Connexion, the Throne, the Crown, the Sovereign and the King-Emperor. Our greatest friend and right-hand man is Viscount Rothermere, who offered to acquire *Blather* for a million pounds and who was refused because we wanted Rothermore. But forget that. The

154

point is that the *Blather* Loyalty and Devotion is being unfairly strained by certain happenings at Court. *Blather* stands for the Union and for a Strong Hand in Ireland, but it cannot tolerate any interference on the part of any king in the affairs of The Nation's Mothers. This is the *Blather* Attitude. 'Hands off our Irish Family Affairs!' – that is our stern advice to-day. **The payment of the Royal Bounty on twins and triplets simply must cease; and quickly.**

You see? Let us put it another way. HM ignores his Irish subjects, puts a tariff on their cows, and forbids his Princes to come over for the shooting; he then turns round and pokes his finger into the private affairs of Irish Family Life. Has his cake and eats it in other words; has it both ways and burns the candle at both ends.

Blather considered the matter carefully and came to the conclusion that no useful purpose can be served by receiving a deputation. *Blather* resolved to fight the menace with every weapon known to clean-limbed British sport.

We dispatched the following sharp telegram to his Majesty the King.

Please accept filial homage stop cannot stand for triplet souperism stop you will have to stop it stop give it over immediately stop will beat you at your own game stop blather will stop at nothing stop ask dulanty stop too much of a good thing stop aithnigheann ciarog ciarog eile[1] stop.

The following arrived in reply.

King deeply touched by message of loyalty stop always deeply interested in activities of british legion in ireland stop please convey sincere thanks and best wishes to men stop.

You see the *laissez faire* philosophy behind it all? Live horse and you'll get grass. Is it any wonder that the entire fabric of our Western civilisation is tottering, that you have MAs and qualified professional men walking the streets. There are only one or two things that *Blather* takes lying down, and this is not one of them. When we say it, we mean it, and we are saying it through our teeth. Here is our answer.

---

[1] Proverb: One earwig recognises another.

155

THE *BLATHER* SCHEME OF TRIPLET AND OTHER BOUNTIES

Charitable Work	Our Bounty	His Bounty
Twins	18 free copies of the pamphlet 'The *Blather* Attitude on Twins'.	Nil.
Triplets	200 yds of best quality cotton baby-cloth, plus £3 3s. od.	£2 2s. od. only.
Quads	4 lbs. of back-rashers from the *Blather flitch* plus £4 4s. od.	£2 2s. od. only.
Giant Vegetable Marrows	*Blather* free tours to America in the Graf Zeppelin.	Nil.
Earliest hearing of Cuckoo, good golf cards, good scout work and woodlanding, etc.	Illuminated *Blather* Cards bearing the inscription: 'GOOD WORK'.	Nil.

Is your son an ignoramus . . .?

Has your son failed the Clerical Officers again? What, AGAIN? No wonder. How can he possibly expect to pass when he doesn't know the rudiments of English? Don't get insulted. We mean it. Listen to what the great German Hedge-schoolmaster, Dr Otto Kindergarten, has to say about the standard of English in these islands. Dr Kindergarten always speaks his mind. There isn't much of it, and he likes to speak it all. You can trust what he says.

'It is a true but little-known fact,' he says, 'that the English language was first invented by the Abbey Theatre. The degenerate patois spoken by the inhabitants of England, Ireland and Wales bears the same relation to pure English as a horse-trough does to the Blackrock Baths. Unfortunately, the number of people who speak English in everyday life is negligible; and it is only on the

stage of the Abbey that one hears this beautiful language spoken· as it should be spoken. Can nothing be done about this scandal?'

Yes, Doktor. Everything possible will be done to educate the Great Ignorant Public. By us. In the first place, we are frankly delighted to see that the Civil Service Commission is putting its foot down and insisting on a reasonably high standard of Abbey English. But that is not enough. Growing Lads must be encouraged, by simple attractive lessons, to speak proper English so that when they come to sit for their exams, they won't be a Trial to their Fathers. We give below the first lesson of our great series. It is specially written in the form of a dialogue between three persons, so that three Growing Lads can get together and give each other hell.

In addition, the student can win valuable prizes by reciting this piece at any decent Feis. We have done it ourselves.

FOR BARNEY'S SAKE,
READ THIS!

Shaun: Good morrah, Peadar.

Peadar: Good morrah, Shaun.

Shaun: It is a grand day, Peadar, thanks be.

Peadar: Musha, aye indeed, it is that, surely. Would you have the filling of a pipe of the good hard plug, forbye?

Shaun: Indeed now, and perhaps I have. Let you draw that stool of the three legs into the good blaze of the hand-won turf and let the steam rise in clouds from your drenched trousers, forbye.

Peadar: Thank ye kindly. A murrain, surely, upon these crickets that leap and leap with many leaps upon the hard flagstones of the hearth.

Shaun: Indeed, and many murrains upon them. But who comes with the soft padding foot-fall, like the fall of twilight on a purple hill? Surely it is Phelim of the Bogs? (*Enter Phelim of the Bogs. As a matter of fact, the dirty rat has been there all the time.*)

Phelim: God bless all here. Have·ye heard the news, the black, black news from the North?

Shaun and Peadar (*together*): Nothing have we heard for many

157

days but the drip-drip-drip of the rain as it drips, and the sighing of the wind as it sighs.

Phelim: Indeed, troth, good cause has it to sigh. For last night, at the grey coming of the twilight, the redcoats seized a poor Croppy Boy as he watered his stag in the glen. O, woe, woe, woe!

Peadar: Alas, alas, poor Yorick.

Shaun: The pity of it. The pitiful pity of it is heavy on my heart this day.

Peadar: A bitter black curse upon these Redcoats, surely.

Shaun: And a red curse, too, say I.

Phelim: Aye, troth, and fifty pink curses with knobs attached be upon them this day.

Shaun: Och, och, ochone, alannah. Och, och, ochone.

Peadar: Alas, alas, poor Yorick.

Phelim: O, woe, woe, woe.

Your ignoramus of a son?
... What of his future? ...
For that matter, what of
his past? ...

That young scion of yours, what of his future? We meant to take you into a corner and ask you about him ages ago, but all the corners were occupied by corner-boys and we failed to find a vacant one. Hence the delay. You have no doubt decided not to send him up to the 'varsity, as that would entail his going about in the cold weather with no overcoat, only a scarf around his windpipe, and he is too delicate for that. The question, then, is to decide on a Career or a Trade. Below, our printers have generously agreed to print our survey of some of the existing openings.

Road-surveyor

The business of a Road-surveyor is to survey existing openings on the roads and to arrange for them to be filled up with basic slag and metal and screened dressings and whatnot. He is also

158

charged with preventing the farming community from making pot-holes in the roads with their pots. The roads in Ireland are the best in the world. That is what a road-surveyor says.

County councillor
There is no salary attached to this occupation, but if your son has inherited your own talent for fiddling with the gas-meter, the question of salary is not important. As most of the Board-rooms are dreary places in the winter, the first essential quality is capacity for heat, or for engendering heat. When the atmosphere becomes too heated, the candidate must be capable of producing a 'breeze'. It is also necessary to ask someone at every meeting whether he is prepared to repeat that filthy lie outside and take the thrashing of his life, or would he prefer to have his face put in there and then. It is also essential (a) to ask the Chairman to resign; (b) to allege that the Department is treating the Council like a pack of schoolboys; and (c) to ask the Chairman to resign.

The Civil Service
This was invented by the Civil Service Commission, Upper O'Connell Street, who jealously guard it and retain the serial rights in Europe and the USA. In the Administrative Grades, intelligence and sound judgment are essential. Candidates deficient in these qualities must produce evidence of a University education.

Cowboy
A lucrative but somewhat overcrowded profession. Candidates must be able to throw a sombrero in the air and riddle it with a six-shooter, give the slip to the Sheriff's posse and leap the Grand Canyon on a Shetland mare. Cowboys can always get a living punching steers in Ringsend, or holding up the Tullamore stage at Tyrrellspass. In time of trouble, a cowboy must know to make for the badlands, huh! Cowboys who wish to practice rustling cattle can do so by rustling silk in the privacy of their bedroom.

Journalism
There are no openings in this profession at the moment, as all our posts are filled.

159

Farming

In this calling there is always plenty of room at the top of the tree, as it is necessary to keep a sharp look-out for Guards. Candidates must be practised in the handling of the cross-cut, must be able to drive a car and make a witty after-sale speech in the Pound. They must also understand how to make poteen and grow barley, and know what is meant by the rotation of crops, which is how the barley looks after drinking the poteen. A good farmer never puts on a dinner-jacket when dining. Tails always.

Gombeenism (Gombeenery)

This is Gaelic for Banking & Finance. It is also known as sucking the blood of the poor and taking the bread out of their mouths at the same time. Really skilful Gombeen-men can also manage to bite the hand that feeds them at the same time, feather their own nest and lie curled up with the jaw between the hands, like a dog in a manger. The first essential of Gombeenism (Gombeenery) is that the Gombeen-man must send all his sons and daughters to Trinity or UCD. Modern Gombeen-men must be prepared to lend total strangers £20,000 on note of hand alone without security.

Film-star

Candidates (female) who are very beautiful can make £100,000 per annum on the films. Candidates who are not very beautiful can also make £100,000 per annum on the films, provided they are winsome like Janet Gaynor, or dynamic like Katherine Hepburn. See COWBOY. The profession will not appeal to those poor backward beings who prefer to take off their clothes in private. Big money can be made directing films provided one's name sounds like Rota Schenk or Baryk Zanuk.

DUT Co. bus-driver

The only essential in this profession is to give the bus its head and yield to its gregarious instinct by driving it in a herd with two others everywhere you go, especially on the Dalkey line. Herds of less than three buses together are unheard of, because if buses travelled alone at frequent intervals, suburban dwellers would have an even chance of getting into town, only to be corrupted in

160

the Big City. It is the business of the driver to prevent this at all costs.

National school-teacher (NT)

The noblest of all the professions. Candidates are expected to make financial provision for retirement into a private mad-house in the early forties, as the little rats are sure to win in the end. Candidates must learn to equate the word 'swine' with 'Inspector', and have the sense not to slap the children of short-tempered coal-heavers. Teachers who deal with the older boys are only a secondary consideration.

Gaiety-theatre leading lady

Candidates for this attractive position must hail from across the water and must visit the vast linotype hall in Independent House and say the machines are wonderful, can almost speak, etc. She must also receive her name in type-metal, thank the operator for it charmingly and put it in her bag. Ability to sing and dance need be no handicap.

Match-seller

Handsome living can be made by retailing matches on bridges and other public places in the City. The business yields a ready cash profit of 25 per cent and the business is not subject to Corporations Profit Tax. Candidates may at their discretion be blind and dumb, but not too blind to notice a bad coin and not too dumb to tell the world.

Newspaper-seller

Candidates who are going to become millionaires must begin by selling newspapers in the streets; no millionaire is considered genuine unless he has done this.

You must admit that this is a goodish list from which to choose a career for your young hopeless. If you do not admit that it is goodish, at least admit that it is fairish. If you do not think the selection is sufficiently wide, write to us and we will print a further list next month. In the meantime, send us a photograph of

161

your son, as we are badly in need of a good belly-laugh. If you have no photograph of your son, your own will do instead.

Cavalcade

Mr Eamonn de Valera arrived.

Mr Eamonn de Valera arrived, accompanied by his son, Vivion.

Mr Eamonn de Valera arrived, accompanied by Mr Vivion de Valera.

Messrs Eamonn and Vivion de Valera arrived.

Messrs Vivion and Eamonn de Valera arrived.

Mr Vivion de Valera arrived, accompanied by Mr Eamonn de Valera.

Mr Vivion de Valera arrived, accompanied by his father, Eamonn.

3

From the Irish

'Remember that I too was Irish. Today I am cured.'
CRUISKEEN LAWN
Irish Times, 31 May 1943

Brian O'Nolan had his first prose pieces published in *The Irish Press* at the end of 1931, when he was twenty. They were in Irish, his first language, and he was to continue writing in Irish on and off until about 1960. The five stories and single essay that make up this section can be looked upon as apprentice pieces: as always, presages of O'Nolan's mature work may be seen in material from the beginning of his career. I am grateful to Breandán Ó Conaire for supplying translations of the stories. It is no easy task to put English on O'Nolan's Irish, for he revelled in word-play and parody from the start, and inevitably something is lost in the transition. However, enough remains to give a reader a taste. The final essay I have translated myself.

The Irish question: An old tale from an old lad

The readers of *Blather* will be glad to hear that we are neither negligent nor careless in matters pertaining to the ancestral tongue. In the warm weather it gets dry and the only remedy is a full glass of Frontillan '34. (Don't let that strange word frighten you, reader. That's the French for poteen.) But may the frost kill us! It wasn't to talk about that kind of tongue we took up our pen. Let you have patience. We'll begin again.

The readers of *Blather* will be glad to hear that we are neither negligent nor careless in matters pertaining to the ancestral tongue. The very moment that *Blather* was founded the VIPs of the paper came together and agreed unanimously that it was a great pity that the old tales of our ancestors were becoming extinct as they were. Before you'd have time to redden your pipe they had decided (a) to snatch the old tales and folklore of our ancestors from the mouth of the grave, and (b) to exit immediately and have a drinking session in the public house at the corner of —— Street. A week after that they assembled together again, and it was then, by dad, that the work began in earnest. Five hundred train tickets were purchased, five hundred notebooks and five hundred pencils. They were distributed amongst five hundred young men, who were ordered to disperse throughout the country and collect the stories of the old people. They are now working at their utmost (and at many other things which can't be mentioned here) in every corner of the country where Irish is spoken or whispered, in pursuit of the elders and coaxing stories from them. This tale below was told by a grey bandy-legged ugly-mouthed old man named Laury Mac Lupracaun.

When he was questioned, he said that he hadn't a story and that he hadn't heard a story nor an excuse for a story in all his life. His shirt was then removed (if he had worn buttons on his skin that would also have been removed, believe us), he was bound in chains and one of the men began to lay into him with a split stick.[1] (The stick was perfect when the battering began, but after a while it was seen to be broken.) Well, well! Is there anything in the world, reader, so miserable and pitiable as the crying of an old grey-haired man? It would wring a tear from your eye the roars let out by the poor old boy, and the agitated manner in which he screamed for his grandmother, who had been beneath the sod for twenty years. Yes, twenty years she had been carrying the sods from the bog, a full of a sack of them – but finally the pain made him see that if he didn't know a story that he would have to make one up if he wanted a break. He was then set free, and he began:

Once upon a long time ago, before trousers were worn in Ireland, there lived a king called Slocky Mac Slobber. He had only the one son. Eochy, I am sorry to say, was the name of this son. The son's fame was far greater and more widespread than the fame of the king, because there was not on the face of the earth, nor on the surface of the globe, nor under the blue framework of the sky a lazier man than he. He spent his time,

---

[1] *Maide briste*: tongs; literally, broken stick.

164

from one end of the year to the other, day and night, and each hour of the clock between those two occasions, lying on the flat of his back, eating and drinking, and when the notion would take him, drinking and eating. He used to lie on a fine soft bed of feathers, and nothing on earth could budge him out of it. He slept at night, but remained awake during the day. The nobles of the royal family would always be gathered round the bed, attending on him, and inventing amusements for him, as is the custom to do for the son of a king.

By the side of his bed was a table covered with delicious savoury food of every sort in existence. And there were fruits there as well, apples and gooseberries, and large leather bags full of watercress, and decorated silver platters full of blackberries, and gold-hooped barrels full of whortle-berries gathered on Slemish, and marble buckets full of red and dark berries. And on the other side of his bed was another table with hundreds of bottles on it, and every bottle of them full to the neck with dry smooth poteen made by the distillers who used to make poteen on Slieve Gua, and there did not exist at that time better poteen-makers in the country. And under the bed were thousands of bottles. And all of them used to be empty.

The young prince spent twenty years in this manner reclining on his bed, and it was contented, comfortable, agreeable and cheerful the soft blanketed life he had, eating, drinking, debating with wise men, and listening to music and to the harmonising of his harpers. But now and again a mournful frown came over his countenance and he would say in a morose, tearful, despondent voice, 'Oh woe is me! Are there no birds with softer plumage on them that a new bed could be made for me, because this bed is damnably hard!' And an anguished cry of lament and sympathy would then rise from the company, pitying the poor fellow.

In the summer when the red pate of the sun was high in the sky and the birds raving in the woods, wheels would be put beneath the bed and the young prince conducted out to the orchard so that he might see the sky and the trees and the other things which do not grow in the inside of a bedroom.

But after some time the king perceived that it was not natural for a person to be stretched out on his bed for so long, and, in a manner which he himself did not understand, he came to realise

165

that his son was perhaps slightly indolent. He pledged one thousand pounds to the first person who would entice the prince from his bed. Many people came and departed again but not one of them bore the reward away. Whiskery long-bearded men from the back of the hills came, fierce large-limbed men of unusual strength, and they attempted to drag the prince out of the bed by force. But they did not succeed.

'Devil a foot nor a toe will I lay on the floor again as long as I live,' said the prince, and he summoned his male nurse, and a great stack of oat-bread and a big bowl of steaming tea was brought in for him, and he set about meal and munching; the men then understood that it was no use, and they departed. The following day a skilled harper from the County Meath arrived, and he began to play lively airs with vigour, hoping to beguile the prince from his bed, for there wasn't a second person on the face of the earth who could hear his music without doing a dance. But –

When the old man had come this far in the story one of the men asked him Did He Think They Were Eejits, or What Sort Of Nonsensical Rubbish Was This, and another man asked was He Looking For A Fight and if he was Step Out On The Road and I'll Give You A Skinful. However, when the old man proved to them that his pockets were empty and that the homespun clothes on his back weren't worth a blade of grass they allowed him to go home. But do not be befuddled, reader. As long as a drop of whiskey remains in the bottom of a glass, those men will not forsake this noble task. If you are a grey-haired person or an eighty years oldster do not attempt to flee or go into hiding from them. And when they arrive, have a story ready for them, or if you prefer, two excuses,[1] as two excuses equal one story. Have that ready and you're in no danger.

[1] The word in the original is *leithscéal* which means 'excuse' or 'apology', and literally 'half a story': *leath* = half, *scéal* = story.

An insoluble question

Once upon a time there was an old fellow, who was honest, charitable, wide-girdled and even-tempered – in short, an exceedingly good person. He was so ancient that he was well able to remember the great historical events which came to pass in Ireland a hundred years before, and he spoke Irish of a strange and awkward sort – the amount of it that he had – whose like is not to be encountered outside the *Book of the Dun Cow*, and often not even in that book either. He had a stoop in his back and he always used to carry a blackthorn stick in his claw; he was stout, well-nourished, with two eyes twinkling lively beneath his white brows, and he wore neither collar nor tie but had a monstrous long white beard flowing down from his two ears on to his breast – enough fine fur to stuff a pair of pillows! The person who would understand the nobility of the elderly and the respect to which they are entitled would take a second look at this specimen. He was too good.

The old fellow lived with his son in a house, and (since we are telling a story in Irish), it was a small whitewashed house in the corner of the glen. Not far from his house was another in which a growing young lad lived with this family. The youngster was increasing in wisdom every day, and becoming astute and inquisitive.

One day he took his father aside and asked him a question – a great question that had been lying heavily on his mind for a long time.

'When this old fellow is in bed,' said the lad, 'does his beard be under the bedclothes, or does it be out in the open with the blankets tucked in underneath it?'

'That's a big question,' said the father, 'and I haven't got its solution. But go and ask your mother.'

This the lad did.

'I couldn't tell you that,' said the mother, 'but I have an idea that his son will know. Go over and put the question to him.'

This was done. The son was an affable fellow, who hadn't any guile in him, no more than his father. He reflected.

'I have slept in the same bed as him,' said he, 'from the time I

167

was as small as yourself, and if I were to be flayed alive on this spot I couldn't answer that question – but here he is coming in now. Ask him yourself.'

The question was put. The Oldfellow contemplated deep and hard. He scourged his sluggish languid mind, and twisted and shook his memory. He closed his eyes and visualised himself lying in his bed. He tried his utmost, but, alas, it was no use.

'I don't know,' he said simply. He felt sad and ashamed that he could not solve such an easy question, after all he had seen of the world.

'Come back tomorrow, little man,' said he, 'and I'll have the answer to your question.'

'Thank you,' said the youngster.

The day departed and the night arrived. The Oldfellow headed for bed. He put on his nightshirt and his sleeping bonnet, he snuggled himself down cosily, put his head on the pillow, arranged the bedclothes compactly and carefully under his beard, and lay there trying to sleep. But he did not lie there for long. His chinbone began to itch, with a firm fiery itch. His neck began to get sore and his ears warm; the bedclothes were irritating his beard. Isn't it foolish my old head is tonight, he thought, and me without my beard under the blankets as it has been for forty years. Angrily he put the clothes over the beard and again tried to sleep. Within a minute, however, he was again at a loss: he was truly wretched, in pain and torment. Had twenty crows been attempting to build nests in that beard, they wouldn't have caused him more distress.

'Damn!' said the Oldfellow.

He controlled the fit of anger that was coming over him, and made an attempt to remedy the situation. He placed half the beard inside and half the beard outside; he lay on his face; he lay on the hair itself; and he put his head completely under the bed-clothes. But each solution was worse than the previous one . . .

The Oldfellow sat up and pondered gloomily to himself. Then he decided that it would be a good idea to get up and make a strong cup of tea, and to put the boy's question completely out of his mind; afterwards he would go back to bed, and only just when he had almost fallen asleep, would recall the question.

168

'I will make a cup of dark, mysterious, uncharted tea,' said the Oldfellow.

He rose and located the dark stairway leading down to the kitchen. Thus it happened that he continued walking the floor without the floor being there: the beginning of the stairs and the conclusion of the floor was that place. He descended like a sack of flour. He broke his neck and split open his skull, and his soul sundered from his body.

That youngster is still living. He goes to school, acquiring education, and that question still remains in his heart, unsolved. He will presently understand that all knowledge is not to be found in the books, and he will put the question to some other old fellow; and if the worst comes to the worst he can wait until the arrival of his own beard (if such is destined for him) and banish the deadly doubt from him for ever.

But maybe God will give him sense.

Good luck and bad luck

'Do you see this watch?' said I.

'I see it,' said Old Greyhead.

'Well,' said I, 'there is a peculiar story connected with it. It's my opinion that there isn't another watch of the same make in Ireland or Aran today. It is an ancient heavy gold watch and it has an attribute which no watch made these days has. Not a minute has it lost since I got it, and my father told me that it only lost half a minute during his lifetime, and that half minute was lost because my grandfather wound it a little too tightly when he got it from his father as a boy, before he was accustomed to it.'

'My own watch is better than that,' said Old Greyhead.

'Hold your tongue and don't ruin my story,' said I. 'Well, when I was young and had little sense, there was one day and I was badly in need of money (I believe I was in love with a girl and longed to buy a present for her). Unfortunately for myself, an unpropitious inclination came upon me to bring my noble and ancient timepiece to the man of the three orbs, and to acquire a

169

generous sum of money for it. There was heavy gold in it, not to be found in any other watch. I would not accept a penny under twenty pounds.

'I put the watch apprehensively in my pocket and repressed the shame which was rising in my breast, and out I went in the evening twilight, proceeding towards the shop of the three orbs. I laid my heavy yellow friend on the counter and asked for twenty pounds. The shopkeeper scrutinised it, and without much delay placed it back in my hand. "It is not our custom," he said mockingly, "to purchase broken objects."

'My heart leapt in my bosom! What's this? I put the watch to my ear, the watch which had not lost a minute in one hundred years. Not the slightest sound was coming from it. It had stopped. I walked out of the shop like a toper on a Saturday night. What had I done that this calamity should befall me? . . .

'I put the watch aside for a day, and timely relief arrived in the matter of the money. The watch was in no danger now, and I felt that it ought to be put in order. I lifted it up and my heart jumped alive again when I heard the tic-tic coming from it as smoothly as ever it came. The dear little instrument was back to its old form. I almost gave it a lump of sugar as a reward . . . I still have the watch as a result of that little hesitation. Have you ever heard of anything as fortunate and as strange as that, Micky?'

'Of course I have,' said that son of a mother, 'Undoubtedly. When I was young (and that's neither today nor yesterday) I was short on sense and I was discussing nuptial matters with a woman. The affair worsened, and one spring morning the two of us were standing in the presence of the priest. When the question would I take her as my wife was put to me, my tic-tic halted. My voice got the better of me. I could not enunciate a word. My tongue failed me. I was dumb, out and out dumb, dumb completely. The question was put a second time, and the same silence ensued a second time. A fit of crying seized the girl and she was taken home.'

'And what happened to you?' I asked.

'Me? I was laid on my back, my shirt was opened, and the man yonder told the man hither to give me some air. Another intelligent man procured a bottle of whiskey.'

'And was it long before you got the voice back?'

170

'By my life it wasn't. Inside two minutes I was able to speak.'

'And what did you say?'

'"DON'T PUT WATER IN IT!!!" The rogue was trying to destroy the drink. That was as lucky a thing as happened in this world.'

'You weren't the only lucky one that day,' said I.

Woe to the lovelorn

From the day he was born Big Gogarty had the cream of common sense. Everybody knew that he was an honest, balanced intelligent individual, the last person to lose the head even if the whole world went bananas; his friends knew his value and had great affection and respect for him. That is the first trait of Gogarty's with which we wish to acquaint the reader.

In addition to that, he understood money and financial matters and, although he was not miserly in any way, it was not his custom to spend or lose the least penny without good reason. He never bothered with the women, hadn't a predilection for the jar and he didn't smoke: he was too sensible. That's the second talent.

However, with the passage of time all things change. Big Gogarty was returning home one winter's evening and he addressed the young boy who used to sell newspapers on the street corner, as it was his custom to buy the Daily from him – this Gogarty was a clever and wise character. He bought a paper.

'A word in your ear,' said he, 'have you a good belt around your trousers?'

The youngster stared at him in sheer wonder.

'I haven't,' he said finally, 'I've braces.'

'Well,' said Gogarty, 'the belt is better, more wholesome and more effective. Here is a good leather belt for you . . . a small present for Christmas.'

The young fellow accepted the belt without another word. He didn't understand the story but it wasn't his wont to spurn destiny. 'I'll get sixpence for it tomorrow in the House of the Three Orbs,' said he.

Gogarty went home in a bus. When he was approaching the

end of the journey he rose and spoke to the official who was in charge of the bus.

'Your trousers aren't hanging correctly,' he said, 'perhaps you would like a belt?'

'My trousers are all right,' said the official angrily.

'Even so,' said Gogarty, 'perhaps you have a headstrong mischievous son. Here's a good leather belt for you. You can make your son hum with it, or wear it yourself. Your trousers aren't all right!' – and he leapt out of the bus into the darkness of the night.

(Permit me now to continue the course of our story in the newspapers. Here below are some short extracts from them.)

The Committee came to order. A letter from the Government was read saying that the position which was vacant should be filled without delay. The name of MacCarthy was accepted as meat supplier for the Poorhouse. A letter was read from Mr Gogarty Esq. in Dublin offering two hundred belts for the men in the Poorhouse. The belts were accepted and gratitude was expressed to Gogarty.

Dunc—— Feis (Cultural Festival). There was a meeting of the Committee and it was arranged that the Feis would be held again this year. A letter was read from Mr Gogarty Esq. offering twenty Irish leather belts as a prize, and he was heartily thanked.

The Committee of the Royal Society for the Clothing of the Naked Savage Blackmen Overseas assembled, the Dowager de la Mer-O'Hickey in the chair, and one hundred leather belts were gratefully accepted from Mr Gogarty Esq.

Saturday, at the Church of St Michael, were married Francis ('Frankie') Gogarty, son of Tiny Gogarty and his late wife, and Mary ('Maisy') Taylor, daughter of Mr Taylor and his wife, of Beltfort. Honeymoon on the Riviera.

Envoi

Mary's father, Mr Taylor Esq. himself, intends to sell the shop and live at his leisure until the day he dies. Perhaps he doesn't wish to continue with the shopwork without Mary there to assist him, or perhaps she sold so many belts that he was provided with sufficient riches. We don't know. But Mary will make a good wife

172

for Gogarty. He would be buying belts until the present day, his fingers trying out the leather and his two eyes fixed on the woman's face, but for the fact that she uttered the necessary word...

Honeymoon, as we mentioned above, on the Riviera super-vivant.

The narrative of the inebriated man

He was a small pleasant non-irascible man and I wouldn't have given him a second glance were it not for the fact that he was vehemently and furiously conversing with a strect lamp. It seemed to me he was drunk and that it would be a good thing to guide him home. I accosted him: 'What's the meaning of this or what's the matter with you!' said I. 'You ought to be in your bed instead of loitering like this in a state of intoxication about the city. You should turn your back on the public-house and return to the family fireside – a nice sensible person like yourself – and take an interest in some hobby, the gramophone or fret-work...'

'GRAMOPHONE!' He looked intently at me with two eyes which had an infernal wildness in them – two venomous red flames.

The drunk man's tale
'Wait a minute,' said he, 'till I tell you my story. It will make you sad if you're a human being at all . . . One clear Spring morning ten years ago I heard the woman's voice for the first time and unless my memory is deluded I considered that it was a good voice she had, a voice that would develop satisfactorily with care and practice.

'It appears that a similar resolution resided in the bosom of the damsel herself, as the practising commenced the very next day and it continued strenuously without cessation or interruption, without respite or pause, for ten years. I am still here but I am not the same man, alas, who used to be there at that time ... I used

173

to have a consuming interest in music then, and I won't say that I didn't strike up the fiddle now and again in the solitude of the night – may I be forgiven for it.

The single-tuned woman

'But the damsel yonder. She lived in the house across the street from my house. Annie Laurie was the first sound I heard on wakening, and Annie Laurie was the last syllable that rent my heart and me going to rest; and the clock said Annie Laurie-Annie Laurie till morning. "After great diversion comes dejection." The great diversion was over yonder from dawn till dark, and as I live, it was me who suffered the dejection, the oppression, the frenzied stupefaction, the fit of wrath, the rancour. I believe that the wheezing of death in my throat would have been more melodious to me than those goading words, Annie Laurie.

'Had matters continued so, I knew that melancholy and loneliness would come upon my soul, that I would become sick at heart and sparse of reason. What happened? I was shaving myself one morning when I became conscious of some other air being rendered. Methinks my pretty comely damsel has a new song – may prosperity follow her – she is making progress.

The man's voice

'Subsequently I recognised that it was the voice of a man. Down the stairs with me. The music was emanating from the house next door to my house, on the right hand side. The song finished and a voice said that they were "going over to the Royal Hotel, Blackpool, for dance music". And they went . . . and majestically and gently, but waxing in power by the minute, the high voice of the woman said that Maxwelton Braes were bonn-ee.

'A year passed and another transformation came upon the world. There was another house next door to mine, on the left hand side, and I heard one morning, over the clamour of Annie Laurie and the shindy of the other man, that it was being announced to the world that a gentleman was about to give a "Talk" on the "Decoration of the Modern Sitting-Room". Another interval passed. Annie Laurie was still alive, so alive that I imagined that the flower of second youth was upon her.

Daventry was coming in doing its level best on one side and Radio-Paris was looking after the revelries on the other side. A barrel-organ used always be audible in the neighbourhood, that and a piper whose ear and whose pipes were far from true, unbeknownst to himself.

'Talks'

'Well, indeed,' said I, 'that is bad tidings. What did you do?'

'Bad news without any doubt. I wrote to the Minister for Posts & Telegraphs. He said that he intended to initiate "Talks" on the wireless giving advice to the public, which would ease the situation. Maybe they would, "TALKS my granny," said I. I procured a long sharp knife and I believe that I dispatched the two men who were so enamoured of the radio (one poor individual had a family of eight). I was about to put Annie Laurie to rest for good when I remembered that it was time for me to be on my way to the Conference at Lausanne.'

'The Conference?'

'Yes. Don't you recognise me? I'm Napoleon Bonaparte!'

'Indeed, you're right,' said I, a little dismayed. 'Wait till you see my fine knife.' The red eyes were twinkling like stars at Halloween.

'I'll see it tomorrow,' said I, moving off as rapid as my feet would carry me.

A bijou: A bon mot

In every language that has ever been spoken there are to be found words of great value which have had neither mention in books nor attention from lexicographers. Be that as it may, they are in the mouths of people whenever they voice their thoughts, and they are as essential as whiskey is to a glass.

Those who rely on the intelligence gained at their father's knee, as opposed to the artificial skills available in the school-house, understand the nobility of these words, and they give great thanks to God that they possess words of this calibre to impart exactitude and neatness to their speech.

175

The good people who speak Irish in Donegal use such a word: a word that has a strength, an efficiency and an ambiguity not to be found in any other; it contains question and answer (according to how it is spoken), depression and love, melancholy and joy; within it are the loneliness of night and the light of the sun, the laughter of youth and the disability of age. 'WELL' (*BHÁL*) – THAT'S THE WORD WE ARE TALKING ABOUT.

A silly little word, the reader may say, a word that was unwittingly stolen from English. Perhaps so; but a theft of that sort is lawful, says Aristotle, if the thief bestows upon it a special delight and beauty when the thievery is done, and this word in Irish has a power and a beauty which are never to be found in English.

Take, for example, the man of the house who comes home one afternoon tired and weary, and not wanting conversation:

'Well, well,' he says. His wife knows what's up, and gives the one permissible answer.

'Oh, well, right enough.'

Or, for example, take two people who meet on the main road one rainy day. They speak.

''Tis a soft day.'

'Well, it is.'

That's a 'well' of another type, far more powerful and effectual than 'alas', 'assuredly' or 'indeed'.

Youth is greedy: offer an apple to a young lad and ask him the question:

'Would you like an apple?'

'Well!' he will say, i.e., 'very much.'

Go visiting by night, to where there is revelry and a five-noggin bottle on the table taking the sting out of life; there you will hear calm contented converse that you will appreciate if you understand it:

'Well, well,' says the man of the house.

'Oh, well,' says another man.

'Well, indeed.'

'Right enough.'

'Well, well, well.'

'Oh, well?'

'Well.'

The mouth that is silent is sweet; the mouth that is half-silent is sweeter, with just the one soft, blessed word slipping out of it from time to time.

Whether this fine word is to be found in Connacht or in Kerry or in Ring I do not know, but, during these times, when Irish is daily growing rarer, it would be a good plan to put the word (with all its nuances) onto gramophone discs, and to cause it to be used throughout Ireland, for when the day comes – may the evil thing be far off – when Irish has vanished from the country, there would be one word remaining that would demonstrate the wisdom, the history, the provincialism and the daemon of our forefathers in every parish.

That's another job for the government.

4

At Swim-Two-Birds

'Honestly, if I get sufficiently drunk over Christmas I'm going to read that damned book for the first time. Those birds must have some unexpected stuffing in them.'

Letter to Timothy O'Keeffe, 18 Dec. 1965

On 4 January 1939, Brian O'Nolan wrote a letter to *The Irish Press*:

Dear Sir,

I have been shown an entry in your College Notes in Monday's *Irish Press* in which the authorship of a book called *Swim Two Birds* is attributed to me. Your information apparently derives from a rumour spread by two gentlemen called Sheridan and O'Brien who charge me with the authorship of a book of this name or something similar. The cream of this elaborate 'joke' is that the supposed book is anti-clerical, blasphemous and licentious and various lengthy extracts from it have been concocted to show the obscenity of the work. I have joined in the joke to some extent myself but I naturally take strong exception to the publicity given by your paragraph, which associates me by name with something which is objectionable, even if non-existent. I must therefore ask you to withdraw the statement. I would be satisfied if you merely mentioned that a graduate mentioned in your last Notes is not the author of any book mentioned and has in fact no intention of publishing any book.

On 13 March 1939, *At Swim-Two-Birds* was published under the pseudonym 'Flann O'Brien'. The back of the jacket, however, attributed the book to O'Nolan. In the months coming up to publication the author excised and amended some sections of the novel. Thanks to the work of the Flann O'Brien scholar, Susan Asbee, it is possible to include here three of the missing or altered passages:

A conversation

(Brinsley and the narrator are in the narrator's bedroom.)

– When we get our degrees, I said, we might get a teaching job from the Christian Brothers.

– If we're lucky. Holy God isn't it a fright!

– The only way to make money, I said, is to make it in a lump. One horse, one bank robbery, one book, that is all you want. Once in a lifetime is enough.

– The book would be a better proposition than the horse, he answered, if it's the sort that depends on the horse being an overrated animal. Where is the nearest good bank?

– The sort of book I mean, I explained, is one with a cover and printed pages, a storybook, you know. Are you writing anything?

My hand was in my pocket resting on the pink sheaf of my typescript.

He said he was not, using an improper expression.

– You should, you know, I said.

We paused in unison.

– How is that business of yours going? he inquired.

– I do a little every day, I said, after meals.

I then tendered an explanation spontaneous and unsolicited concerning my own work, affording an insight as to its aesthetic, its daemon, its argument, its sorrow and its joy, its darkness, its sun-twinkle clearness.

Nature of explanation offered: It was stated that while the novel and the play were both pleasing intellectual exercises, the novel was inferior to the play inasmuch as it lacked the outward accidents of illusion, frequently inducing the reader to be outwitted in a shabby fashion and caused to experience a real concern for the fortunes of illusory characters. The play was consumed in wholesome fashion by large masses in places of public resort; the novel was self-administered in private. The novel, in the hands of an unscrupulous writer, could be despotic. In reply to an inquiry, it was explained that a satisfactory novel should be a self-evident sham to which the reader could regulate at will the degree of his credulity. It was undemocratic to compel characters to be uniformly good or bad or poor or rich. Each should be allowed a private life, self-determination and a decent standard of living. This would make for self-respect, contentment and better service. It would be incorrect to say that it would end in chaos. Characters should be interchangeable as between one book and another. The entire corpus of existing literature should be regarded as a limbo from which discerning authors could draw their characters as required, creating only when they failed to find a suitable existing creation. Could anyone devise a more abandoned villain than Claudius? Assuming the genius required to do so, would it be possible to justify the waste of space and effort involved in establishing his villainy before he is in a position to proceed to the crime proximately required by the plot? Was it not simpler, it was asked, to say that Mr James Hunter, gentleman, the villain of the piece, was in reality Claudius of Hamlet q.v.? That would acquaint the reader with the worst and preclude mountebanks, upstarts, thimbleriggers and persons of inferior education from an understanding of contemporary literature. Conclusion of explanation.

– That is very interesting but it is all balls, Brinsley said. Do you mean that a character in a book should have a day in his destiny and be the captain of his soul?

– Certainly, I said.

– Do you know, I don't think that's new, he said.

– And what's so very old about it?

– It's the sort of thing that occurs to everybody but nobody bothers to try it out. Do you know what I mean? It wouldn't stand the light of day. As a matter of fact I thought of it myself.

– You're a great man altogether, I said.

– But I did. Two years ago.

– Well never mind about that. I had some queer ideas myself two years ago. Here is a wad of my recentest prose.

I proffered a wad of my precise typescript, bent in double, pink-tinted. He took it without delight.

– Where did you get this? he asked.

– Sit down and read it, man, I said.

– I have a lecture, you know. Can I take it with me?

– Yes. But listen till I tell you. It's about the legendary Finn. He's a suitable man for a role in my story. Therefore he gets the

180

job. That stuff is all irrelevant – it's just for atmosphere, you know and so on. Are you listening to me?

– I am. I thought of it all two years ago.

He went away with my paper in his hip pocket. Cold listless rain was streaming without noise against the windows. Wet boots were leaving dismal smears about the floor and my surroundings appeared to me to bear a futile aspect. I made my way wearily to the street. In Leeson street I was depressed by desultory tramcars in the distance. I entered the post-office, emerging later to post a letter and walk homewards.

Name and address on letter: V. Wright, Esq., Wyvern Cottage, Newmarket, Suffolk.

Memoir on the Pooka's father, the Crack MacPhellimey

Fergus ('The Pooka') MacPhellimey, a species of rural demon, was born of respectable but poor parents in the County Cork, in 1876, a year memorable for the ravages of potato scale and shepherds' scurvy. His father, known far and wide as The Crack MacPhellimey, was a hard working devil-tinker who attended fairs for the purpose of seducing farmers' boys from righteousness by offering them spurious coins of his own manufacture which (by means of a secret chemical process) had the effect of rotting the pocket or mattress which contained them and imparting a contagious dry tetter to the human body – the object of the traffic being to make the afflicted boys utter curses and ungodly maledictions. He also retailed a line of magic shoddy of grey herringbone pattern with a faint red check, the peculiar quality of the fabric being that it dissolved into an evil smelling grey slime on coming into contact with water. This material he sold chiefly to the farming class in the west of Ireland, a district subject to incessant rain. The Crack was a familiar figure in his green coat of Irish poplin reaching from his neck to his heels and was welcome at any gathering on account of his sober and industrious habits, his skill as a fiddler, and his inexhaustable stock of anecdotes, rebuses and topographical poems, not a few of the latter being in the Gaelic language, an idiom he commanded with sweet charm. What brought him his greatest fame, however, was his skill as a dancer. His long poplin coat (was) worn chiefly to hide his slightly clubbed foot and consequently his feet were not to be seen when he danced, but their clump on the flags of a kitchen floor (was) so true and rhythmic that it was an unfailing delight to all present, and his easy accomplishment of the most intricate steps gave rise on more than one occasion to the opinion that he had three feet at least beneath the coat or maybe four. Even his spurious coins, distributed unobtrusively when the night was far advanced, did little to reduce his welcome when he appeared on his travels at the end of a year, for the full course of the tetter (provided the rashes were not treated with brown-bread poultices), was only six months and ten days. He also received honour by reason of the generous treatment he gave his wife, one of the Brannigans of Rush.

It happened that Fergus was born in a deserted piggery early in the morning. A country gentleman, passing by on horse-back, chanced to look into the piggery and noticed a hoof and a hair-tail protruding from a heap of soiled straw. Dismounting, he approached and woke the Crack MacPhellimey, who was asleep in an upright posture at a nearby wall, the back of his head being towards the east. The gentleman, who was one of a far-seeing and provident disposition, produced his costly wash-leather purse and offered two and fourpence for the foal, explaining at the same time that his wife was with child and that he would require a horse for his son in about six or seven years time. Perceiving that the offer was a generous one inasmuch as he did not own a foal, the Crack accepted it courteously. It was only when he withdrew the straw that he discovered that his wife had given him a son: a creature of human form covered with a soft yellowish down similar to that worn by chickens of the Rhode Island breed. The Crack then became subject to the pangs and pride of parenthood. Conclusion of memoir.

182

Mail from M. Byrne

I am just back from Galway where life goes very slowly but scarcely slowly enough for a man of my slothful habits. My granny's house is a grand place entirely. When I arrived off the bus I was asked what I would like for my tea. I said a rasher and egg and went to bed afterwards. When I got up the next morning, it was still raining and I had another rasher and egg for my breakfast. There were no papers so we sat watching the grey downpour of the rain on the cowering hillside. After about an hour like that my granny said what about a cup of tea? This was accepted then the tea was made with a great fuss of crockery and cooking. At one o'clock my granny said it was time for a midday cup of tea and who would have some. We all withdrew our gaze from the downpour and took the hot cups in our hands and drank it with conversation and enjoyment. Just at half two we had our dinner, a very tasty piece of lamb served with cabbage, potatoes and plenty of hot tea. Afterwards I smoked by the window and mused and read an old book of Dickens. Time was resting heavy on me till four o'clock when I heard the snap of the caddy-lid and knew that the tedium of the day was about to be relieved. I took the hot cup and laid aside my book and took my part in small-talk as it jumped quickly from one simple thing to another. Just at half-five when the oil lamps had been trimmed and lit and put in place, my granny asked what about a little drop of tea? The pot was still hot near the hob where it was always kept and the tea was made without delay. Paddy from Redmond's across the way came in through the rain with a load of parcels and I talked to him by the fire till tea-time. There was home-made currant bread for tea with jam, and rough country butter. At about then a strong cup of tea was made for everybody to mark the entry of these friends of Maggie's, one of them was just home from America where she had done some nursing. At about eleven when I had heard about three hours talking I thought I would go to bed and pray for fine weather so I had my supper of raw onions bread and tea and went up the steep stairs with my hot-jar in one hand and a candle in the other. I did not look what was in the jar but I can guess.

Brinsley was here and told me about the book, it will be very good if you can bring out the idea that Trellis is neurotic and may be imagining all the queer grotesque stuff and that he is not above going out in the street in his night-shirt. Just suggest it very subtly and leave them all to draw their own conclusions – was Hamlet really mad and so on. It would not do to present him as an ordinary lunatic struggling against creatures of his own imagination, that is too worn out, like then he woke up as an explanation for some otherwise inexplicable situation. It is a *pity* though that the madman theme is barred because I could give you a lot of tips about those gentlemen from my visit to the home at Nauheim. (Digression: You heard about the loonie that confided to the visitor that he was King of England. How do you know you are says the visitor. Because God Almighty told me so in a whisper one night, says the loony confidentially. You're a bloody liar, says a voice from the other side of the partition, I never said any such thing.) The greatest madmen of course are quite harmless and were never locked up in their lives. One man I knew thought he had a glass bottom and was afraid of his life to sit down in case he'd break it. In other subjects, however, he was a man of great intellectual force and could accompany any man in a mental ramble through the labyrinths of mathematics or philosophy or any other brand of truth so long as he was allowed to stand up throughout the disputations. Another man I knew was perfectly normal and well-conducted except that he would in no circumstances turn to the left and had a bicycle so constructed that it could not be turned in any direction except to the right. The simplest walk in such circumstances required an unusual amount of forethought and planning, and an unexpected visit to a strange house (which would have to be approached from a direction giving a right hand turn in at the gate) might result in an all-night walk of twelve hours duration before the patient could get home again, for there could be no question of going back the way he came. Others are subject to colours and attach undue importance to articles that are blue or red or white merely because they have that tint. Some are much exercised by the texture of a cloth or the roundness or angularity of an object. Numbers, however, account for a great proportion of unbalanced humanity. One man will rove the street seeking motor-cars with numbers that are divisible by seven. A poor German that I knew was very fond of three and made every aspect of his life a thing of triads. He went home one evening and drank three cups of tea with three lumps of sugar in each cup, cut his jugular with a razor three times and scrawled on a photograph of his wife with his dying hand goodbye, goodbye, goodbye.

5

Henrik Ibsen and Patrick Kavanagh

'Quite suddenly a small dog has appeared in my mind. He is clearly the property of some deceased mandarin. His coat is clipped in the manner of the east; his waist is clipped nearly naked, fantastic pantaloons of hair are made to clothe his legs. He runs rapidly around my head, searching vainly for mice. Suddenly he has grown old. Pathetic white moustaches girdle his old jaws. He lies down.

The walls of my memory have been decorated free of charge by Mr Jack Yeats. Every night without fail there is a display of fireworks –

The Plain People of Ireland: Where?

Myself: Inside in me head.'

CRUISKEEN LAWN
Irish Times 2 December 1942

In 1940, Brian O'Nolan, with the assistance of some friends, invented a new art form: the 'Letters Controversy'. We reprint here selections from two manifestations of the genre. The conventions of this new creative vehicle were simple: (a) that letters should be written under spurious names to the editor of a newspaper, and (b) that they should have only the most tenuous connection with reality. R. M. Smyllie, Editor of the *Irish Times*, allowed the carry-on, not only because it provided entertaining copy free of charge, but because, as news of the con-troversy spread, the paper's circulation grew. It was as a direct result of these letters that Smyllie offered O'Nolan a regular column – *Cruiskeen Lawn*. Readers may like to try to identify which ones were written by O'Nolan: it is not easy. One woman who protested that her name had been used without permission was in turn accused of being an impostor!

The first letter is quite innocent:

The Three Sisters

Sir,

Is it asking too much in these days of paper shortage to ask for space in which to issue a plea for greater support of the exquisite production of Tchekov's masterpiece, *Three Sisters*, being given by Lord Longford's company at the Gate Theatre?

One often hears it said that Dubliners will support a good play when it is offered to them; but this theory was not borne out by the many empty seats visible the night I visited the play.

Yours, etc.,
D. C. Barry
34 Lower Leeson St., Dublin

On June 3 there appeared a letter signed 'H.P.' blaming the lack of attendance at the Gate Theatre on the Irish love for American films, and on pro-Gaelic xenophobia among the few intellectuals. F. O'Brien responded:

Sir,

I was interested in 'H.P.'s' saucy letter of yesterday commenting on the poor attendances at the Gate Theatre's presentation of *The Three Sisters*. He is right when he suggests that overmuch Gaelic and Christianity, inextricably and inexplicably mixed up with an overweening fondness for exotic picture palaces, effectively prevents the majority of our people from penetrating farther north than the Parnell monument. Heigho for the golden days I spent as a youth in Manchester! In that civilised city we had Chekhov twice nightly in the music-halls; the welkin rang all day long from non-stop open-air Hamlets in the city parks, and the suicide rate reached an all-time high from the amount of Ibsen and Strindberg that was going on night and day in a thousand back-street repertory dives. One politely mentioned one's view on Dick Wagner when borrowing a light from a black stranger, and barmaids accepted a chuck under the chin only when it was accompanied by a soft phrase from Pirandello. Nowhere in the world outside Sheffield could the mind glut itself on so much buckshee literary tuck.

187

Hard as 'H.P.' may be pressed, I think I can claim to endure more agony than he from having to live in Ireland. Looking back over a lifetime spent in the world of books, I think I have reason to be despondent. I was one of the first readers of John O'London's Weekly, and can claim that I have never seen an American moving picture. As a lad I knew Ibsen. He was a morose man, bovine of head at all times, and formidable of stature when he was not sitting down. He was objectionable in many ways, and only his great genius and heart of gold saved him from being excluded from decent society. Once I noticed at table that there was dandruff in his tea. Swinburne and Joseph Conrad were also frequent visitors to my grandfather's place, and their long discussions on George Moore were a fair treat to listen to. The recollection of these evenings around the rustic tea-table in the back garden is still almost acutely pleasurable, and is like a fur on the walls of my memory. I break no confidence when I say that when my grandmother and Mrs Swinburne repaired upstairs to leave the men to their game of weighty words, it was for a puckish diversion undreamt of by the tea-distended titans they left behind; laughable as it may seem, there was stout in the wardrobe. I often smile to think what my grandfather would have said had he known. The ladies, indeed, were well out of it, for few would credit the row that developed when Swinburne and Conrad got down to it, with my grandfather, nothing if not courageous, breaking an odd lance with them. At dusk, Coleridge would sometimes look in on his way home for a final pipe, and more than once the burly shape of Lord Macaulay was known to grace the gathering.

I do not think that old men like 'H.P.' and myself can expect to do much to stem the tide of Gaelic barbarism in Dublin, but if he thinks it would do him good I am prepared to correspond with him on the subject of Joseph Conrad. I need scarcely add that 'Conrad' was only a pseudonym (or pen name), for that seafaring man hailed from a far land which has since encountered still another of the slings of destiny. The only alternative seems to be to pay the vanished past the tribute of a silent tear.

Yours, etc.,
F. O'Brien
Dublin

Sir,

I feel compelled to attract attention to certain inaccuracies in a letter addressed to you on the 3rd inst, by Mr F. O'Brien, in which the writer assumes an easy familiarity with Ibsen and his contemporaries. Mr O'Brien may well be an old man, as he says himself, and judging from the pedestrian quality of his style, I see no reason to question his probity on this score; but this is one occasion when mere senility cannot be accepted as an excuse for ignorance. He has painted a word-picture of the great man that reflects very little credit either on Ibsen or on himself, and it is partly to clear the name of my favourite playwright, and partly, let it be added, to test Mr O'Brien's honesty, that I charge my pen to reply.

My own father had very distinct recollections of those pleasant summer days when he, Ibsen, Swinburne, Lamb, Macaulay and the rest of his *coterie* foregathered on the lawn at Hawleigh, Surrey, to engage in intellectual converse. And I think I can disclose, without giving scandal, that it was something a little bit stronger than cups of tea, as Mr O'Brien says, that decorated the wicker-work table before them. Ibsen's courtly manner and air of good breeding made him stand out, even in that distinguished company. The suggestion that he once befouled his tea with the dandruff cascading from his magnificent head, apart from being in rather bad taste, can at once be dismissed as a figment of Mr O'Brien's overworked imagination – 'a false impression proceeding from the heat-oppressed brain'. Ibsen, as my father knew to his cost, never indulged in anything but cocoa, since stronger beverages were inclined to make him sing out of tune. And as for the disorder of the scalp alluded to, he could not have possibly been a martyr to this complaint, since he was as bald as a coot. His superb leonine (*sic*) head was crowned by the most cunning transformation ever created by the famous *coiffeur*, Antoine, of the Boule Mich.

In this connection, my father used to tell an amusing story about the dinner given at Hawleigh to celebrate the publication of *Clive of India*. As usual, Ibsen insisted on helping the guests himself. It was when serving soup that he leaned too far over the tureen, and the assembled literati were horrified to see the toupee slide from his head, to be lost from sight in depths of the

189

steaming borsch. With a readiness of wit that never failed him in a crisis, my father took down a finely-wrought toasting fork that hung over the fireplace, fished out the recalcitrant wig and, with a slight bow, restored it to its delighted owner. It was at this juncture that Ibsen uttered the timely *mot* about hare soup, which converted what might have been an embarrassing incident into an occasion of the utmost jollity.

Mr O'Brien's casual reference to Coleridge's dropping in to Hawleigh 'for a final pipe' tempts me to remind him that at the time of which he writes Coleridge, then aged six, was scampering about, a barefooted gamin among the oyster beds of his native Colchester. I am afraid that, in spite of his large reference library, F.O.B. is thinking of Coleridge Taylor, the composer, who first won prominence by picking out (with one finger) the air of his 'Petite Suite de Concert' on Chopin's piano in Valledemosa, and who ended his days filling the exacting *rôle* of Mister Bones in a negro minstrel performance on the foreshore at Margate.

F.O.B.'s final *gaffe* lay in the suggestion that Joseph Conrad was not, in fact, a full-blooded Irishman. This ugly innuendo can be dictated only by the writer's implacable hatred for all that is Gaelic and good. Let Mr O'Brien keep off the subject of J. Conrad if he knows what is good for him. Should he attempt to sully his illustrious name with sly gibes and scurrilous allusions, I think I am safe in saying that there are others besides myself prepared to speak their minds. '*De mortuis*, etc., etc.'

Yours etc.,
Lir O'Connor
Dublin

Sir,

As the last surviving link with Wordsworth I might be excused for ignoring the extraordinary letter from Mr L. O'Connor which appeared in your issue of Saturday. Not everybody, however, can have recourse to the golden luxury of silence. Those who have lived – as I have – in what I may call an old-world garden, walled by twelve-and-sixpenny novels heaped eight feet high, have a solemn duty to discharge. Even if Mr O'Connor's hodge-podge of fiction and half-truth touched but lightly the memory of

190

my friends of another day, it is all the more imperative that he should not be allowed to go unanswered. One does not ignore the dead mouse in the cheese sandwich merely because it is a very small mouse.

I do not know what to make of Mr O'Connor's claim that his father was present at those gatherings around the rustic tea-table. I cannot recall any person of that name, nor can I find any record of such a person in my papers. Conrad occasionally appeared with a serving-man, who had the strange task of straightening out his master's hammer-toes when the heat of dialectics engendered cramp. So far as I remember, this man's name was Sproule. Then there was the notorious gamekeeper introduced by my own intemperate grandmother, but his stay was so short that he may be ruled out. Who else is there? Can it be that Mr O'Connor, in his anxiety to besmirch the name of great men, does not hesitate to do a major violence to his own? If he is serious in his statement, then his father must be looked for among the ranks of those great masters of English prose; for I (thank heaven) was too young at the time, and my grandfather was past caring. A stranger claim than this has surely never been advanced in a public paper. It will come as a stark shock to Lord Longford to know that his theatre may contain any of these evenings a brother of the three sisters. Certainly I would put nothing past Chekov.

Mr O'Connor's reference to the toupee incident will give fair-minded readers a general indication of his reliability. His account is ludicrously garbled. In the first place, Lamb was not present at all. Secondly, it was Ruskin who took the wig out of the boiling soup, and, indeed, gave the rest of the gathering an adroit hint as to how the incident should be treated. Pretending to have noticed nothing, he deftly ladelled the sodden article on to Ibsen's plate, and mentioned that anybody who thought the soup was too hot could go into the house and add cold water to it in the bathroom. Ibsen, cunningly taking his cue, tasted the soup and pretended to burn his mouth. Then he rose and disappeared into the house, as Ruskin was made the recipient of quiet words of congratulation by his colleagues. Ten minutes later, Ibsen reappeared with an empty soup plate and explained away the wetness of his replaced hair by some stupid remark about having

191

been out for a stroll and encountering 'a bit of a shower up the road'.

I may permit myself to be amused by Mr O'Connor's suggestions that I did not know that Ibsen wore a wig. Probably the fact is better known even than Keats's predilection for brawn. My reference to the dandruff in Ibsen's tea sprang, not from ignorance, but from a very full knowledge of the liberties this *savant* took with his head. In fact, he had six or seven wigs, each with ever-lengthening locks, and these he wore successively in an attempt to simulate the way of nature. When he had reached the last wig, a creation of tangled luxuriance truly leonine, he would throw out odd remarks about having to get his hair cut. Very shortly afterwards he would appear again in wig number one. He was probably not the first to think of this trickery, but he went even farther (and, incidentally, farther than the frontiers of good taste) in his pretence that his hair was genuine. He regularly purchased canisters of what I took to be synthetic dandruff and dusted himself liberally with this substance about the head, neck and shoulders. Ruskin, who rarely got the better of any argument with Ibsen, swore to me privately that the stuff was genuine camel's scurf, imported at great expense from the Far East. If it was, heaven knows what awful oriental plagues we regularly sat down to tea with.

It occurs to me that Mr O'Connor's letter is not intended to be taken seriously. Very well, if it is, but if the presentation of a serious play by Chekov in the Gate Theatre is to be made the occasion for oafish jokes, then the sooner we get into the war the better. By our neutrality we are seeking to preserve something pretty dirty, something that was unknown, thank heaven, in my own day.

Yours, etc.,
F. O'Brien
Dublin

Sir,
In struggling to solve the riddle of my ancestry Mr F. O'Brien has unwittingly stumbled upon the truth, and has all but 'let the mouse out of the sandwich', to cite his own amusing idiom. It was

Ruskin, he says, who salvaged Ibsen's transformation from the samovar of smorsgaard that night at Hawleigh. Tirra, lirra, by the river, how innocent you are, Mr O'Brien! But, of course, it was Ruskin! And by the same token, it was none other than Ruskin, who spent most of his free evenings reading snippets from *Sesame* to Mr O'Brien's grandmother, who used to sit for hours on end, glassy-eyed and still drinking it all in. Were it not for the fact that this charming and cultured lady had already given her hand to another I am convinced that Jno. would not have hesitated to make the proposal that would have made F.O.B. my own nephew.

However, it was not to boast of my antecedents that I elected to joust with Mr O'Brien, but to clear Jos. Conrad of the charge of being a wop. Josephine Cumisky or Joseph Conrad as she was afterwards called, was born and spent the earlier years of an exciting life dreaming the hours away on the gentle slopes of the Galway mountains. Cool, slim and unhurried, this lissom slip of a girl had the sea in her blood, and willingly, nay eagerly, she answered to its call. On these stolen trips into Galway's dockland how she used to revel in the salty yarns and coarse oaths that poured from the lips of the dark-bearded sailors who lounged about the coal wharves. Little by little she acquired proficiency in the argot of the sea, and soon she was as foul-mouthed as the lowest stevedore that ever battened down a hatch. Her plans were all but made. A strong growth of superfluous hair beneath her lower lip, which in a man would probably be classified as an 'imperial', helped to make the deception possible.

Then one summer's night she ran away to sea, signing on as a humble heaver aboard a coal boat bound for distant Wigan. Her master's ticket soon followed, and the name of Josh. Conrad became an object of respect in every gin-palace from Bermuda to the Barbary coast. It was in Singapore that she met Georges Sand. The years had left their mark on Josephine Cumisky. No longer cool, slim nor unhurried, it was a warm-hearted, buxom matron that won the affection of Sand, tired out by a life spent tuning Chopin's grand piano. The ceremony which united them was a simple affair, the Service being read by Capt. Conrad himself in a chop suey joint in the European quarter. The rest of my story is common history. How they came to live at Hawleigh

193

as paying guests with Ibsen and my father waiting on them hand and foot. How Sand's tuning key came to take its place with his wife's goatee over the massive fireplace in the dining hall, where, I understand, they may be seen to this day on payment of a small pourboire to the guide. And with what *otio cum dignitate* they whiled away the evening of their lives, surrounded by the pledges of their mutual affection.

My proof-reader has drawn my attention to a few minor *errata* in my notes on the Ibsen school. Whilst they scarcely detract from the sense of the text, in the interest of strict accuracy, I had better correct them. For 'borsch', therefore, read 'bosh'; for 'toupee' read 'tepee', and, of course, for 'Lamb' read 'Bacon'.

Yours etc.,
Lir O'Connor
Dublin

Sir,

I see that Mr O'Connor has written another letter to your paper without giving any clue as to whether he intends himself to be taken seriously. This rather vitiates the whole discussion, and makes me doubt whether he is worth my time.

It is interesting that he claims to be a son of Ruskin. Nowadays too many people, by mere reason of an inherited surname, seek to shove themselves into positions of prominence, where they can win themselves considerable quantities of potatoes, not to mention golden opinions from all concerned. It has become fashionable to claim privilege merely because one is well whelped. Public life in Ireland today abounds in this baneful nepotism. Mr O'Connor pins the name Ruskin in his button-hole in the hope that he will be known to the present generation of the great masters of English prose. No doubt, that will be a consolation for being unknown to the Registrar-General.

As a lad I knew Ruskin. He was a frequent caller to my grandfather's place, and so impressed us all with his dainty personality that I cannot lightly credit Mr O'Connor's suggestion that the man was a whited sepulchre. It was a favourite saying with him that 'it is not what you wear but where you wear it.' Once he exemplified this obscure maxim in a strange way. He appeared one morning in a suit made of blue-striped shirting, a shirt made of thick tweed, a leather tie and shoes of poplin laced up with silver watch-chain. My grandfather expressed polite surprise, but Ruskin laughingly riposted that 'it is not what you wear, etc., etc.' Thereafter we repaired to the garden, and throughout the live-long sultry day no sound was to be heard save the click of the croquet balls and the coarse coughing of the heat-demented finches in the ivy.

Re Conrad, I am not going to enter into a newspaper controversy with Mr O'Connor or anybody else on such a subject. It is news to me that this great gentleman was a lady. Great as my surprise would be if this were proved, it would be nothing compared with the chagrin which Ibsen would endure if he were alive to hear the proof. That unprincipled foreigner spent many hours of his life closetted alone with Conrad, doing nothing more or less than discussing George Moore.

> Yours etc.,
> F. O'Brien
> Dublin

Sir,

I cannot allow to go unchallenged the insinuation of Mr L. O'Connor that it was Ruskin who used to read snippets from *Sesame* to Mr F. O'Brien's grandmother. Mr O'Connor is pardonably confused; it was Carlyle, and the book he read from was not *Sesame*, but *Salome*. I remember those evenings as though they were last night, and though I am naturally rather advanced in years my memory and, indeed, all my faculties are every bit as good as in my prime. So far as I recall, Ruskin came only once to those delightful soirees where the great Norwegian was guest of honour; and on that occasion he was so affronted by Aubrey Beardsley's table manners that he swore a solemn oath never to return. I believe he kept to this oath, though there was a rather nasty rumour floating around for a while concerning a brawl between him and Stephen Crane; certainly Ruskin mysteriously acquired a black eye, and refused to explain what caused it. Zaro Agra, the Turkish George Eliot, refers to the matter in his significant biography of Rupert the Lion-Hearted, but is, unfor-

195

tunately, unable to draw any coherent conclusion from the meagre facts.

It is curious that neither Mr O'Connor nor Mr O'Brien allude to the presence at those care-free salons of the greatest visitor of all: Feodor Dostoyevsky. He it was who kept the table in a constant roar with his rollicking tales of Siberia, and if I live to be a hundred – which won't take long now, alas, time hounds me so with its ceaseless gallop – if I live to that age, I say, I shall never forget the sensation he created the evening he told us who he really was: Flann Doyle, born and raised in Goatstown. Ever since then, on every anniversary of his birth, I make a pilgrimage to the humble public-house, within whose shabby portals his eyes first opened on our unwitting world; and it is always a grief to me to see that as yet no plaque adorns those walls, no mark of recognition shows my countrymen's deep pride in one of Ireland's most illustrious sons. Some day, I hope, the Government will perceive the crime of their omission; and in that glad hour, when justice atones for its neglect and Flann Doyle is honoured as our most immortal novelist, there will, I venture to predict, be joybells rung in heaven.

I am not positive about the facts of Josephine Conrad's life and so cannot speak here with absolute authority, but I doubt Mr O'Connor's statement that she hailed originally from Galway. According to general gossip around my own dinner table in those long-lost years, where Ambrose Bierce and his adopted grandson, Irvin S. Cobb, were inveterate trenchermen, Miss Conrad was a native of Connemara. Her marriage to George Sand was not her first; the records reveal at least three others, one to an English sailor named Jim Lord, one to an American mulatto, and one to a member of the well-known legal firm of Ford, Ford, Ford, Hueffer and Madox. Two of these unions were successful, but the last-mentioned was disastrous and the less I say about it the better. Miss Conrad was extremely touchy on the subject of her marital adventures; I remember her leaving the room in a huff one night because George Meredith and Rudyard Kipling had begun to exchange distinctly coarse pleasantries on that sublime and sacred topic. 'Connemara Josie', as we called her, was a stickler for the decencies, and to the end of her life she was a militant subscriber to anti-vivisection journals, and emphatically refused to come to dinner unless all present laid a careful restraint upon their tongues. Would that such delicacy were more prevalent today.

> Yours etc.,
> Whit Cassidy
> Schloss Vouvray, Killiney, Co. Dublin

Sir,

Having unwittingly provoked this flood of reminiscences, I feel compelled to point out, in the interests of accuracy, that by no conceivable feat of dexterity could Ibsen, or anyone else, drop a wig into a samovar.

It would be just possible, if it were a very small wig and a very large samovar, to ram it in by main force. But, as we are given to understand that the wig was leonine, it goes to show that Ibsen's hair was his own; a supposition that is further strengthened by the fact that Bergen, where Ibsen spent most of his life, is noted for gales of wind.

If your wig was liable to drop off at the dinner-table, it would be impossible to go out of doors in it at Bergen. Ibsen was essentially an outdoor man.

Also I think that your correspondents should make it clear that the Ruskin in question was not the author of *Fors Clavigera*, but his younger brother, who did the boots and knives at Framley Parsonage. He afterwards married my maternal great-aunt, and settled at Monte Carlo. The marriage was not a success.

> Yours, etc.,
> H.P.
> Dublin

Sir,

Allow me to correct one or two misapprehensions revealed in Mr F. O'Brien's recent letter. In the first place, it was not Ibsen who possessed several wigs and took such pains to make them seem realistic – it was Strindberg. Mr George Brandes made the matter clear in his amusing book of memoirs, not yet, unfortunately, available in an English or Irish translation. He explains that Ibsen and Strindberg took an impish delight in posing as one another, and relates that it was actually Ibsen who took the author's call at the first night of *The Spook Sonata*. Evidently, Mr O'Brien and his associates were completely hoodwinked, and this accounts for the faint element of grotesque humour in their story. Strindberg never could resist the temptation to clown around, as the eminent critic, James Hunter, used to tell me repeatedly over his Pilsener at his favourite Montmartre restaurant, 'The Plucked Crow'.

Mr O'Brien is also mistaken in dismissing contemptuously the gamekeeper his grandmother so obviously adored. This very gamekeeper gave his name to a symphony by the Connemara composer, D. H. Lawrence, better known as the Sheik of Araby. And he was also, as I remember him admitting modestly to Samuel Butler, Arthur Rimbaud and myself, a natural son of Walt Whitman.

May I plead for greater accuracy in your newspaper, and fewer aspersions on our fragrant culture.

Yours, etc.,
Paul Desmond
Dublin

Sir,

Mr O'Brien may wish to know that the reason for Ruskin's anger, when asked to explain the black eye, was because Ruskin's injury was so obviously caused by *The Stones of Venice*.

Now why should it be deemed impossible for Ibsen's wig to fall into a samovar? It is understood that this particular vessel was a tartar sanabar made from the shell of a mock turtle. It is now used as a pot for a cactus plant in the Majorca cottage where Chopin resided with George Sand.

Mr Whit Cassidy's reference to Dostoievsky is most appropriate. Has not George Moore written in the preface of Dostoievsky's *Poor Folk*: 'The least critical cannot fail to perceive that these letters are unlike real letters, that they bear no kind of resemblance to the letters that might have passed between a half-witted clerk and a poor girl over the way.'

Yours,
Oscar Love
Blackrock, Co. Dublin

Oscar Love was an incurable writer of letters to the *Irish Times*, and his name is to be seen in the correspondence column as late as 1966, His trademark was the more or less apposite quotation, one of which adorned every letter he wrote. Who he really was is in doubt.

Sir,

I am no book-worm. Nor, for that matter, am I one who goes in much for highbrow discussions. What am I, then, you will ask? Well, just put me down as a quiet wee body who is far too engrossed in her collection of ferns to find any time for matters outside the realm of her leaf album. For this reason you will understand that I do not profess to follow the precise drift of the debate that my brother, Lir, has been conducting with F. O'Brien *et al.*, but it is all so intensely interesting, don't you think? However, it is not in order to join in my tiny voice in the controversy that I seek the cosy hospitality of your columns.

Frankly, I am a little worried about Lir and the repercussions that all this excitement may have on his general health. For, since the beginning of his rather heroic campaign on behalf of cleaner literature he has locked himself in his library with all lines of communication virtually cut off. Our between-maid, Gumley, who takes in his tray, tells me that he is surrounded by his beloved books and appears to be making a meticulous check of all the literary references made in the letters written by his protagonists. His librarian, Mr Butterly, is away on holidays at Loch Corrib with his butterfly net, with the result that my brother has to lift all these heavy old books down from the shelves himself – a form of exercise which, I feel certain, cannot do his blood pressure any good.

From what I know of Lir, I am convinced that he is willing to shed his last drop of ink in defence of his principles, and for this very reason, I want to make one little suggestion. Before doing so, let me say that never for one moment was I deceived by Miss O'Brien's delicious fooling when she alluded to herself as a stuffy old gentleman. Call it intuition, if you will, but from the very outset I detected in F.O.B.'s letters the sentiments and emotions of a woman like myself, weak, foolish and human. I often wonder what she is like. Is she a middle-aged lady novelist, with the usual military moustache, or is she a 'bright young thing' with shingled skirts and all the other trappings of Miss 1940? Whatever is the answer, I know already that I will take to her the first moment we meet; for 'The Colonel's lady and Judy O'Grady etc., etc.,' as Mr Lever so very nicely put it. Well, that brings me to my idea. What I want to do is this: I want to invite Miss O'Brien, Mr Cassidy, 'H.P.', Mr Desmond and dear Mr Love (what an exciting name!) to have tea with us here in the 'Noggin. Or if the menfolk feel that tea is a little too lame for them I have a little of my own apple wine, which even our gardener is afraid to touch, it goes so quickly, he says, to his head.

In order to preserve the proprieties I will act as Miss O'Brien's chaperone, and in honour of the occasion I will get Lir to show her his collection of daguerreotypes, which he took on his walking tour to Majorca, and with which he usually entertains the infrequent lady visitors to our little place. There is one particularly fine view of Chopin's piano, which bears the caption:

> Here Chopin and Georges Sand
> Used to sit, hand in hand.

Who knows what fruit may spring from this little plan of mine? Perhaps, the intellectual delights of Hawleigh may be tasted once more in this tranquil residential suburb. Perhaps, the ghost of Ibsen may walk again on our own little lawn, bending every now and then over the shoulder of Lir O'Connor to utter some incomparable gem of word-loveliness. Perhaps, the burly figure of Macaulay will be seen once more strolling arm in arm with Whit Cassidy down by the goldfish pond. The air will re-echo to the brisk exchange of puns between 'H.P.' and his pathetic prototype, Lamb; and, perhaps, if he has nothing more important to do, Mr Love might have something to say to poor little me.

> Yours, etc.,
> Luna O'Connor
> La Casita, Sallynoggin

Sir,
Luna O'Connor's gracious invitation to tea is not accepted. Tea is the curse of this country, and Irish cider does not go to the

head. It is much more disturbing. The introduction of tea as a beverage has undermined the constitution of every nation indulging in the vice. Give me beer, dear Luna: it's good for you.

I have pleasant memories of Luna. She was quite a slim lady, with glowing cinematic hair. I first met her in Ebury Street one moonlight night many years ago. I was much puzzled as to why she should leave her Noggin, and I was soon enlightened. From 121 Ebury Street out popped jaunty George Moore. Notwithstanding the deceptive moonlight I recognised him on the instant, for he wore an Aubusson carpet around his neck, and it draped his shoulders prettily.

Now, who but a Luna could deem this a highbrow discussion! What is a highbrow?

Roy Campbell says that he recollects an occasion when a man in Durban delivered a lecture on 'Why I am a highbrow'. His brow was invisible, and his only prominent feature was an enormous posterior, which suggested the following lines:

> There once came a highbrow from Britain,
> Whose praises can never be written,
> So steep rose his high brow
> From his heel to his eye brow
> With a bump in the middle to sit on.

Yours, etc.,
Oscar Love
Blackrock

Exactly one month after Oscar Love had put an end to the *Three Sisters* controversy, the poet and novelist, Patrick Kavanagh, unwittingly started another one, in which the new 'art form' reached its zenith. Reprinted here is an extract from the review that began the fuss, and some of the letters that continued it. Over a fortnight later, R. M. Smyllie, who had himself contributed to the debate under the name of 'The O'Madan', as Editor of the *Irish Times* invited Kavanagh to reply.

Literary criticism

MAURICE WALSH'S NEW NOVEL,
REVIEWED BY
PATRICK KAVANAGH

The Hill Is Mine, by Maurice Walsh (London: Chalmers), 7/6 net.

What is an artist? Can a writer of best-sellers, like Maurice Walsh, be an artist? According to one definition, an artist is one who specialises in new ways of saying nothing. He is more interested in the conveyance rather than in the thing to be conveyed. Usually he has nothing to convey except his own virtuosity. To some extent we may find this sort of empty virtuosity in Hopkins, Eliot, the later Yeats and Joyce, and in nearly all the prose and verse innovators of the past twenty-five years or so. This sort of artist is like a ploughman who has horses and plough, but no land. Not being troubled by the urgency of spring-sowing he has time to speculate on new theories of ploughing. And in this way he is often very useful.

On the other hand, the man with land may have no seeds, and then we have growths of weeds. Literary weeds are sometimes popular. Suspicion haunts the book which sells ten thousand copies. In our world ten thousand perceptive readers is an optimism too large for ears of ordinary credulity. But there is popularity and popularity. There is the popularity of stupid, boring books like *Gone With the Wind*, which hit the fashion, but there is also the eternal popularity of *Don Quixote*, *Gil Blas* or Hans Andersen's *Fairy Tales*.

There is a common denominator of the spirit where the vulgarian and the artist meet. With Maurice Walsh, being a best-seller, it is only fair to look beneath the surface of his work. There may be an artist there.

First and foremost, he is a fine story-teller. He is an artist of theme rather than of form. Sometimes the theme may not be to our liking, but his people live, and anything may be forgiven the writer who can create life.

202

In many of the previous Maurice Walsh novels that I have read there was a little too much of the open-air, boy scout type. The boy scout may be said to represent civilisation at its lowest. The jamboree is the academy of illiteracy. There was also Maurice Walsh's unfortunate weakness for a Scottish setting.

Although in his latest novel, *The Hill is Mine*, he has not escaped this dreadful atmosphere, there breaks through to us time and again the light and integrity of the true artist. And his sense of humour is delightful . . .

Sir,

I doubt if Mr Patrick Kavanagh's standing as a literary critic will be greatly enhanced by his remarkable description (in criticising Mr Maurice Walsh's latest novel) of *Gone with the Wind* as a 'stupid, boring book'; or by his further amazing remarks that 'the Boy Scout may be said to represent civilisation at its lowest. The jamboree is the academy of illiteracy!'

In view of these remarkable and quite unnecessary opinions, it is doubtful whether Mr Kavanagh's gracious approval will actually contribute greatly to the success of Mr Walsh's latest book. I trust that abler pens than mine will deal with the opinions themselves.

Yours, etc.,
'F.L.J.'
Glasnevin, Co. Dublin

Sir,

I am pleased to see that Mr P. Kavanagh's criticism and his recent short story, published in your paper, have received the treatment they deserve in your correspondence column. Decent men, thank God, can still express their views in your paper.

Mr Kavanagh's stuff smells strongly of the Goebbels' midden, and I wonder you allowed it to stray into your paper – which is not supported by guttersnipes or the type of individual who enjoys 'strolls through the sewers', conducted by Mr Kavanagh and his ilk.

People with reasonably clean minds are growing weary of the cesspool-in-the-backyard style of writing. There is a clean-up coming in the world. May I, as an old and devoted supporter of your paper, ask you to make a start – at least in your literary column – to clean out this 'modern' stuff. Some 'Jeyes' and 'Keating' would be useful.

Yours etc.,

N. S. Harvey

Ashdale, Cloughjordan, Co. Tipperary

There were many letters along these lines before the ubiquitous Oscar Love made his contribution, complete with quotation:

Sir,

Mr Kavanagh made one error in his literary criticism. His critics have made a dozen. Mr Ahern has not laughed so much since he attended a bottle party in September, but I expect that Mr Kavanagh has laughed, too.

My disapprobation was tempered with gratitude for many arresting reviews by Mr Kavanagh. It is not difficult to believe that 'F.L.J.', Mr N. Harvey and Mr Ahern confine themselves to 'the Hundred' Best Books. As these have not been read, I make a brilliant suggestion. Let Mr Kavanagh compile a list of the hundred worst books. These will be devoured by most of his critics. It is evident that not one of these critics has read the works of William Carleton, James Stephens or Samuel Lover. When the widow says to Rory: 'There's not a finer thing in the world than a dhrop o' whiskey to drive the sickness from your heart' – how these literary scouts must tremble!

Unlike Mr Jones, I have not corresponded with the German Youth, but if his foreign correspondence was equalled by his present purposeful plunders he might hesitate before re-opening communications when peace dawns. Mr Jones may be humane, but he is unable to see through intensive scouting. 'F.L.J.' explains – Civilisation at its lowest is represented by the 'human robot'. So we are to make the robot a boy scout. I thought the object was to change that charming beast, the boy, into a cute little devil.

I cannot say that my critics are correct in stating that German boys were compelled to work. In the public reading racks of many little towns in Germany I saw coloured posters of harvest scenes. These were pictures of boys aiding in harvesting. At the foot of each poster there was a portrayal of a mother and children. Volunteers were urged to come forward to help the farmer. At Oberdollonder I witnessed a group of boys draw lots by a musical test for those who would assist on the farms and those who could go hill-climbing. Incidentally, those boys themselves cooked a meal that would astonish our Boy Scouts.

The boy in Germany has no such outlet as the gambling mania for his activities, and so has more thought of citizenship.

'F.L.J.' states that it would not be a good deed to help a farmer. Is labour so plentiful? In America entire colleges visit farms to carry on the work of the control of noxious weeds.

Mr Harvey's reference to Jeyes and Keatings, Mr Ahern's bottle murder and sudden death, together with 'F.L.J.'s' 'frowsty tripe', consumed while Mr Jones shuffles his pack of cards, indicate that they are fit scoutmasters. An improved outlook might develop by reading Baby's Debut –

> So bidding you adieu
> I curtsey like a pretty miss,
> And if you blow to me a kiss
> I'll blow a kiss to you.

Yours, etc.,
Oscar Love
Blackrock

Sir,

May I contribute a few experiences and ideas to this very interesting controversy?

I have met some Boy Scouts, and, my! was I disappointed. My tricycle chain had become unstuck near the Scalp, and I thought myself in clover when round the bend came some Scouts in little, short trousers. I called to them but only one answered, a rough, French-looking fellow wearing a beret, who shouted 'Howdye, sister.' Thank goodness, I was always independent and was able to settle the trouble myself.

Early last year I was in Germany, though I suppose one shouldn't say that; so many people think one a 5th Columnist on such little provocation. Anyway, there I met many of the Hitler

Jugend. It is quite untrue that Hitler doesn't let them speak to strangers. I found them clean, companionable, and I can assure you that I had only to raise my hand to have my tricycle mended every day. There is one big difference actually between them and the Scouts, and, strangely enough, no one in this discussion has mentioned it. The Jugend never, or hardly ever, have hair on their legs. Yes, really. It reminded me so much of what a dear, facetious school friend of mine used to say as something rather *risqué* about Empire Roman boys – that they *plucked*.

Of course, I'm only a girl; but I do think Mr Kavanagh, whose homely articles I enjoy ever so, should not annoy all our uncles and aunts by saying such startling things about institutions. Once in London I met such a nice boy in the Tube and brought him back for tea, but he ruined everything by telling Aunt Charlotte (I was living with her at Bayswater) that he thought all RAs were fools and their work *tosh*. 'I didn't catch your name, young man,' she said, 'but please do not visit my house again.' And, though I tried ever so hard, she remained implacable.

Mr Harvey reminds me of my Uncle Robert – so stern. I used to watch him sitting for hours with *The Times*. He never read it, preferring to snooze, the sweet old dear, but he said it made a good impression on the servants.

Lastly, might I make an appeal to those of your readers who are older and more worldly-wise than me. I know such a nice boy in the Navy, but he tells me such queer stories. I'm sure Mr Harvey wouldn't approve of them (I've never let Uncle Robert hear any of them, not even the one about the fishmonger's daughter, though Aunt Charlotte calls it droll). Ought I to stop writing to him, or should I wangle a visit to London for his next leave! He has promised; but, there, how I do run on.

Yours, etc.,
Judy Clifford
Holme, Burnaby, Greystones

While this controversy was in full spate, Patrick Kavanagh's poem, 'Spraying the Potatoes', appeared on the literary page, complete with misprint. Flann O'Brien's name soon appears:

Sir,

At last, I said to myself, the Irish banks are acknowledging the necessity for hygiene. My eye had lighted on the heading 'Spraying the Potatoes' and I had naturally enough inferred that our bank notes were being treated periodically with a suitable germicide, a practice which has long been a commonplace of enlightened monetary science in Australia. When I realised that the heading had reference to some verses by Mr Patrick Kavanagh dealing with the part played by chemistry in modern farming, my chagrin may be imagined. I am no judge of poetry – the only poem I ever wrote was produced when I was body and soul in the gilded harness of Dame Laudanum – but I think Mr Kavanagh is on the right track here. Perhaps the *Irish Times*, tireless champion of our peasantry, will oblige us with a series in this strain covering such rural complexities as inflamed goat-udders, warble-pocked shorthorn, contagious abortion, non-ovoid oviducts and nervous disorders among the gentlemen who pay the rent.

However, my purpose in writing is to intervene briefly in the Donnybrook which has developed in your columns on the sub-ject of literary criticism. First, I think it is time somebody said a seasonable word on this question of sewerage. Mr Harvey, who lives in the honky-tonk ridden West End of Cloughjordan, accuses Mr Kavanagh of preoccupation with 'middens', 'back-yard cesspools', and of seeking to conduct the public through the city sewers. Irish newspapers and periodicals have published many thousands of articles in which the work of Irish writers has been associated with sewers, sewer-rats and sewage, and to a lesser extent with muck-raking and other operations usually carried on on sewage farms.

So much for the readers, or, if one may term them so, the anti-writers. Now if we turn to the writers, we find that the same boot is also on the other foot. In his latest book Mr Seán O'Faoláin talks about things which emerge from sewers, and likens the east-wind that blows occasionally in the Republic of Letters to 'the drip of a broken pipe'. Other writers have frequently invoked the image of the humble sewer rat when dealing not only with the public, but with each other. In fine, the writers and anti-writers indiscriminately accuse each other of being sewer-minded and both classes roar 'Yah! Sewer Rat!' with equal venom. To say the least of it, this is confusing. One would imagine that anybody who can read or write in modern Ireland asked for nothing better than a quiet evening down a sewer, moving an idle oar down the dark streams, browsing in quiet backwater with a drowsy angler's eye on the plunging rats, 'wine-bark on the wine-dark waterway'. Probably Mr Harvey thinks that, when Mr Kavanagh lays down his Homeric fountain-pen for the day, he strolls out into the street, opens a manhole and disappears for the evening; or that when two intellectuals talk about walking down O'Connell street, they mean wading down the magnificent vaulted Gothic sewer below the street. At this rate any house agent who hears a prospective client inquiring particularly about the plumbing and drainage of a house will know that he is dealing with a literary bird. Certainly, if it is true that our native intellectuals foregather in the sewers, there must be serious congestion. If there is a Carnegie library in Clough-jordan, there must be a terrific crush in the most fashionable cesspool.

As regards boy scouts, I agree with Mr Kavanagh. The idea is one of the most pernicious of our British importations. All boy scouts seem to be warts in the process of becoming prigs. At a time when any normal young fellow should be learning how to hold his own in a game of three-hand solo, the wretched boy scout is learning absurd blue-sea rope-knots and – of all things in a land where the *coillte* have been *ar lar* for centuries – trail-finding and woodlanding. They are also encouraged to do one good deed a day, notwithstanding the well-known axiom that it's only by doing noble deeds all day long that life can become one grand sweet song. It would fit these youngsters better to learn to find their way across the city *via* the sewers. Then they would have some prospect of growing up to become great writers.

Few will support Mr Kavanagh in his unsympathetic judgment of *Gone With the Wind*. A book that has won for its author many thousands of tons of tubers cannot be dismissed so lightly. There are many people of the writing class in Ireland who cannot regard seriously any book which has not been banned for obscenity, and which has not involved all concerned in catastrophic libel suits. This may be all very well as a general rule of thumb, but there must be exceptions. There are still people in the world, thank heaven, who can relish a good wholesome story well told. To be curled up with a good book of an evening is one of the few simple pleasures left to us. To me and Mr Harvey, I mean.

Yours, etc.,
F. O'Brien
Dublin

Sir,

After an *Irish Time*less fortnight at loach-progging in the upper reaches of the Aunagawen, I return to find the kids with their gloves off and even the lassies a'heavin' literary bricks into the fiction-fight. Plunged thus *in medias res* I find the issues obscure, but there is no mistaking the larned lingo which our leisured juniors lay by for such rainy days; it carries the unique accents of the derivative little disciples of Ditchwater.

What matters it if Mr Kavanagh leaves his dandelions to grow hoary-headed in his potato-beds in order that he may impugn the guaranteed circulation of the blood?

Reck we aught of Mr Montgomery and his atrocious synthesis of the Thrasonical Yeatsian Tradition with Holy Living and Holy Dying?

And why the pink-wailed obscurantism of Sister Clifford? Is it that her tricycle so circumvents her scalp that she must needs make the Jugend the buttend of her entendre?

Who can say? But before the critics and the critics of the critics play Kilkenny cats in your columns, and before Patrick pours more Paddiana in the Pennypots (vid. column *ibidem*), permit me to remind them, one and all, that they will need fertilisers rather than spraying-stuff before they can parade with any pride the weak drills of their Verschen-gartens.

I can hear you murmur, Mr Editor, 'Let the little Tiger Tims trounce each other. The Battle of Waterloo...'

But I say, Regular Fellers me eye! These are the little doses of salt which constitute the social solvent of our day. Barking the bushes in Fairview Park and playing banker on the ledges of the Loop-Line columns!

A nice state of things it is, to be sure. And what would Franciscus Parvus say were he with us now? Well do I remember

209

one August Monday in Harcourt Street Station when he borrowed a match from me in order to do public execution on a volume of Anita Loos. That was in the 1920s – and his chrysostoned prophecy anent our canine destiny is still working itself out.

While not wishing to qualify one iota of the assertions made in the foregoing paragraph, I am prepared to concede that there were mitigating circumstances in the case of Kavanagh, who, after all, ploughs a lonely if somewhat arid furrow. But Love and Judy are the limit, and now we're bound to find the Cork twin brethren in the Punchbowl and O'Brien's hatchet striking sparks out of the cowled lamp-light at Purcell's Corner. Not that one would mind were it not that the war-fever spreads automatically to their undignified elders and soon, Mr Editor, unless you put a sock on them, Fleet Street will resound to another battle of the Books, and the crisis will extend to the now senescent patrons of Duke Street.

Mr Editor, sir, this is my first and last effort at appeasement. If my policy of conciliation fails to mop up their Quink, then have at them and let loose my black-webbed Swan!

> Yours, etc.,
> Jno. O'Ruddy

P.S. Did you ever read such nonsense as that which characterises the concluding stanzas of the fifth canto of N.C.'s 'Colleen of Clonmacnoise', and what by way of charity can be said for the cheap fallacies of Mr Oscar Love's political science in *Thrimmenkraft* (now fortunately out of print), recognised almost at once as a love-child of Mrs Beeton?

P.P.S. I would commend to Miss Clifford a further and more careful perusal of my *Time of the Woollen Sleeve*, an autographed copy of which I am willing to present to her if she meets me with a recognisable Michaelmas daisy in her upraised right hand between half-seven and the Pillar, some Sunday in the middle of next week.

> Again, Yours, etc.,
> Jno. O'Ruddy
> Raheny

210

Sir,

I fear that you and I have been made victims of a particularly stupid practical joke. As to which of us is the greater dupe, I will allow you to decide for yourself from the facts as I present them.

This morning in the library I was browsing over a first edition of Sorensen's *The Osmosis-Diffusion Dielectric*, when I was informed that there was a deputation awaiting me with a request for an audience. As these deputations usually comprise the crofters and tenants from the estate, who come armed with rakes, pitchforks and scythes when they wish to discuss some obscure clause in the tithe laws with me, I took down my father's old elephant gun from its accustomed place over the fireplace, loaded it with some nick-nacks from my desk and bade them enter. Imagine, therefore, my astonishment when I found myself confronted by what I can only describe as a gaggle of earnest young men, whose bizarre attire, together with the heavy beards which they affected, immediately betrayed them as pals or butties of some literary bun-fighting faction or other.

Their request was a strange one. Would I take up the cudgels, or, to be more accurate, the old vacuumatic, in defence of one of their number? They knew full well, they said, that never had the prosiest little poet or the most prosaic minor novelist appealed for my help in vain when struggling beneath the heel of the critic. The world 'heel' they used with advertence to its newer shade of meaning. Would I, in short, address a few lines to your journal in aid of a Mr Patrick Kavanagh, in the calves of whose legs a pack of Wolf Cubs and Brownies were delightedly burying their imperfectly matured fangs. I replied that to the bibliophile like myself every minute spent away from the company of my beloved books represented sixty golden seconds gone down the waste-pipe of time, but rather than see the pen vanquished by the jack-knife or the whistle lanyard I would give the matter my attention. At that juncture I discharged my game piece through the window as a hint that the interview was at an end, and musingly watched them retreat in disorder.

Since then Butterley, my librarian, and I have searched every shelf and combed every catalogue in quest of some of this Mr Kavanagh's work. I have skimmed through *The Utility of the Horse*, by Paul Kavanagh; *What to do with your Pulsocaura*, by

211

Pietro Kavana; *Yoga and Rheumatism*, by Pav Ka Vanna; *I Was Stalin's Chamber Maid*, by Pamela Kay Vanagh, and a score of others by authors whose names approximate to that of the man whom I set out to vindicate. At the end of six hours' research I was forced to give up. Sir, in the entire compass of a library which, I should add, is the largest collection of books in any private establishment north of a line drawn from Williamstown to Cabinteely and passing through Glasthule, there is not one single work from the pen of Mr Kavanagh!

Butterley has just drawn my attention to some lines, entitled 'Spraying the Potatoes', which appeared in Saturday's issue of the *Irish Times*, purporting to issue from his nib (or should I say 'his nibs?'). This hardly could be said to help the case of Mr Kavanagh himself. The phrase 'potatoes', which recurs in his little burlesque, may be good Runyon, but, believe me, it is very poor Kavanagh, and smacks more of pool-room, crap game and pin table than does it of the Blackrock Literary Society.

No, Mr Kavanagh, I am afraid you have no claim upon my patronage. Until such a time, therefore, as you or some of your admirers can furnish me with convincing literary proof of your existence, I cannot in all conscience take up your case.

Yours, etc.,
Lir O'Connor
La Casita, Sallynoggin

Sir,
I should like a few moments alone with Mr Brown; he might not be so cock-a-hoop later. I have always understood that his *forte* was the internal combustion engine; instead I discover that he assumes a specialist's knowledge of Boy Scouts and purity.

I am an old woman, but at least I have reared two boys and managed to live quite happily with a husband for thirty-seven years. What grigs me is that Mr Brown is so repetitious on the subject of boys and purity – as if he were acting a part or learning all about purity for the first time from that little paper hanger we hear so much of lately. It seems to me that Mr Brown explains why Miss Clifford was unsuccessful in her attempts to pick up Boy Scouts. All I can say to her is – stick to your naval boy and his

212

queer stories. At least, he may have some guts. Did purity and temperance get the British Empire?

On Sunday I was at tea with my neighbour, Lir O'Connor, a man I haven't much use for normally because of those interminable reminiscences, but, leaning back in his Madras chair, he said: 'Crowd of little namby-pambies; pansies.' Then he started off again about Ruskin and the toupee.

Would my two sons be much use now if I had mollycoddled them with short trousers and 'don't do this' and 'beware of that'? These Mr Browns are nothing but titivators of their own repressions. At least Mr Harvey admits that he likes to hide himself and read Bawdy Smollett, and, apparently, through sheer diligence, has found passages in Shakespeare overlooked by me. All I hope is that Mr Brown does not confine his Bible reading exclusively to the Book of Genesis.

Mr O'Brien seems to fancy himself a wit. Possibly he is, but he has no balance. If he had, he would not try to provoke Mr O'Faoláin, who, despite his name, present residence and Cork parentage, has inherited part of the vasty tradition of West Britonism to which, thank goodness, I am a generic and spiritual heir. Mr O'Brien would probably like to see boys in kilts, which are one degree earlier and more mollycoddle than short trousers. Anyone who talks of 'British importations' always wants everyone to wear kilts and speak that unschooled language talked by the Vigilance Committee and vanguard Civil Servants.

One of the beauties of Ireland for an old woman like me is that it never changes. Poor Miss Clifford cannot find boy friends now; when I was her age I had to live permanently in Paris and Baden-Baden. I think that Mr Kavanagh, with his intimate and sympathetic knowledge of the youth of Ireland, would bear me out. He stands for something, for real men and women. Mr Brown and the other friends of Boy Scouts belong to the Geneva milk and water school with their 'let's ban this' and 'don't publish that'. They have shares in distilleries, but no whiskey in the house, and the worst cooks in Europe – if they are not on vegetarian diets.

Yours, etc.,
(Mrs) Hilda Upshott
The Grange, Sallynoggin

213

Sir,

Having been absent from home on a literary pilgrimage to the tomb of Nat Gould, I missed the opening spasms of the correspondence, which, with exquisite delicacy, you have entitled 'Literary Criticism'; so I am afraid I do not know what it is all about. Somebody told me yesterday that it derives from Mr Kavanagh's review of a novel by that admirable story teller, Maurice Walsh, who is one of the kindest and most modest of men. He also happens to be one of the most successful novelists of our time; and I should imagine that on the subject of 'potatoes' in the Flann O'Brien sense of the term, he could give some sound advice to all the boys and girls who have been horning in on this controversy. Mr Walsh makes money by his pen. Probably that is why he does not write letters to the *Irish Times*. I have read the book that started all this to-do, brouhaha, schemozzle, and what not; and it is pretty good, to my untutored way of thinking. If any of your correspondents could tell a story like the bold Maurice, he, she, or it, as the case may be, would not need to worry any more about the weekly tuber crop. So much for the congeries of booksy-boys, pansies, nambie-pambies (*pace* (Mrs) Hilda Up-shott), escapists, fly-boys, Cissies, Conchies, Wolfcubs, retired Sanitary Inspectors, acidulated spinsters, uplifters, Sundowners, hieratic humbugs and ex-TDs who have been wasting so much of your space.

Now for the sewer rats. There was a time in this country, in the dear, dead days beyond recall, when every newspaper controversy, on however high a plane it might have started, inevitably finished up by the interchange of the epithet 'Castle hack' among the protagonists. At a later stage of our national development, your correspondents tended to stray into a discussion regarding the validity of Holy Orders; and now by a series of easy and graceful transitions, we find ourselves led gently, but inexorably, into our municipal drain pipes.

My poor friend, Maurice Walsh! Little did he think, when writing *The Hill is Mine*, that his work would inspire so many of his artistic compeers to cry in eager union: 'The Sewers are Ours'. I cannot follow Flann O'Brien into the pungent purlieus of the septic tank, where, apparently, he and his boy friends take their vespertine ease, as Gogarty would have it. I am too old for

214

that sort of thing now. Besides, although I am strictly, almost passionately neutral, I believe there is a war on – a fact which does not yet seem to have reached the whimsy-whamsy boys of the contamination squad.

Yet, as dear old Quintus used to say, *dulce est desipere in loco*, even if the *locus in quo* should be the Gothic vault of which Fräulein O Brian – or should it be nic Brian – writes so feelingly. Is there any other country in the earth; is there any other capital city in Europe, where, in the middle of a world war, grown men and women would be writing about 'Literary Criticism', and pontificating anent the prose style of a sewer rat? There is not.

And, in a way, it is a pity. For after all it is better to be arguing about books than about the Battle of Benburb, or where you were in 1922. But Seán O'Faoláin has a lot to answer for, having been responsible for that unhappy remark about the drain pipes. Yet, Seán is a first-rate writer. And I don't mean maybe. Now, having begun five consecutive sentences with conjunctions, thereby offending against the canons of your leading article style, I had better wish all the crazy gang a very good day, and subscribe myself, with the appropriate number of knobs. Yours, etc. (why etc., I never could understand, but you always do it),

> (The) O'Madan
> Chateau Egout, Stonybatter, Co. Dublin

Sir,
Musing with my friend Angela Triptripe the other evening on the perils of perils and it is the purest thing I know musing with Angela Triptripe on the perils of perils. It was a lovely evening I remember Anna Livia P. spilling along as usual and all those beautiful white bare legs as far as the eye could see Angela however said you take things too seriously but you mustn't not in Dublin you mustn't City of grey bricks like Louis MacNiece said like he didn't say where only the poor still love it's cheaper than potatoes and the rest call each other rats so really they should know.

But I said What can I do Angela you poor Triptripe do you think I should have never been born not that it matters. You're quite right said Angela though of course that goes for the whole

215

shooting match only definitely it seems a pity what with all the nice round Towers and who made them anyway? True for you I said and Fair enough. Like there are a lot of reporters about the place said Angela and also the gentlemen from the *Irish* (*sic*) *Times* and of course they all say they can't get it printed or the Censor won't let them and more boloney. True for you I said and Fair enough.

Yes said Angela then but you should be wise and mind nobody pulls your leg And mind your own I said or they'll be pulling that or maybe I will myself Yes a lot of monkeys said Angela only you couldn't pull a pinkeen out of the Dodder you poor sap. Maybe not I said but I could write a letter to the papers Ha Ha said Angela you're pulling my leg now are you? Oh no I said I couldn't do that only South American Joe could do that, but I could write a letter to the papers to stop all letters to the papers, I could write it in Block capitals. What is this said Angela the walrus and the Carpenter? Block capitals won't stop them you poor fish. Only South American Joe can stop them, only South American Joe. And then and there with Anna Livia P. purling and plaining along Angela broke into song winning great applause and some coke and tubers from the hedgerows And she sang

> South American Joe. He's your man.
> He's the man that can can can
> He's got his gun and you're on the run!
> South American Joe. He's your maaannn.

> Yours, etc.,
> Ewart MacGonicle
> 43 Morehampton road, Dublin

Miss Lambkin, of Ventnor, Sandycove informs us that she is not the author of a letter which appeared in our correspondence columns yesterday bearing the signature 'W. R. Lambkin'. We deeply regret any inconvenience that may have been caused to Miss Lambkin.

Sir,
I have been asked by those anxious for my literary reputation to dissociate myself from a letter appearing in your columns on

216

Wednesday. The letter appears to be from my address, and is signed by a Mr Ewart MacGonicle.

I dissociate myself with enormous relief. On this occasion I have had the dubious pleasure of watching Mr MacGonicle floundering down the bannisters, as of hearing him stutter something about 'winding up little balls of yarn'. But I have never sat at meat with him. He thinks he is a Kafkaesque bird. I don't. I take a poor view of him.

Unfortunately, a lady, by name Miss Triptripe, seems to be trailing this fellow. She came around last evening bawling he had her ruined, and in the next (breath) that, indeed, he never. I am sorry for her, but she must get off my doorstep. Whichever of her stories be correct, obviously Mr MacGonicle is fitted only for the company of 'civilisation at its lowest'. And what's that, will anyone tell me? I hint darkly there's more than poor Scouts in it. Some I could name, too. Heiling – sorry. Hailing about all over the shop. I have it in for them.

I know you will regret any inconvenience I may have been caused, Mr Editor. Forget it, pal.

Yours, etc.,
'South American Joe'
Dublin

Sir,
The time has come when I can no longer remain silent. I had hoped to live the rest of my days in harmonious retirement, contented with the memory of my one assault upon your columns back in the era of the celebrated Ibsen controversy; but, alas, the cause of justice, love and sex equality has summoned me once more to the arena wherein all evil dreams are mended and the heart is soother in verbiage and the botanic flamboyance of the endless equivoque. Today, sitting at my study windows and letting my aged eyes rove as of yore through the panorama of lake and tree and mountain, I realise the hour has struck when I must relinquish awhile the burden of my lifework – *A History of the Wheelbarrow in all its Aspects* – and so, setting aside my half-completed manuscript of volume seven, I return again to the jostle of the market-place and brave for, perhaps, the last

217

occasion the raillery of O. Love, my virtual (and, doubtless, virtuous) neighbour.

The question, as I see it – and tossing aside all the smoke-screen flimflam concerning Boy Scouts, political theorising, the condition of agriculture and the hygenic aspect of great literature – is in reality an absurdly simple one. I will say nothing about Mr Patrick Kavanagh's refreshing enthusiasm for the bicycle as a means of transport – poets are entitled to go into transports over anything they please, and I well remember Algy Swinburne's secret craving to ride down Putney High Street on his grandson's little scooter. Better times, better manners, as Lord Lytton Strachey used to say; and I can never quite put out of my mind the picture of Rupert Brooke on the merry-go-round at Hampstead Heath one rainy summer's day – grasping the mane of his hobby horse with throbbing, sticky fingers and raising his high soprano in characteristic glee. In the imperishable apophthegm of my young contemporary, Mr Louis Bromfield, 'it takes all kinds to make a world'; and there can be few among us who would have it otherwise.

With this fact before him, then, it would be a churl, indeed, who would seek to tarnish the splendour of our Celtic heritage. I cannot too strongly emphasise, or in too formidable terms decry, when the issue has become so clearly vital to our nation and our age. Hart Crane, a poet himself, stated in 1931 that this was no time for poets; but 1940 is not 1931; and all the ink in Christendom can scarcely dry the feathers of fiery Pegasus while there is yet a clear Pierian stream to take a bath in. Foreigners may hurl at us the jibe that we fiddle while Rome burns, but posterity remembers Nero and his lovely music when the tuneless screaming of the burnt has faded totally from aural ken. In this, as in so many matters, there can be no shrinking when the kettledrums peal. Nelson, after all, was not a Dublin man.

Yours, etc.,
Whit Cassidy
Stava Pollyanna, Ultima Glasthule, Co. Dublin

218

Sir,

The last thing I remember Lorna said to me: 'Did you put out the cat? . . .' Then I heard her saying: 'You never told me you were after writing to the paper, John. I caught sight of your name when I was going to light the stove. Then I read the stuff about you wanting to make an AP with that Judy. Don't you know she was in service with Mrs Flann O'Brien in Ticknock, but gave notice on account of the bad drains. What would you be making an AP with the likes of her for?'

'ARP it was,' I said. 'I wanted to see her about a septic tank.'

Lorna appeared somewhat mollified. She said she hoped some Boy Scout would do something about the poor tank if it really was septic.

'There was a man called to see you today,' she went on. 'Butterley was the name. He said he wanted the loan of your *Abracadabra Curiosa* for Mr O'Connor. So I said that was an expensive book and had he anything in writing. "No," says he; "I guess I'm a fake," and, with that, he just melted into thin air fornint me. Janey Mac, I'm not the same since.'

The next morning in Moore street Lorna met Mrs K., who said herself and Pat were having a quiet evening on board the sludge-shifter at the Pigeon House when they saw Butterley riding their cock albatross on a reconnaissance flight over the Bull Wall. They raised their sharp helliloos and Hibernian ululations to stop the thief, and two Garda Baby Spitfires went up in pursuit. The raider made his escape, but not before his tank was badly punctured, and he was seen making what appeared to be a forced landing in the general direction of the Nose of Howth, with dense clouds of dark smoke pouring from his mount.

Although our unicorn, by reason of his organic structure, cannot be regarded as an unclean animal, Paddy often spends hours in our back garden in silent communication with the beast. He arrived the other evening with an ass and creels, seeking consolation for the loss of his albatross, and he sat for a long time on the stone outside the back door, feeding mangolds to Archie, and throwing absent-minded handfuls of corn to Peggy, our pet Phoenix. Subsequently he withdrew to the greenhouse, and on his return triumphantly showed us a dissertation of forty thousand word jewels in prose on the subject of my prize pumpkin, while his three book reviews intended for publication in next Saturday's *Irish Times* (*Sewercide*, by Flann O'Brien; *Knicknax*, by Judy Clifford, and *Green Grazier*, by Niall Montgomery), had all become magically metamorphosed into *rima cantata* sonnettes electrotranscribed with asinine l'envoi and burdened with the usual butter and eggs and a pound of cheese. And parachute roses across the moon, earless and unabashed.

It seems that I'm mixing with doubtful company, I soliloquised, as I continued my anabasis to put out the cat.

Yours, etc.,
Jno. O'Ruddy
Raheny

Sir,

I write again chiefly in the hope that, by adding to the demands on your restricted space, I may assist in crowding out Mr Love, who must surely have another letter containing still another quotation on the way to you by now.

Your superior correspondent, The O'Madan, says that he cannot follow me into the pungent purlieus of the septic tank. I did not say anything about septic tanks, which are only makeshifts for houses in unsewered country districts. (Indeed, I know one County Cork intellectual who always calls his septic tank 'the library'.) If The O'Madan means that he is too fat to negotiate our city manholes, I can direct him to a large outfall grating near Ringsend, which is large enough to admit a bus-load of literary toadies. If Ringsend seems too far from home, he can try getting down the manhole head first, because I find that bottle-shoulders usually go with corpulency, and even the staidest gentleman will develop a surprising talent for contortion when he finds himself head first half-way down a manhole and stuck fast. And, while I am at it; would not 'Sewerealists' be a handy label for our native smut-and-libel boys? I cannot help wondering what poor old Coleridge would think of it all.

A word of warning to the Irish nobleman should he decide to take the header and trust to the sprightliness of his stomach

220

muscles. *'Facilis est descensus Averno, sed revocare, hoc opus, hic labor est.'*

> Yours, etc.,
> F. O'Brien
> Dublin

Sir,

moving been has correspondence entire the which in direction the be to seems it because backwards question the putting am I? about talking are they what idea remotest the have, columns your in themselves spread to allowed been, leniency great very your of result a as, have who, correspondents literary your of many how wonder I.

> Yours etc.,
> 'Lanna Avvia'
> Dublin

Sir,

Your correspondent, 'Cu SO_4', is worried about the position of the wasp described in Mr P. Kavanagh's poem, 'Spraying the Potatoes', published in your issue of the 27th ult.

Another appreciative reader of poetry is perturbed by the thought that the blossoms of Arran Banners, described as blue, are in reality white. It is doubtful if poetic licence permits such an inaccuracy as this, and I think Mr Kavanagh should severely reprimand his Muse for not having consulted the Department of Agriculture's leaflet on potatoes (sent free on application) before inspiring him.

At the same time I consider that Mr Kavanagh's effusion could truly be described as 100 *per cent* modern poetry were it not for the small *percentage* of intelligible statements with which it is contaminated.

> Yours (in solution), etc.,
> Na 2 Co3
> Dublin

Sir,

'By thy wildgaze I thee gander.' Higgin caps rejoyceing with ackemma scout bottle and small irish times passing. Hoops laugh and five pere saint guzzle. Haw, haw, and lord frocken frocken. Landsender. O Kultur! O Knocknee and hairy airs! Sewer they sawn down my scout trees for poteen still and shin toasters. Me feather bed bare for fourmaster and master pan warming. Ochone, acorn, me scout lads be woodless, be mastless, be mindless, be the powers curt and iveagh shorts hairs I have them. Me black boat, me red deer, me gold eagle, me brown wolf. Alack for them all and me tram tracks fast going. But me scout lads, me oak harts, me feather bed tarzans. Me jam bores and peace doves be the short hairs I'll keep them, the prods and the papes of them. Hale civilisation.

But me plays boys, them poet gets, them spud spraying buzzards, them flann footed bly blows, be the jeyes fluid I'll flay them. Sewer as grass grows every manhole with scout poles I'll plug them. Every bust boy I'll dust up with me scout lads good deeding. In me pigeon house salt bottom muck dump I'll plant them. Heil civilisation.

Yours, etc.,
F. McEwe Obarn
Bahnhofplatz, Golden Ball

Sir,

Now that the sewer-rats have almost done with the remains of Privy Councillor Kavanagh, perhaps you can find a tiny nook in your columns where a certain timid, wee mouse of a person can express her views. And who is this outspoken mouseling, you will ask with interest ever a-growing. Why, none other than your own small Luna, of course, who is probably the most indignant little body in the whole of Sallynoggin this day, but let me begin at the beginning. This morning I arose to greet the rosy-fingered day in a mood of ungovernable whimsy. The air was fragrant with the burgeoning bougainvillea, and Aeolian music assuaged my ears as I flung open the casement. Out on the lawn the lightly-draped figures of Anderson, Stanford and Ridgeway, my three favourite woodland deities, were tripping through the intricacies of a

222

Terpsichorean measure. Wreathlets of asphodel adorned their hair, and beneath their down-light feet was the sun-drenched jasmine. Then there sounded out the silvery tinkle of a faërie bell and the dancers disappeared into the foliage in a fine flurry of their draperies. Up the crazy pavement came the satyric figure of our elfin postman, playing on his miniature Pan pipes and blowing out his moustache into a delicious wee fan in doing so. Gumley, our Tweenie, ran out eagerly to meet him and adroitly avoided the out-thrust cloven hoof, with which he attempted to trip her up. A faded copy of the *Irish Times* done up in pink ribbon changed hands, and then the old ruffian tore down the garden path, happily pursued by our elfin Pekinese, Mr Jno. O'Ruddy.

Well, from the very moment that I opened that paper, which I should explain was Tuesday's issue, all the sun-pleasure and flower-thoughts faded from the furious mind of your little friend. Sir, you have wronged my brother, and in doing so have directed poor Luna's feet into the Slough of Despond. You had the downright effrontery to publish a letter from Mrs Hilda Upshott, of The Grange, Sallynoggin, in which she quotes certain aphorisms that fell from the lips of Lir on the occasion of a recent tea-party in this house, worded in such a way as to suggest that she actually sat down at the same table as my brother and myself.

Lest your unkindness in fostering this preposterous libel be unwitting, let me explain that Upshott, or 'Uppie' as she is known below stairs, has been the bane of my brother's life ever since the day he accidentally lodged half a pound of buckshot in the nape of her husband's neck. Old Sam Upshott was chief gamekeeper on the estate since my father's time, and his passing on was spoken of with regret by those of us who knew him as a true and faithful servant, and one who knew his place, which is more than I would care to say of the girl he left behind him.

The circumstances surrounding his demise were commonplace enough. It was 'the twelfth', and some of Lir's sporting friends insisted on dragging him away from the companionship of his books, replacing the finely tooled copy of Donderlein's '*The Saturnine Encephalopathic Syndrome*' into which he had been dipping, by a light fowling-piece of my father's which had been rusting in the gun room for nearly twenty years. Once away from

223

his library and out in the open air the scholar became lost in the eager huntsman, with every sense on the *qui vive*. When I say 'every sense' I am, of course, only speaking figuratively, since the fact that he had forgotten to bring along his pince-nez left him rather imperfectly equipped for the chase, and, as it happened, it was this very self-same oversight that was ultimately responsible for spoiling the entire day's sport for the Nimrods. As you know, we O'Connors are apt to be somewhat impulsive at times, so that the first sight of feathers in a spinney over near Foley's Folly Lir let off a magnificent left-and-right with a delighted: 'My bird, if I am not altogether mistaken!' Imagine his annoyance when on searching the brush he found, not the plump corpse of a pheasant, but the mortal remains of Samuel Upshott, with a hole the size of a turnip through the quaint old deerstalker's cap that he used to affect. Although the incident cast a blight on the day's outing, it speaks well for my brother's sense of humour when, instead of becoming moody over the bird he thought he had brought down, he hid his disappointment with the remark: 'Poor Sam, fine fellow! But, unfortunately, fine fellows don't make fine birds.'

The newly-created widow behaved rather badly over the whole affair, I thought, pointing out that while a few shillings can procure a brace of game in the open market, the acquisition of a suitable helpmeet is a horse of a very different colour, a fact of which nobody is more acutely aware than myself. However, sooner than have any unpleasantness, my brother gave to Upshott and her children the south-west gate lodge, to be held in fee-simple until one of the boys is old enough to take his father's place in our employment. This property is known among the tenants on the estate as 'Kill o' the Grange' or, more familiarly, 'The Grange', on account of the little cemetery adjoining the kitchen garden, in which rest the various gamekeepers to the family who gave up their lives in the interests of sport.

Furthermore, we allow Upshott to perform certain chores about the house so as to prevent her from thinking that she is sponging on our hospitality. Armed with mop and pail, her ponderous figure can frequently be seen swabbing out the conservatory or dusting out the blue-room. It was probably while on such a menial mission as this that she overheard the conversation

224

which she had the unpardonable impertinence to communicate to a public newspaper.

Finally, then, Mr Editor, since you, for your part, have contrived to disclose the skeleton in our family cupboard, I trust you will have the manliness to publish in full this disclaimer. This woman's unwelcome attentions towards my brother have convinced me that if there were fewer Upshotts in this world there would be fewer of their more modest, retiring sisters spending their evenings with stamp album and fern book, and I, for one of them, might not now be signing myself

Yours, etc.,

Miss (alas) Luna O'Connor

La Casita, Sallynoggin

Sir,

Now that the ball is over, it may be no harm if I address a few words to the stragglers on the gallery steps.

In my review of Maurice Walsh's *The Hill is Mine* I referred to the empty virtuosity of artists who were expert in the art of saying nothing. Ploughmen without land. One of my critics said it was a wistful remark, and, maybe, it was; but if ever a critic was proved right, all round, by his critics it happened this time. It is to be feared that the diletanttish disciples of Joyce and Eliot are no more a credit to their masters than are the followers of Lord Baden-Powell and Margaret Mitchell. I am referring chiefly to the undergraduate-magazine writers who reached the heights of epic literature in a balloon filled with verbal gas. It was all very adolescent, though at times faintly amusing.

As I write these words a feeling of deep pity comes over me – the pity that is awakened by the contortions of a clown's funny face, or when listening in to a certain radio situated just less than 1,000,000 miles from Athlone. There is tragedy here, and I, for one, am shy to bring these literary scouts and touts to a raw awareness of their tragedy. Too soon they will know the misery of literary men without themes, poets without burdens, ploughmen without land. Such grief has Higher Education brought to simple-minded, decent fellows, who might have developed in happiness as Corporation workers in actual sewers.

I hardly expected boys like these to realise that the predicament of the wasp in my poem was due to a misplaced full stop. Some people may say that I have taken the thing too seriously, but life is a serious business. These silly letters are significant, because, as I have suggested – or have I? – the face of truth is often most truly reflected in the mirror of folly.

On the serious letters I do not intend to comment here.

Yours, etc.,
Patrick Kavanagh
Dublin

(This correspondence is closed. – Ed. *I. T.*)

6

The Bell

The sunlight is wan filtered deceptive dirt, like diluted cider. It sits like some gaudy industrial waste on the harlot town, imbuing the grey platter-faced houses with a sinister luminance. Like the time we went down the ochre mines in Avoca, poor George was alive then and Fanny wasn't born yet. And your man Jim fell off the third ladder and lost the candle and Sissy began to squeal and cry with fright. And now she's married away in far-off California, maybe never to return to Ireland this side of the grave. She was only a little slip of a girl then. I wonder does she ever remember the day we went down the mine and the fun we had when we were all together. Does she remember the picnic in Woodenbridge and the time I pranced around the field with a bully-beef tin on my head for a hat?

Lord when I think of those times!

CRUISKEEN LAWN
Irish Times, 6 May 1942

In October 1940, Seán O'Faoláin, the indefatigable novelist, historian, polemicist and Corkman, founded *The Bell*, a literary/political journal which was to be of considerable importance in the maturing process of the young Irish state. The magazine stood against the insularity of thought that, in the opinion of the more enlightened intellectuals of the day, was suffocating Ireland, and fought the censorship of books on religious and moral grounds. Foreign cultural and political matters were widely discussed in *The Bell*, but an attempt was also made to describe with dispassion Ireland's own position, and its social traditions and habits. Although in the *Cruiskeen Lawn* column Myles was to mock Seán O'Faoláin for his Corkness, and the anti-censorship lobby for its pseudo-intellectual trendiness, he wrote for the magazine, as Flann O'Brien, the following three articles, descriptive of life in Ireland at the beginning of 'The Emergency'.

Going to the dogs

It was at Manchester in 1926 that the dogs started their interminable and hopeless pursuit of the toy hare. The success of the sport was instantaneous and new tracks sprang up rapidly throughout the country. The following year the new game came to Ireland and seemed to fill perfectly a void which (in the absence of horse-racing at night) had existed in the spiritual and intellectual consciousness of the people. Early in 1927, the National Greyhound Racing Company was formed in Dublin by the late Hugh McAlinden and Joseph Shaw of Belfast, J. M. Collins and P. O'Donoghue of Dublin, James Clarke of Ballybunion and H. B. Hobson of Manchester. The spread of the sport was made easy by the device of installing the gaming machinery around the edges of existing football grounds rather than acquiring and equipping entirely new centres. The Irish company obtained options on Celtic Park in Belfast and Shelbourne Park in Dublin, each a well-known soccer ground. The first meeting at the Dublin ground was held on the 18th of May. The Irish Coursing Club, which had enjoyed long-established authority on all matters relating to coursing and greyhound breeding, took control, issued licences for the establishment of tracks and then fixed a cold, unblinking, supervisory eye on every man and dog concerned. Greyhound racing grew quickly to a big thing.

In Dublin, a second track not inferior to the first was opened at Harold's Cross and many of the bigger country towns soon found that a track was an essential amenity. At present there are as many as twenty-one recognised tracks in the country and perhaps twice as many unofficial 'flapper' tracks. The latter, of course, are frowned upon heavily, and owners who are found running their dogs at them behind disguises qualify for penalties deadlier than anything known to the GAA. Nevertheless, it is recognised that these humble venues can be valuable training grounds. Many a retired aristocrat who had brought honour to his country at the London White City would confess, if he could speak, that his early days on those forbidden campuses were the happiest days of his life.

The demand for good dogs is so insistent that a considerable

228

breeding industry has developed in this country during the last ten years. In normal times, it is estimated that greyhounds to the value of £500,000 are exported every year. Greyhounds seem to flourish here no less than horses. The two Dublin tracks are regarded everywhere as the display centres of top-notch dog-dom. Any dog who distinguishes himself on either of them attracts the immediate interest of the moneyed English fanciers who never tire of looking for an animal who is good enough to bring home one or other of the succulent sides of bacon which are on view at the 'classic' London meetings – the Derby, the Laurels, the Gold Cup, the Pall Mall, or the Golden Collar. Fancy prices have been paid for Dublin dogs in the past. Bally-hennessy's Sandhills was sold for £1,000 and had won more than £5,000 in stake money for his owner in less than a year. Future Cutlet cost his London owner £550 and in thirteen months had won £6,000. The legendary Mick the Miller had earned £10,000 when he retired, and as a youngster had changed masters in Dublin for £700. As against such as these, it is also true that large cheques were drawn for many other dogs who turned out, so to speak, to be black sheep.

Let us take a tram to Shelbourne Park. This place is nicely situated (as a guide-book would say) between a gasworks, a tidal river full of old buckets, and a sort of dockland hostel where sea-going tramps lie up for intervals to have oil-cake, maize and the like extracted from their stomachs. Nonetheless, it is a neat clean place, enlivened by sea-breezes and an antiseptic tarry aroma thrown out gratis by the gasworks – wholesome breathing for man and dog. At the gates you are invited to pay the company either 3/6 or 1/3. Many people (those who follow the cloth-cutting adage) reflect that the difference of 2/3 might, if invested judiciously with the books, represent £1 later on, and accordingly enter by the cheaper door which leads to 'the outside', otherwise the exterior of the inside. Unlike nearly all horse venues, the cheaper enclosure at a dog-track usually affords a perfect view of the racing and has a very large selection of good bookmakers. The only difference is that it does not have the start or the winning-post and does have a larger percentage of shiny suits. The winning-post is of no interest because all experienced patrons seem to be able to judge what the result of the race is going to be before it is half over, even when the winner is still nosing his way through the back of the pack.

The books arrange themselves conventionally on each side of the course facing the stands and try to sell as many tickets as possible. The trend of the market in the inside enclosure is telegraphed by tick-tack men to the books in the cheaper place. The betting is brisk because there is a new race every fifteen minutes and considerable activity is necessary if all one's money is to be risked before racing is over. There are usually six or seven races, one or two of them over hurdles.

A noticeable thing about Shelbourne Park is the great number of women who attend – not the dressed-up type who loiter about horse-tracks obstructing people who have work to do – but earnest ladies who have no thought of anything but the dogs. Bookies will tell you that many of them are shrewd backers and do not work in shillings. The 'regulars', male and female, have their own peculiarities. They occupy the same place night after night, move always in the same group and give their money to the same bookmaker. They always seem to wear the same look of depression or elation at the end of the evening's business, no matter how much they have won or lost. There are many 'characters', 'cards', people who are different from others in some mild entertaining way. Yet when the lights go out, the starting bell clangs and the dogs come streaking round the track at forty miles an hour, they are all suddenly reduced by the tension of the spectacle to uniform pin-points of attention. The instant the race is over, they disintegrate into their multiple diversities, all reassuming their distinctive eccentricities as readily as one puts on a garment – the shrugging spasms, the gawky eye, the trick of interminable muttering.

There is a familiar friendly relationship between the book-makers and the punters. A punter who wants a slightly better price than what is ruling will not be refused if he cares to make a point about it. A nod occasionally takes the place of green notes when a regular wants to play with what he hasn't got. Disputes are unknown because the bookies prefer to pay rather than humiliate a customer by proving he is wrong. A very consider-able reputation is enjoyed by such fearless layers as Joe Mirrel-son, Billy Walsh, Tommy Burns, Jack MacFarland, Con

230

McGrath, Michael O'Donoghue, Harry Leddy and many others. Their chalky bags are the repositories of ruin and opulence and they fill their god-like office with efficiency, dignity, and great affability.

I remember one evening not so longer ago noticing a man I knew from the County Monaghan eating in a city restaurant, accompanied by three other young men in blue suits and salmon-coloured caps. When I asked what had them in town, they said they were up with a dog and a considerable sum of money in notes. I implored them to tell me no more and in due course made my way to Shelbourne Park. There I happened to meet another man who had for many years impressed me by the singular regularity with which he lost his money on unsound betting transactions. In his earlier days, he had devised a system entirely from his own head which enabled him to lose his money many times more quickly than was possible with the assistance of ordinary bad luck. He was now content to lose heavily on single bets instead of yielding to any catastrophic doubling-up neurosis, but he assured me that things could not be going worse with him. From his shabby and ill-nourished appearance, this seemed to be a fact. I gave him a quiet word of advice about the last race and then carefully lost him in the crowd.

The dog was unknown and the betting closed at sixes and sevens, which means that the price was very satisfactory, not disordered. The crowd thought that some other dog could not possibly be beaten and I watched the traps nervously as the hare came bobbing down the straight to the start. My own dog seemed to emerge miraculously through the grating of his trap before the others were released and to have shot round the first bend before there was any question of a race at all. When the others had gathered themselves into a pack and set off in pursuit, my own dog was almost in sight of home and he was probably well on his way back to Monaghan with the salmon-coloured caps before the other dogs were caught. Going out, my arm was taken by the shabby gambler. He thanked me with the simple words of a man who rarely finds it necessary to thank anybody. Then he drew my attention to the race itself. Never, he swore, had he seen anything so exciting, so heart-pounding, so full of the colour and fire of hard clean racing. What could be more cheering to the

231

heart than to see six or seven lithe thoroughbreds streaking round a track with fair field and no favour, no hard feelings if your fancy loses provided the best dog wins? Was there anything in the world finer to watch than a race between those grand animals, hurtling onwards neck and neck to a fierce finish? To his dying day he would remember that great race.

I refrained from mentioning that there had been no race to speak of, knowing well what a good win can do to a man's head. I noticed that his face was beautiful, shining on me with the clean luminance of a better world. If he had died at that moment, he would have gone straight to heaven. It goes to prove that how you leave Shelbourne Park is more important than how you enter it. If you leave it with the feel of strange greasy notes in your pocket, you will find it a wide clean fine place, magnificent well-appointed stands on each side and grass of an unusually green hue in the centre. Attendants in spotless white coats (which have been subjected to a patent antiseptic process) will be around you retrieving benign-faced hounds from an innocent after-race frolic. All around you handsome men and women will be walking with quiet dignity to their gleaming cars. They will be dressed in cool expensive linens and will carry in their faces the mark of clean living. A cool breeze will temper the genial evening.

But if you happen to depart leaving all your money in the bag of a bookmaker, you will be appalled at the dreariness of your surroundings. Thunderous clouds will be massed above the ramshackle stands, ready to vomit their contents on you when they get you away from cover. Loathsome dogs, their faces lined with vice, will leer at you in mockery. Your demoniacal fellow-degenerates, slinking out beside you, will look suspiciously like drug addicts. Every one of them will have lost his entire week's wages notwithstanding the fact that he has a wife and seven children to support, each of whom is suffering from an incurable disease. There will be a bad smell in evidence, probably from the bucket-strewn river. If you notice any odd patron walking out jauntily, it will be safe to infer on such an occasion that he has given himself the needle behind the grand-stand.

At Shelbourne Park and at every other park, there are two ways of it, and the pity is that you cannot be at the choice of them.

232

The trade in Dublin

In the last ten years there has been a marked change in the decor of boozing in Dublin. The old-time pub was something in the nature of an Augean stable (it is true that Pegasus was often tethered there) with liberal lashings of sawdust and mopping-rags to prevent the customers from perishing in their own spillings and spewings. No genuine Irishman could relax in comfort and feel at home in a pub unless he was sitting in deep gloom on a hard seat with a very sad expression on his face, listening to the drone of bluebottle squadrons carrying out a raid on the yellow sandwich cheese. In those days a definite social stigma attached to drinking. It was exclusively a male occupation and on that account (and apart from anything temperance advocates had to say) it could not be regarded as respectable by any reasonable woman. Demon rum was a pal of the kind one is ashamed to be seen with. Even moderate drinkers accepted themselves as genteel degenerates and could slink into a pub with as much feline hug-the-wall as any cirrhotic whiskey-addict, there to hide even from each other in dim secret snugs. A pub without a side-door up a lane would have been as well off with no door at all.

Up to recent times the only improvement was the bar parlour, a dark privacy at the rear where any respectable bowler-hatted gentleman from the countinghouse of a large drapery concern could tinkle in peace at his hot mid-day whiskey. Such places were clean and comfortable enough, though often equipped with forbidding furniture of the marble-topped and iron-legged variety usually found in morgues and fish-shops. Latterly, however, we have had the Lounge, the Lounge Bar, the Select Lounge, the Oak Lounge, and Octagonal Lounge, and still more refined booze-shops called brasseries and butteries where obsequious servers in white coats will refuse point-blank to give you beer, even if your doctor has certified under his own hand that you will drop dead after one glass of spirits.

It is in such places that one can perceive in its full force the Reformation which has been spreading throughout the public-house congregations. The old-fashioned curate, the drinker's

233

confessor and counsellor, is disappearing. His honest country face, his simple black clothes, his coatlessness, his apron and the gleaming steel armbands on his shirt-sleeves were almost supernatural symbols which invested the lowliest pub with a feeling of being-with-friends, a homeliness which many men fail to find in their own houses. He was the repository of every grain of knowledge which could be gathered from a lifetime of other people's drink-loosened conversations. In one small head he could contain an incomparable compendium of every known fact about politics, women, the GAA and, tucked away in a separate compartment by itself, a thesaurus of horse-lore not entirely to be independently unearthed from the Form Book or the Calendar. Sensing the innate spiritual character of his calling, he served humanity well in his licensed parish.

The white-coated server who has ousted the curate in some pubs may be taken as a sign of the decline of faith. The Irish brand of humanity, expansive and voluble, is hardening and contracting under the hammer-blows of international mammon, dealt through the radio, press and cinema. Among the stupider section of the younger generation a shabby and rather comic 'smartness' may be discerned, even in the simple task of dealing with a bottle of brown stout.

Their cinema-going has taught them the great truth that William Powell does not walk up to a counter, bellow for a schooner or a scoop and ask Mick whether the brother is expected up for the match on Sunday. William is modern and drinks out of glasses with long stems in a cushioned corner with his doxy. His many imitators (what could be more flimsy than an imitation of a flat two-dimensional picture-house ghost?) have insisted on something similar, since they, too, have to go out with Myrna Loy. The Select Lounge has been the handsome answer of the trade in Dublin.

Today there are many of these lounges in the city, even in those areas which people living elsewhere call 'tough quarters'. Some are very good, many are curious travesties of what may be regarded as the publican's conception of paradise. The better places are quiet and comfortable, softly lighted, and a boon to any sensible, tired person who wants a stimulant without being jostled and who does not concern himself with social trends or

234

think that a well-dressed woman in a pub is an outrage that imparts a sourness to the drink.

The other places afford a pathetic insight into the meaning attached to the word 'modern' by many publicans. They think that it means just tubes – tubular chairs, repellent alike to eye and seat, tubular lighting, tubular effects in decoration. Those who have been to prison immediately recognise the lamentable simplicity of the decor and the severity of the furnishings. The ugliness of such a tavern cannot be completely offset by the fact that most of the customers appear to be film-stars or that the man who serves you is a bell-hop from New York.

Here let us digress to touch upon a very important irrelevancy. The lower orders (non-car-owners and the like) are excluded from all these lounges, sometimes by an impudent surcharge on the already extortionate price of drink, nearly always by outlawing the pint, which is the only cheap nourishing light beer that can be had. Although probably more than half of the money amassed by any publican has been made from selling pints of porter, the pint-drinker is rigidly confined to his outer corral, far away from the heat and the soft seats; he never even sees the fancy clock that has no numbers on its face, only a dot for each hour. Some publicans, equipped with the odious sham-gentility which money earned by astute trading confers on humble folk, justify this nonsense by a process of reasoning too tortuous to record. One well-known argument is that 'the lads would not go in there if you paid them'. In a country which is held to be democratic and in which writers and labourers are on the same economic plane, it is an impertinence which should be challenged by some public-spirited person at the annual licensing sessions, if only to make 'himself' explain his quaint social theories in public.

One wonders what Mr James Montgomery would think of it all. Mr Montgomery is one of the select band of Dublin gentlemen who knew the Dublin pub-life of the old days and who contributed his own big share of whatever ambrosial vitamin made that generation of drinkers and thinkers immortal. (We cannot help wondering, myself, the printer and the Editor, where a compliment can also be a libel.) Other veterans, happily still encounterable, are Seamus O'Sullivan and famous Martin Murphy of the Gaiety Theatre. If they could be persuaded to tell

235

the tale (or 'write it down' in the manner of people who summon their neighbours for using unmentionable language) they could fill *The Bell* for many issues with material that would make it a standard work of reference for anybody who wants to dig under the calloused skin of Dublin.

They could tell about the beginnings of the United Arts Club, conceived in Neary's snug (or maybe in MacCormack's of South King Street) by the boisterous Count Markievicz. If you turn into Chatham Street today and mount the stairs inside the Neary hall-door, you will find yourself in a seductive den (Select Lounge is the correct term) probably never dreamt of by the Count. Here the authorities had the sense to employ a real artist, Miss Bradshaw, rather than a distant Japanese technician, to enliven the walls with pictures.

The only other public-house that comes to mind in this con-nexion is Higgins's Waterloo Bar at the bottom of Waterloo Road. Here the far-sighted proprietor, who also owns another pub in Pembroke Street and in person resembles Kreisler, had the enlightenment within him to retain Mr Brendan O'Connor to design his lounge and Mr Desmond Rushton to leave his mark upon the walls. The result is a combination of utility (functional something-or-other architects call it), comfort and restraint – but no pints. All sorts may be seen here of an evening, front and rear.

> Sometimes carters slacken rein,
> Sometimes exiles come again,
> Or a pilgrim you will see
> On the way to Mellary.

Davy Byrne's in Duke Street, the Bailey Restaurant nearly opposite, and the underground Bodega in Dame Street are licensed tabernacles sanctified by the past attendances of people with names like Orpen, Gogarty, Griffith, Murphy, Furlong, Montgomery, McKenna, even Joyce, not to mention the Toucher Doyle, the Bird Flanagan and his relative, the Pope. (Who will pretend that these are not ordinary surnames that can be borne by anybody?) All three still open their doors at ten o'clock and possibly shelter today the makings of a second fame – the same again. They are run by new if cognate personalities and none has found any necessity to have recourse to the blandish-merits of the Select Lounge. The premises bear openly the marks of their departed guests, like traces of fresh stout found in a glass by a policeman after hours; but they still look prosperous, not like banquet-halls deserted.

The bar of the Ormond Hotel and Barney Kiernan's down the quays were other centres of intellectual sodality. Barney's was a dim and venerable backwater where an argument could be pursued hour by hour without interruption, with casks all around to receive the resounding fist. Fanning's of Lincoln Place had and has a similar fame. Some of the distinguished guests in Fanning's, guzzling the uniformly good drink, will tell you that the intransigence of the distinguished boss's political beliefs can sometimes lend an unwelcome uniformity to his conversation.

Today, as in the past, birds of a feather tend to flutter into the same snug. Grogan's of Leeson Street and Higgins's of Pembroke Street are noted for the punctilious attendances of students from 'National'; Trinity students have their names marked on the roll at Davy Byrne's. Mulligan's in the narrow street which runs alongside the Theatre Royal caters for painted ladies and painted men – the theatrical kind, often straight from the stage. Most people connected with show business make their way here, and Mr Mulligan has recently provided a new Lounge for their further entertainment and approval.

The Palace Bar in Fleet Street is the main resort of newspapermen, writers, painters and every known breed of artist and intellectual. Porter is served willingly everywhere in the house, and in fancy tankards. The clients range from the tiniest elfin intellectual to a large editor, alive and in good condition. Looking at the editor, one frequently sees the left hand flung out as if in demonstration of some wide generous idea; actually, however, it is merely a claw in search of a cigarette, a modest tax that is gladly paid by listening neophytes. The editor is unconscious of this mannerism; he is king in this particular Palace and merely exercises a ruling-class prerogative.

The partitioning-off idea which dominates the scheme of the lounges at Doran's of Marlboro' Street and O'Mara's of Aston's Quay seems to attract clients who have weighty secrets to exchange – lovers and the like. The Scotch House on Burgh Quay is famous for the mellowness and good colour of its whiskey and

237

civil servants. It was stated officially recently in the newspapers that the Dolphin Hotel is noted for its 'sporting crowd' and 'racing people'; whatever about the horses, it abounds in suede shoes and jackets with two splits. Probably the oldest licence and the oldest pub in Dublin is the Brazen Head Hotel, an old coaching-house down the quays, one-time resort of Robert Emmet and the United Irishmen. Here the most random spit will land on ten centuries of antiquity. 'Professional gentlemen' as they are called by landladies – doctors, lawyers, architects and that ilk – do a lot of their drinking in the Metropole. The Red Bank, the Wicklow Hotel, the various Mooney's, Madigan's of Earl Street, and McArdle's of South King Street are popular with all creeds and classes.

When many of Ireland's staid rulers of today were younger and on the run, they ran sometimes towards Rathfarnham, frequently in the Parnell Street direction. Devlin's, Kennedy's and Kirwan's in that thoroughfare were places where Miss Ní h-Uallacháin was served without question, even though the lady no longer lived in her guardian's house and was wanted by the police. Michael Collins often drank a bottle of stout in the bar of Vaughan's Hotel. In Dan Dunne's of distant Donnybrook, as Batt O'Connor relates, he once, leaning back, touched a hanging bell-push with his head. The man of the house promptly cut down the bell-push and proudly showed it afterwards to customers as his most famous and cherished possession. Not even the jagged wire can be seen today, for Time, that bedfellow of all publicans, has erased the whole public-house.

At ten o'clock on week nights and at half-nine on Saturday the tide ebbs suddenly, leaving the city high and dry. Unless you are staying at a hotel or visiting a theatre, you may not lawfully consume excisable liquors within the confines of the county borough. The city has entered that solemn hiatus, that almost sublime eclipse known as The Closed Hours. Here the law, as if with true Select Lounge mentality, discriminates sharply against the poor man at the pint counter by allowing those who can command transport and can embark upon a journey to drink elsewhere till morning. The theory is that all travellers still proceed by stage-coach and that those who travel outside become blue with cold after five miles and must be thawed out with

238

hot rum at the first hostelry they encounter by night or day. In practice, people who are in the first twilight of inebriation are transported from the urban to the rural pub so swiftly by the internal combustion engine that they need not necessarily be aware that they have moved at all, still less comprehend that their legal personalities have undergone a mystical transfiguration. Whether this system is to be regarded as a scandal or a godsend depends largely on whether one owns a car. At present the city is ringed round with these 'bona-fide' pubs, many of them well-run modern houses, and a considerable amount of the stock-in-trade is transferred to the stomachs of the customers at a time every night when the sensible and the just are in their second sleeps. Coolock, Tallaght, Templeogue, Santry, Lucan, Ballydowd, Cabinteely, Shankill, Fox-and-Geese and Stepaside are a few of the villages where there is revelry by night. Stepaside in recent years has been notable for the engaging personality of Mr James Whelan, who has now, however, forsaken the dram-shop for the farm. The Lamb Doyle's nearby, cocked high up near Ticknock, was a favourite point of pilgrimage of a summer Sunday for the boys of Casimir Markievicz's day. It is still there, though under new and female management.

To go back to the city: it appears that the poor man does not always go straight home at ten o'clock. If his thirst is big enough and he knows the knocking-formula, he may possibly visit some house where the Demand Note of the Corporation has stampeded the owner into a bout of illicit after-hour trading. For trader and customer alike, such a life is one of excitement, tip-toe and hush. The boss's ear, refined to shades of perception far beyond the sensitiveness of any modern aircraft detector, can tell almost the inner thoughts of any policeman in the next street. At the first breath of danger all lights are suddenly doused and conversation toned down, as with a knob, to vanishing point. Drinkers reared in such schools will tell you that in inky blackness stout cannot be distinguished in taste from Bass and that no satisfaction whatever can be extracted from a cigarette unless the smoke is seen. Sometimes the police make a catch. Here is the sort of thing that is continually appearing in the papers:

239

Guard — said that accompanied by Guard — he visited the premises at 11.45 P-m. and noticed a light at the side door. When he knocked, the light was extinguished, but he was not admitted for six minutes. When defendant opened eventually, he appeared to be in an excited condition and used bad language. There was nobody in the bar but there were two empty pint measures containing traces of fresh porter on the counter. He found a man crouching in a small press containing switches and a gas-meter. When he attempted to enter the yard to carry out a search, he was obstructed by the defendant, who used an improper expression. He arrested him, but owing to the illness of his wife, he was later released.

Defendant – Did you give me an unmerciful box in the mouth?

Witness – No.

Defendant – Did you say that you would put me and my gawm of a brother through the back wall with one good haymaker of a clout the next time I didn't open when you knocked?

Witness – No.

Justice – You look a fine block of man yourself. How old are you?

Defendant – I'm as grey as a badger, but I'm not long past forty. (Laughter.)

Justice – Was the brother there at all?

Defendant – He was away in Kells, your worship, seeing about getting a girl for himself. (Laughter.)

Justice – Well, I think you could give a good account of yourself.

Witness – He was very obstreperous, your worship.

Witness, continuing, said that he found two men standing in the dark in an outhouse. They said they were there for 'for a joke'. Witness also found a empty pint measure in an outdoor lavatory and two empty bottles of Cairnes.

Defendant said that two of the men were personal friends and were being treated. There was no question of taking money. He did not know who the man in the press was and did not recall having seen him before. He had given strict instructions to his assistant to allow nobody to remain on after hours. There was nobody in the press the previous day as the gasman had called to inspect the meter. The two Guards had given him an unmerciful hammering in the hall. His wife was in ill-health, necessitating his doing without sleep for three weeks. A week previously he was compelled to send for the Guards to assist in clearing the house at ten o'clock. He was conducting the house to the best of his ability and was very strict about the hours.

Guard — said that the defendant was a decent hard-working type but was of an excitable nature. The house had a good record.

Remarking that defendant seemed a decent sort and that the case was distinguished by the absence of perjury, the Justice said he would impose a fine of twenty shillings, the offence not to be

240

endorsed. Were it not for extenuating circumstances he would have no hesitation in sending the defendant to Mountjoy for six months. He commended Guards — and — for smart police-work.

Not many publicans, however, will take the risk. If they were as careful of their souls as they are of their licences, heaven would be packed with those confidential and solicitous profit-takers and, to please them, it might be necessary to provide an inferior annex to paradise to house such porter-drinkers as would make the grade.

The dance halls

'Jazz-hall' dancing may appear to be a harmless enough business, however unimaginative. Many of our clergy do not think it is and several of the Solomons of the district court are quite certain that it isn't. The dance hall was unknown before the last war and the prevalence of the craze today may be taken to be a symptom of a general social change that is bound up with altering conditions of living and working. Today there are roughly 1,200 licensed halls in the 26 Counties, accounting for perhaps 5,000 dances in a year. Golf and tennis clubs, Volunteer halls and the like do not require a licence. In all, it is a fair guess that 10,000 dances are held in a year, an average of three a day. In terms of time, this means that there is a foxtrot in progress in some corner of Erin's isle throughout the whole of every night and day. This is hard going for a small country. Is it appalling? Is it true that the rural dance hall is a place to be avoided by our sisters? Is it fair to say that Ireland is peopled by decadent alcoholics in pumps?

In 1935 the Public Dance Halls Act was passed. It was designed to control dancing – by then a vast industry and a country-wide neurosis – and to wipe out abuses bearing on everything from sanitation to immorality. The problem itself and the operation of the Act have occupied pages of newspaper space since. Bishops and judges have made strong comments. Satan has been blamed personally. There is, however, no great uniformity in outlook or conclusion. Here are some reported pronouncements, picked more or less at random. Probably very few of the pronouncers have ever paid fourpence to swelter for four hours in an insanitary shack.

Some time ago the evil of commercialised dance halls was so great that the Government felt bound to legislate. This legislation has been a dismal farce. It is the opinion of many that it has done more harm than good. – *Most Rev. Dr Gilmartin*

The Act was the most excellent passed since 1922. It only required a very modest quota of sweet reasonableness and goodwill to work it. – *District Justice Johnson*

The provisions of the Public Dance Halls Act, 1935, were unworkable and had been recognised by the Bench as unworkable. – *District Justice Little*

There is one agency which Satan has set up here and there in recent years that does incalculably more harm than all the others we have mentioned. It deserves to be called after his name, for he seems to preside at some of the dark rites enacted there. We have in mind the rural dance hall, owned by a private individual, run for profit, open to all who pay, without any exception of persons, conducted with no sort of responsible supervision. – *Most Rev. Dr Morrisroe*

He saw no harm in a well-conducted dance. It was his wish that people in Raphoe Diocese should get as much innocent recreation as possible and make the most of their opportunities. For that reason he was very pleased to see such a fine new hall being provided in Letterkenny. – *Most Rev. Dr MacNeely*

They were disposed to think that if the dance finished at midnight on a fine night, people would not be inclined to go home but would walk around the country. – *Solicitor Lisdoonvarna Court*

All-night dancing should be abolished completely. No licence should be granted to a hall which is contiguous to or within easy distance of a public house.[1] – *Rev. R. S. Devane, SJ*

In order to satisfy himself as to the suitability of a place proposed for public dancing, he would require that elevations and sections of the premises, accompanied by a block plan showing the position in relation to adjacent buildings, be lodged with the chief clerk of the court, and that certified copies be supplied to the Superintendent of the division concerned. – *District Justice Little*

[1] But is there any such spot in all Ireland?

242

The Galway Hospital Committee have passed a resolution drawing attention to the prevalence of sexual immorality as shown by the number of illegitimate births in the Galway Maternity Hospital and stating that it deplores this departure from the Gaelic tradition of purity, caused, in their opinion, by the lessening of parental control and want of supervision at dances and other amusements. – *Irish Independent*

I am in position to state that the vast majority of unmarried mothers have met with downfall under circumstances remote from dance halls or dances. – *Dr J. F. O'Connor, Macroom*

Illegitimate births in the 26 counties, 1929: 1, 853; 1939: 1, 781. – *Returns of the Registrar-General*

Father Devane is anxious to know how far dance halls set up a restlessness that causes girls to emigrate. He wonders, too, how far dance halls lessen 'the strenuous efforts so vitally necessary in the present agricultural crisis'. He asks why there are so many dance halls in Donegal. You follow Father Devane with your coat off. You ask no questions. You tie up dance halls and emigration and make the dance hall nearly as all-embracing a source of evil as the British connection, and hint darkly. . . . There is a background to the dance hall. Take Donegal, the black spot. Social life in the crowded areas there is a grand affair. Dancing played its part. During the winter there were endless excuses for raffles – a dance till midnight at 3d. a head. The schoolhouse was used for big nights. The parochial hall was there, but there was always too much style – and the charge was high 'to keep out the rough'. The raffle and the schoolhouse are no more. The parochial hall is still a pain in the neck. So the local dance hall arises. It does not come in. It grows. Nothing so natural to these areas is bad. To be sure, 'nothing human is perfect'. The men who built these halls are just neighbours to the boys and girls who attend them. The girls don't emigrate in search of dancing or glitter, but in search of wages. Many Donegal girls come to Dublin. Some get quite good wages. But they don't stay in Dublin, although Dublin has dance halls galore. They feel lonely in Dublin, so they go to Glasgow where hundreds of neighbours have made their homes . . . – *Peadar O'Donnell in a letter to the* Irish Press

An application on behalf of Rev. Fr. Monaghan, CC, Killanny, was made for extension of a licence for dances at a carnival.
    Justice Goff – This is a marquee. I am afraid I cannot. – *Irish Independent*

When District Justice Walsh was told that a dance licence for a Milford hall was lapsing as the hall was being converted into a cinema, he said: 'That is worse. At least the dancing money is kept in the country.' – *Irish Independent*

Let us visit some of these 'vestibules of hell'. If you want to go to a dance in the country, you buy a copy of the local paper and turn to the dance page. This, so to speak, is the countryman's leader page. Only after reading every word of it does he penetrate to the coursing notes and after that a long time may elapse before he reaches the customary holocaust involving those 10,000 Chinese coolies.

Judging rural Ireland by these dance blurbs, one would imagine that the entire population are returned emigrants who spent their lives in the neon-spangled honky-tonks of the tough San Francisco waterfront. However congested the district it is one long list of dances, monster dances, grand annual dances, stupendous carnival dances, gala dances, cinderellas, excuse-me's, even an odd 'Irish and Old Time' for the cranks. Only the odd name of man or place gives a pathetic clue that there is some make-believe in progress and that the newspaper is *not* one of the English language sheets of abandoned Shanghai. You are asked to dance out the Old and dance in the New 'to the haunting strains of Mulvaney's Rhythmic Swingsters'. What do you make of 'Farmers annual dance (cocktail bar)'? Personally, I see no reason why our ruined farmers should not wear tails if they want to, but they have been misled if they think it is necessary to forsake good whiskey or beer for lethal noggins of chemical gin. 'Lime, flood and spot lighting installed for the occasion by the Strand Electric Co., Dublin. Carnival Hats, Novelties and Gifts for Everyone. A Night of Laughter, Gaiety, Fun and Surprise.' *Where?* In TUBBERCURRY! This notice appears in the paper upside down and the reader is finally warned that the dance 'will be as crazy as this advertisement'. At the Mayo Mental Hospital Staff Dance 'the floor will be specially treated for the occasion', while that other dance in Fethard will be in aid of 'noteworthy object'.

Taking rural Ireland to include the towns, there are three or four kinds of dances. For any dance costing over five shillings, you must put on what is known as 'immaculate evening dress'. You are on the border-line when you come down to 3/9. A surprising number of young men own a passable dress-suit and work-a-day rags, with absolutely nothing in between except football attire. I have heard of dancing men being married in their evening clothes.

The dress dance in the country is run by those of the white collar and the white soft hand – clerks, merchants, doctors – and is usually taken locally to be a proof of progress or culture. When the plain people see handsome men in 'immaculate' evening clothes alighting from fine motor-cars and disappearing into a Town Hall that seems temporarily glorious and reborn, they know well from their cinema that there is city devilry afoot. Inside, however, the scene is very familiar. Think of an ordinary good dance (say in the European quarter of Shanghai) and then divide everything by two. The lighting is poor and the place is too hot. The floor is of thick planks (it was put there to accommodate a welcome for Parnell) and the knots will tell through the city man's shoddy pumps. The band may be good or bad. Bands vary enormously for this reason – *a dance is regarded as successful according to the distance the band has to travel.* For the best possible dance the band would have to come from India. This is the great immutable law that determines the local prestige of every event. A Committee is doing pretty well if they can get a band from a hundred miles away. What is regarded as a good band in the country will have 'own electric amplification' but may lack a piano. Their tunes will be old and grey and far behind the whistling repertoire of any diligent cinemagoer. 'Good-night, Sweetheart' is still a rage in the west.

Nearly every male who goes to dances likes drink and takes plenty of it. Some people may think this is an offensive statement but it is the plain truth. It is often a case of little by little. There is no evil intention. It starts with a few half-ones merely to get into form and after that the reveller is on his way, even if he doesn't know where he is going. This part of the evening's work is performed in an adjacent hotel or pub. Nearly every pub is entitled to serve a toothful to 'travellers' but in practice very few of the locals fail to obtain suitable filling for their teeth. It is an old custom.

This custom carries with it an odd accomplishment that no stranger can acquire. It is the craft of going out for twenty

245

separate drinks to a pub 400 yards away without ever appearing to have left the hall at all. It is a waste of time seeking to solve this puzzle by observation. If you are a lady, you can dance every dance with the one gentleman, talk to him unremittingly in the intervals and yet you will notice him getting gayer and gayer from his intermittent but imperceptible absences. If, on the other hand, you are a man who is seated in the pub all night concerned only with honest drinking, you will observe the complementary miracle and wonder how the inebriate in tails manages to satisfy all the requirements of his partner in the hall without ever appearing to leave the pub. There it is. I can offer no explanation.

These dress dances are not very interesting. They have scarcely any relation to 'the dance hall scandal', 'the jazz mania', or any other popular explanation of the decay of our country at the present time. The real thing is the cheap dance where the price of admission ranges from 3d. to 1/6. To arrive at some idea of this, you must divide that recollection of Shanghai, not by two, but by high numbers that go higher as the price comes down. Most of the halls I have seen are old school-houses or new timber structures with a tin roof. There is no means of ventilation save the savage and heroic expedient of the open window. There is no attempt at having a proper dance floor, even where the hall has been built *ad hoc*. Light is provided by large paraffin lamps suspended from the roof, less frequently by incandescent paraffin installations on the walls. The music may be supplied by a solitary melodeon or piano-accordion, with possibly a fiddle and drums. Dance music as such is almost unknown. What seem to be vague recollections of Irish airs are churned out in an interminable repetition and nearly always bashed into a desultory three-four time that usually sounds very alien to what was intended by our ancestor. Even when a modern dance tune is attempted, it is played straight with no attempt at syncopation, and, being necessarily played from hazy memory, it sometimes finds itself mysteriously transformed into 'Terence's Farewell to Kathleen'.

The dancing itself is of the most perfunctory order. If the hall is small and the crowd enormous (and this is the normal situation) the parties quickly lock themselves into a solid mass and keep shuffling and sweating for ten minutes in the space of a square

246

foot, like a vast human centipede marking time. If the hall is roomy and the crowd small, the dancers shuffle about in great circles and can travel a considerable distance in the course of an evening. If a lad cycles twenty miles to a dance and twenty miles home and does another ten miles in the hall, he is clearly in earnest about his dancing.

Just as the success of a dear dance depends on the extra-territoriality of the band, no cheap dance can be said to have succeeded if the door of the hall can be readily opened from without after the first half-hour. The crowd inside must be so dense that an entire repacking and rearrangement of the patrons is necessary before even the blade of a knife could be inserted through the door. When you do enter, you find yourself in air of the kind that blurts out on you from an oven when you open it. All about you is an impenetrable blue tobacco haze that is sometimes charged with a palpable fine filth beaten up out of the floor. Whether standing or dancing, the patrons are all *i bhfastódh* [Editor: i.e., 'in a clinch'] on each other like cows in a cattle truck, exuding sweat in rivers and enjoying themselves immensely. Nobody is self-conscious about sweat. It rises profusely in invisible vapour from all and sundry and there is no guarantee that each cloud will condense on its true owner.

There are certain general considerations which apply to all these dances. The girls always predominate and usually pay their own way. Behind the upright throng one can sometimes glimpse a low flat row of sitting people who look as if they were painted or pasted on the walls. Once there, they seem to have no chance of budging till the dance is over. There is always an official charged with accomplishing a hospitable rite known as 'looking after the band'. Late in the night there are signs on him that he has been looking after himself, but the boisterous revival of the 'musicianers' towards the end of the evening will prove that he has not made undue depredations on the trust fund. For a dance of any importance (say, a shilling dance) the average farmer's son will permit himself a half-pint of 'parliamentary whiskey' on the hip and will not hesitate to lace his blood with judicious nips of poteen if the stuff is to be had. The liquor is consumed in breath-taking gulps in a place apart and is never openly flaunted. Scenes of open or riotous drunkenness are rare. Notwithstanding

247

any cloakroom that may be provided, complete with attendant, the general tendency is to bring the overcoat into the hall. No tax is payable on any dance that costs anything up to 4d. Tax and licensing provisions are evaded by calling a short dance a 'practice' or a 'dance class'. Where supper is provided, the beverage is always tea, never a nourishing or cooling draught like home-made lemonade. If a committee can rise to the swirling device that throws pretty and romantic coloured lights throughout the darkened hall, they are entitled to call their functions 'gala dances'. There are fine big halls here and there where dancing is attempted on a reasonable basis – the big converted railway shops at Dundalk, for instance, or the shirt factory building outside Buncrana.

Irish dancing is a thing apart. There is perhaps one *céilidhe* held for every twenty dances. The foxtrot and the Fairy Reel are mutually repugnant and will not easily dwell under the same roof. Very few adherents of the 'ballroom' canon will have anything to do with a jig or a reel. Apart from the fact that the Irish dance is ruled out in most halls by considerations of space or perspiration, there is a real psychological obstacle. It is a very far cry from the multiple adhesions of enchanted country stomachs in a twilight of coloured bulbs to the impersonal free-for-all of a clattering reel. Irish dancing is emotionally cold, unromantic and always well-lighted.

One occasionally encounters the barn-dance. This is the 'mind the dresser' business held to the tune of a lone Raftery in a farmhouse kitchen, to celebrate a wedding or an American wake. Most of the dances are sets and half-sets based on English figure dances and introduced to this country in the seventeenth and eighteenth centuries by the landlord class. There are also boisterous versions of Irish dances and an odd invitation to talented individuals to 'oblige' with solo items. Curiously enough, this sort of thing is beginning to smell of the stage Irishman.

Some district justices have a habit of taking leave of their senses at the annual licensing sessions. They want Irish dancing and plenty of it, even at the most monster 'gala dance'. They believe that Satan with all his guile is baffled by a four-hand reel and cannot make head or tail of the Rakes of Mallow. I do not think that there is any real ground for regarding Irish dancing as a sovereign spiritual and nationalistic prophylactic. If there is, heaven help the defenceless nations of other lands.

Little need be said about dancing in Dublin or Cork. In Cork nearly all the fun is concentrated in the spacious and well-run Arcadia. Dublin has six or seven hotel-halls where the all-important 'refreshment' facilities are available and some sixty other halls where there is dancing several nights a week. In addition, every junta of goodtime folk who care to register themselves as a sports or social club can dance and drink almost without restriction. In theory, only members can join in this diversion but in practice anybody can pay and enter. At 1 p.m. on Sunday morning these haunts are crowded with ill-slept revellers in search of healing ale.

Yes, strange and beautiful sights you will see at a dance in Dublin. Even a district justice, happy and mum, surrounding with his righteous tissue a sizzling tank of malt. That dance, however, does not cost threepence. The entry-fee is 7/6 or half a legal guinea.

Characteristically, as well as contributing to *The Bell,* Myles parodied it in *Cruiskeen Lawn*:

No, this is not from *The Bell*

My agent in London has notified me that he has managed to buy up for next to nothing a job lot of inferior oil paintings – a mangled pheasant sprawling on its back on a dark table, with rosy apples glinting in the background, and so forth, in the mode that is only too familiar. In due course each of these pictures will receive my signature, inscribed in suitable vermilion paint in the bottom left-hand corner. Then they will be thoroughly washed and sent to the Academy. When they are accepted, exhibited and praised, I will wire my agent to ransack the junk-shops for more rubbish, and tell him he can run up as high as thirty shillings for anything that could be said to resemble any of our notable native personalities. If he knows his business I will be an Academician in ten years, and possibly will be run for Pres. if the gangs there fall out.

On and on

According as my agent produces darker and queerer stuff from the back-street hovels of the East End, the critics will refer to my stimulating experiments in colour timbre, my essentially Celtic concept of the spectrum, my model way with pigments, and the emerging of the astonishing crisis of my artistic dialectic in practically pitch-dark monkey-work with brush and trowel. People will say that I have that queer thing, genius. I will probably conduct classes and pander to the insatiable craving to be lectured, which is the distinguishing mark of all morons. All for a price, of course.

I recognise that all this means corduroys, a nodding familiarity with diplomats, foamy-mouthed, pipe-smoking, and great mouthfuls of desperate jargon about the interpretative function of painting, the invalidity of unintellected representationalism, the hellish loveliness when you have had it explained to you by Roger Fry.

But one moment

I admit, of course, that you occasionally come across a painting from which you start back almost frightened by the queer, but authentic, incomprehensibility of it. Here, you say, is something that devolves, not from Krondt, Liebz or the Munich group, but from that myopic, almost intuitive, awareness of naturalistic cosmic function. Here is something, you add, that Yeats himself might have acknowledged without remorse. Then you walk around with the queer picture in your brain all day, vainly asking yourself whether you are really mad. We used to say in Cork that the sterility of Dublin conversation could only be attributed to the vast number of low-grade Corkmen who had migrated there, though our own preoccupation with *mittel-europäische* symbolisms and our hard cross-country walks with the Professor left us little time for lighter fancies.

Rubber snouts and the Western man

On the southern quays (where one first came to grips with Proust) there lives an old lady called Sheelihuddy. Out of old lorry tyres she fashions little snouts for synthetic fox furs, which are imported from Russia and sold up and down the country as the real thing. Now here we have something fine, something taut and memorable. A rubber snout, hacked out with an old knife in a riverside slum, may seem a poor thing. Yet it has distinction, it possesses elegance, it pleases, *because it has its place in that corpus of traditionalism and indigenous diacritica which add up to the Ireland that we know.* Take the snout in your hand and note the cunning perfection of the stipple, the precision of the twin nostril vents. Here, you say, we have something that is *real,* something divorced from Japanese formalism, something heroic and occidental, expressive of Cork, if not of Ireland. Like it or dislike it, but do not ignore it, and, above all, do not drop it on the floor.

Bell-idiocy

In a recent issue of *The Bell* I notice an article on (shhh!) the Censorship Act. It is prefaced by an editorial note which says that 'there is hardly an Irish writer of repute, many of them Catholics, who has not been banned by the Censorship Board'.

Here, I think, we have bunkum of a dimension that is grandiose. I know many good Irish writers who have not been banned. Have we reached the stage where a writer is considered to be 'of repute' because he has been banned?

The fuss that is made about the Censorship in certain quarters makes me laugh. The rule is that you must make a scathing reference to the Censorship at every possible opportunity in speaking or writing. Give the impression that it is a purely personal scourge, a thing that is destroying you, subjecting the 'artist' in you to diabolical torment. Then you are made as an Irish intellectual and eligible for your first corduroys.

About a year ago I read a report of a meeting held by people with some name like The Friends of Irish Intellectual Freedom.

251

Most of the time was occupied by harangues about the necessity for repealing the iniquitous Censorship Act. The worthies did not disperse, however, until they had adopted a resolution calling for an immediate ban on the importation of the anglicising and demoralising English newspapers.

This may be funny, but it is also true.

7

Poems in Translation

By God it's not for nothing that I call myself a pal of Jem Casey.
At Swim-Two-Birds, p. 107

Brian O'Nolan's MA thesis, 'Nature in Irish Poetry', written in Irish, was divided into two. The first part was a discussion of the genre, often couched in circumlocutions newly minted by O'Nolan to convey literary concepts that the Irish language had not yet satisfactorily tackled. The second part was an anthology of Irish nature verse, going back to the days when the language was as different from modern Irish as Geoffrey Chaucer's English is from Jeffrey Archer's. Particularly in the early days of the *Cruiskeen Lawn* column, his enthusiasm for the subject was alluded to, and he would occasionally include a translation of some piece that particularly appealed to him. *At Swim-Two-Birds,* too, contains many pieces of Middle-Irish verse. These are translations, to be sure, but they are also half-parodies of the work of Standish Hayes O'Grady, whose masterwork, *Silva Gadelica,* made accessible for the first time much of O'Nolan's thesis material. An essay by Flann O'Brien, affectionately commemorating O'Grady, his mentor and butt, acts as a preface to this (perhaps) complete collection of O'Nolan's published verse translations:

Standish Hayes O'Grady

Standish H. O'Grady died on this day 25 years ago. Most people, if asked what they knew of him, would mention *The Flight of the Eagle* or *The Coming of Cuchulainn.* This, however, would have annoyed the great man. 'Let me intimate,' he once wrote, 'since I am often tantalised by having a kinsman's good work attributed to myself, that my trade mark (without which no goods are genuine) is either as on the title page of this book, or thus in full – STANDISH HAYES O'GRADY.'

Standish Hayes plied a much more difficult craft than did

Standish James, and the goods he left behind were more laboriously produced. He was a worker in the field of Irish studies, but one of an unusual kind. He combined with profound learning other qualities of humour and imagination which enabled him to deal with early texts in a lively creative way that lifted his work far out of the repellent rut traversed by most philologists. Whether his head was smooth or hairy, he had no place among the fogeys –

> Bald heads, forgetful of their sins,
> Old, learned, respectable bald heads
> Edit and annotate the lines
> That young men, tossing on their beds,
> Rhymed out in love's despair . . .

His originality and agility of mind bubble up in the prefaces to his works and are reflected in the curious and charming English which he devised in an effort to render to the student the last glint of colour in any Irish word. Dr Hyde has described it as 'half Latin, half early English phraseology, subtly inverted and highly Romanised; as: "he was a covetous and unconscionable man who, though it were but a solitary scruple whether of gold or of silver that he heard of as possessed by any in his country, would by force of arms make his own of it" (fer sanntach díchuibsech atacomnaieside, ocus cin co cluined acht mad aenscrupal óir no airgit oc duine ina thír dobeirid ar éicin chuice féin).' Occasionally the queer English seems to acquire a peculiar luminance of its own, casting a ghostly charm over passages which read pedestrian enough in the Irish. In 'The Little Brawl At Allen' (which seems to have been a sizeable affair): after 'a fermentation of anger took Goll' and 'the parties fell unrelentingly to bone-splitting each other', we read that 'an ill place had it been for feeble invalid, or delicate taper-fingered woman, or aged senior of long date'. Usually, however, he gets not only the exact meaning of the Irish but the atmosphere and emotional content. Translating O'Hussey's well-known Ode to Maguire, he writes, 'To me it is an ache that Hugh tonight is in a stranger land – by operation of the armed vociferous clouds' displeasure lies under lurid glow of bolt-fraught lightnings flashing thickly. We hold it a calamity that in the province of Clann Daire our well-beloved is couched betwixt a coarse, cold, wet and grass-clad ditch and the imperious fury of heaven.'

O'Grady's best-known work was *Silva Gadelica,* published in 1892, a miscellany of medieval Irish texts, with an accompanying volume containing a translation, notes and a breezy preface in English. The Irish volume has another preface couched in the old Irish of the texts and embodying the editor's own genealogy: he laments the apathy of the Irish people in relation to their literary heritage and urges the necessity of making an effort to see whether there is yet time for them 'some fragment or particle of the knowledge and culture of the ancients to preserve henceforth free from extinction and unending loss, with the day now in its late-going and the melodious mother-tongue all but ebbed away . . . (blogh ná blúire éigin d'ealadhain agus d'ollamnacht na sean do thárrtháil feasda gan bádhadh gan buan-chailleamain ós anois as dol i ndéidenaighe do'n ló agus an teanga bhinn mháthardha beag nach tráighte)'.

O'Grady's next most important work was his Catalogue of the Irish MSS in the British Museum. This work was never finished, but 672 pages of it have been printed. The first 327 pages are devoted to History, Law, Lexicography and Medicine, and the rest to Poetry. The Catalogue contains extracts from the more important manuscripts, and with O'Grady's unrivalled knowledge of all relevant historical records and traditional lore, teems with information on words, events and customs. The whole work is highly readable and diverting and has been described as being in itself a most valuable introduction to Irish literature.

His first publication appeared in 1853 when he was twenty-one, and affords interesting evidence of the degree of erudition he had attained even at that age. It consists of passages from a poem dealing with the travels of Donnchadh Ruadh Mac Conmara, the poet, with examples of the poet's own work, and with translation and notes. It contains the text of a letter of introduction, or 'pass', given by the poet to Richard Fitzgerald the Brave in 1759. Such documents were common among the educated classes, being used as 'passports' in regions where the writer was known and had influence with the natives; they were frequently availed of for displays of fine language. There is probably no printed record of such a document outside O'Grady's work.

In 1857 he published the text, translation and notes bearing on 'The Pursuit of Diarmuid and Grainne' (with a zestful preface) and 'The Lamentation of Oisin'. Then, after a gap of thirty years, he published a commentary on Kuno Meyer's edition of 'The Battle of Ventry', doing sundry violences to that savant's reputation as a scholar. This may be found in the Anecdota Oxoniensia. In 1888 he edited 'King David and the Beggar' and an interesting narrative poem, 'The O'Dobharchon', dealing with a man who was turned into an otter and had to dwell at the bottom of a lake. His next work was *Silva Gadelica*. Besides the Catalogue, he left another unfinished and partly printed work – text, translation and notes of *Caithréim Thoirdhealbhaigh,* a history of the Norman wars in Munster.

O'Grady was born on 19 May 1832. His father was admiral O'Grady, brother of the first Viscount Guillamore. He spent his youth in the colourful Shannon country. The country people in the barony spoke Irish in those days, and it was in his wanderings among them that he contracted his admiration for the beauty and precision of the language, and the beginnings of a vast knowledge of traditional data bearing on place-names, local monuments, folk customs and tales current among the people on historical cataclysms like the siege of Limerick. As a youth and already an accomplished and correct speaker of Irish, he was sent to Rugby to receive the education deemed essential to his class, and came back from there in due course to Trinity College, where he went to work at once on the manuscript collections. He came to know John O'Donovan and Eugene O'Curry, and also Joseph O'Longan, the last of the old-time scribes. At Trinity he tutored James Godman, of Skibbereen, who subsequently became Professor of Irish in the University. After the appearance of *Silva Gadelica,* he received the honorary degree of D.Litt. from Cambridge. There his extraordinary range of knowledge enabled him to hobnob on equal terms with scholars who had devoted their lives to other studies. He was at home with the obscurest Orientalist. He died at Hale in England, and was buried at Altrincham Churchyard.

In *Silva Gadelica* he delivers himself of several characteristic thrusts at self-righteous people who have at one time or another expressed their distaste for the Irishry. '*Silva Gadelica*', he writes, modestly, 'is far from being exclusively, or even primarily, designed for the omniscient impeccable leviathans of science that headlong sound the linguistic ocean to its most horrid depths, and (in the intervals of ramming each other) ply their flukes on such audacious small fry as even on the mere surface will venture within their danger.' To this he adds a footnote: 'Thackeray warns Bob Brown the younger that, since the days of Æsop, a desire to cope with bulls is known to be fatal to frogs. As yet no Gadelic batrachian has sought thus to burst himself; *per contra* it were no less instructive than easy to point out how and where lordly cetaceans of philology, enviously invading shallows in which the humble Celtic whitebait sports at ease, lie stranded (as Milton has it) "many a rood in length".'

Talking of a piece which contained peculiar constructions more readily renderable in Latin, he remarks: 'The style is not Ciceronian, it is true; but there is no knowing what Tully might have written had he translated literally from Irish. He would have been none the worse for being able to do so.'

That is a sentiment that can be echoed in respect of more than old Tully. Many sound rubs of this kind are to be found in O'Grady's footnotes. He quotes J. Stanihurst's account of the characteristics of the native Irish:

> The people are thus inclined: Religious, frank, amorous, irefull, sufferable of paines infinite, very glorieux, many sorcerers, excellent horsemen, delighted with wars, great almsgivers, passing in hospitalitie; the lewder sort (both clarkes and laymen) are sensuall and loose above measure. They are sharpe witted, lovers of learning, capable of any studie whereunto they bend themselves, constant in travaile, adventurous, intractable, kinde-hearted, secret in displeasure. . . . They exchange by commutation of wares for the most part, and have utterly no coin stirring in any great lords' houses. . ..

À propos of the last sentence he adds this delightfully irrelevant footnote: 'Writers are fond of remarking either that history repeats itself, or does not repeat itself, according to their exigency. It is safe to affirm that here the former aphorism is the one in point.'

He then castigates Stanihurst for his rancorous attitude to the Irish:

257

Better for him he had tarried with the wild men that never harmed him, or in some of the lands which he visited after them; when he returned, his own highly civilised countrymen rewarded his John-Bullism with a degree higher than any he had taken at Oxford: in fact, on the 1st of December, 1581, they hanged and quartered him.

His gift of combining the real stuff of scholarship with his own irrepressible breeziness is shown well in the following footnote on the levying of tribute:

From the most remote times collection of any kind of dues has in Ireland been a ticklish business; the extraordinary tale called 'The Siege of Cnoc Damhgaire', near Knocklong (county Limerick), is based on king Cormac's attempt forcibly to exact his revenue from Munster, a province which appears to have habitually and successfully been refractory to the monarchs, i.e., kings of all Ireland as distinguished from the five provincial kings. As for the *cíos* 'rent' (so Elizabethans rendered it, and such it means today) or tribute which the *urradha* 'subordinate chiefs' paid to their chief paramount, it had to be taken. In English a chief's *urradha* were called his 'gentlemen': thus O'Conor-Sligo was O'Donnell's gentleman, and continually it needed hundreds of swords and axes (many of whom never saw Tirconall again) to persuade him to his duty. The following again were O'Conor-Sligo's gentlemen: O'Dowda, O'Gara, O'Hara-Buie, O'Hara-Riach, O'Hart, MacDonough of the Corann and MacDonough of Tirerril, who all were just as reluctant to part. The whole theory is summed up in a still lively tradition of the following correspondence (incorrectly given in the Abbé Mageoghegan's *Histoire d'lrlande*): *Cuir chugam mo chíos nó mara gcuirir – mise Ó DOMHNAILL,* i.e., 'Send me my rent, or if not – O'Donnell.' Answer: *Ní fhuil cíos agat orm agus dá mbiadh – mise Ó néill.* i.e., 'I owe you no rent, and if I did – O'Neill.' Fictitious if you will, but typical.

For all his light heart, however, O'Grady does not appear to have been entirely wanting in ideas of personal dignity. His unfinished Catalogue breaks off in the middle of a sentence because he fell out with the Museum authorities and declined to have anything more to do with them. He seems to have had brushes with the staider savants of his day owing to his weakness for erudite multilingual puns and jokes, which were rarely construed in the manner intended by those to whom they were addressed. It is said that he had a violent quarrel with Kuno

258

Meyer over the construction of a few lines of Irish for the *Athenaeum* magazine, and thereafter the two men never spoke.

It is gratifying to record that the Government Publication Office has recently re-issued, by some reproductive process, the Irish text, notes and English preface of *Silva Gadelica*; and the price today is seven-and-sixpence, compared with two guineas forty years ago.

Scel lem duib

Here's a song –
stags give tongue
winter snows
summer goes.

High cold blow
sun is low
brief his day
seas give spray.

Fern clumps redden
shapes are hidden
wildgeese raise
wonted cries.

Cold now girds
wings of birds
icy time –
that's my rime.

Aoibhinn, a leabhráin, do thriall

Delightful, book, your trip
to her of the ringlet head,
a pity it's not you
that's pining, I that sped.

To go, book, where she is
delightful trip in sooth!
the bright mouth red as blood
you'll see, and the white tooth.

You'll see that eye that's grey
the docile palm as well,
with all that beauty you
(not I, alas) will dwell.

You'll see the eyebrow fine
the perfect throat's smooth gleam,
and the sparkling cheek I saw
latterly in a dream.

The lithe good snow-white waist
that won mad love from me –
the handwhite swift neat foot –
these in their grace you'll see.

The soft enchanting voice
that made me each day pine
you'll hear, and well for you –
would that your lot were mine.

Domforcai fidhbaidae fál

A hedge before me, one behind,
a blackbird sings from that,
above my small book many-lined
I apprehend his chat.

Up trees, in costumes buff,
mild accurate cuckoos bleat,
Lord love me, good the stuff
I write in a shady seat.

Clochán binn

Little bell that rings at night
When the weather's a holy fright,
I'd rather hear its summons
Than my foolish woman's.

A dhruimfhionn donn dílis

O Drimin Donn Dheelish,
O cowlet of mine,
The warble-fly's eating
Your silk of the kine.

Cridhe hé

He is a heart, a pet,
He is a grove of nut-trees,
He is a stripling
– Kiss him!

Ach a luin

Ah blackbird, well for you,
Your nesting-place is where you will
Pilgrim that pays no due,
Sweet, soft and magical your bill.

Int en gaires asintsail

The bird that from the sally calls
(melodious bill), its note is choice,
(the sprightly black man's yellow beak)
a nimble tune – the blackbird's voice.

Sgíth mo chrob ón sgríbinn

My hand has a pain from writing,
Not steady the sharp tool of my craft
Its slender beak spews bright ink –
A beetle-dark shining draught.

Streams of the wisdom of white God
From my fair-brown, fine hand sally,
On the page they splash their flood
In ink of the green-skinned holly.

My little dribbly pen stretches
Across the white paper plain,
Insatiable for splendid riches –
That is why my hand has a pain!

Do bhulla, a bhréagóg fhallsa

Your Bull, you lying layabout, it doesn't drive me crackers;
it is a Bull that commands no respect, and not beyant in
Rome was it issued.

You traipse about here and there, bitterer your voice than
henbane; your shape hardly resembling a human, an
apparition of ancient iron.

You impetuous gabbling prostitute, harder far than iron;
how can one estimate a woman of your kind, you fleshless,
sterile spook.

Your skinny pierced belly, woe to him who sees it at
breakfast time; eternally a portent of famine, woman, you
cannot hide your blights from the world.

Protopolitics (extract)

One of the greatest poets in the period bordering on modern Irish
was named Eochaidh Ó Heodhusa (or O'Hussey), and he . . .
conceded that our ancestors believed in magic, prayers, trickery,
browbeating and bullying; I think it would be fair to sum that list
up as 'Irish polities'.

One poem, edited many years ago by Eleanor Knott, takes my
fancy, and I will try to convey it.

When the scene opens we see a group of 30 well-favoured
T.D.s[1] of nephological preoccupation. They are gazing at a cloud
and in due course circulate word among the populace to beware
of this cloud, to dig great shelters in the earth and shelter from it,
because anybody struck by the moisture thereof would forthwith
go off his rocker. Here is one of O'Hussey's verses, with my own
weak gloss:

---

[1] Dáil deputies – Irish MPs.

263

A shluagh an domhain, déanaidh
uamha doimhne i ndroibhéalaibh
(ar lucht eagna an bheatha bhí)
ar eagla an cheatha ad-chluintí.

Now listen lads, please excavate
Forbidding caves most tortuous
(Thus warned those good interpreters)
For fear this shower'll scorch us.

Crying wolf is an old hazard and the idea of being asked to build underground shelters by these professors just made the citizens laugh. It now began to get very dark and the brains trust thoughtfully retired to certain subterranean diggings of their own. The cloud swells, blackens, explodes, and there is true desolation. Then the sky clears and my 30 technical men come up to the surface in the lift to say WETOLDYOUSO! Right enough, they saw that everybody who had remained out in the rain had gone stark mad. They were pleased at their own cuteness, but hold on till you hear what happened:

Gidh eadh, do chuir cáach i gcéill
don bhuidhin úghdar ainnséin,
(dream dhreichmhiolla na ngníomh nglan)
neimhchríonna dhíobh go ndearnadh.

The dauntless lads however conveyed
To this assembled soggarthary
(This beauteous band of peerless act) –
That hiding was derogatory.

Déanaimne aimhghlic amhuil
Sinn féin, ar na feallsamhain,
beag díol na cruinne dar gcéill
ná bíonn 'san uile acht d'einmhein.

We must make batty just the same
Ourselves, the savants then opined:
Poor price the whole world for our wits,
If all men have not equal mind.

You see the extreme cuteness here? Your men realised they had outsmarted themselves by remaining sane and straightaway decided to make themselves mad, knowing the mad majority would regard them as mad if they remained sane. Here you have the genesis of all political scheming. (Don't overlook that phrase *sinn féin* in the third verse!)

The next poem, and the 'Sweeny' sequence that follows it, have been taken from *At Swim-Two-Birds*. The story of Sweeny dates back to perhaps as far as the seventh century, although when it was first written down is uncertain. King Sweeny offends St Ronan, and is condemned, through the cleric's curse, to live the rest of his life as a bird. Flann O'Brien used his own translations of some of this material as a counterpoint to other strands in his novel, but it is, I believe, worthwhile to see the work in isolation. I have altered the order of the poems where this aids continuity.

Finn Mac Cool's poem

I am a bark for buffeting.
I am a hound for thornypaws.
I am a doe for swiftness.
I am a tree for wind-siege.
I am a windmill.
I am a hole in a wall.

I am the breast of a young queen.
I am a thatching against rains.
I am a dark castle against bat-flutters.
I am a Connachtman's ear.
I am a harpstring.
I am a gnat.

I am an Ulsterman, a Connachtman, a Greek.
I am Cuchulainn, I am Patrick.
I am Carbery-Cathead, I am Goll.
I am my own father and my son.
I am every hero from the crack of time.

Saint Ronan's curse

My curse on Sweeny!
His guilt against me is immense,
he pierced with his long swift javelin
my holy bell.

The holy bell that thou hast outraged
will banish thee to branches,
it will put thee on a par with fowls –
the saint-bell of saints with sainty-saints.

Just as it went prestissimo
the spear-shaft skyward,
you too, Sweeny, go madly mad-gone
skyward.

Eorann of Conn tried to hold him
by a hold of his smock
and though I bless her therefore,
my curse on Sweeny.

Sweeny tormented

Sweeny the thin-groined it is
in the middle of the yew;
life is very bare here,
piteous Christ it is cheerless.

Grey branches have hurt me
they have pierced my calves,
I hang here in the yew-tree above,
without chessmen, no womantryst.

I can put no faith in humans
in the place they are;
watercress at evening is my lot,
I will not come down.

As I made the fine throw at Ronan
from the middle of the hosts,
the fair cleric said that I had leave
to go with birds.

I am Sweeny the slender-thin,
the slender, the hunger-thin,
berries crimson and cresses green,
their colours are my mouth.

I was in the centre of the yew
distraught with suffering,
the hostile branches scourged me,
I would not come down.

———

Our wish is at Samhain, up to Maytime,
when the wild ducks come
in each dun wood without stint
to be in ivy-trees.

Water of Glen Bolcain fair
a listening to its horde of birds,
its tuneful streams that are not slow,
its islands, its rivers.

In the tree of Cell Lughaidh,
it was our wish to be alone,
swift flight of swallows on the brink of summer –
take your hands away!

———

Though my flittings are unnumbered,
my clothing today is scarce,
I personally maintain my watch
on the tops of mountains.

O fern, russet long one,
your mantle has been reddened,
there's no bedding for an outcast
on your branching top.

Nuts at terce and cress-leaves,
fruits from an apple-wood at noon,
a lying-down to lap chill water –
your fingers torment my arms.

267

Sweeny's lay in Glenn na nEachtach

Bleating one, little antlers,
O lamenter we like
delightful the clamouring
from your glen you make.

O leafy-oak, clumpy-leaved,
you are high above trees,
O hazlet, little clumpy-branch –
the nut-smell of hazels.

O alder, O alder-friend,
delightful your colour,
you don't prickle me or tear
in the place you are.

O little blackthorn, little thorny-one,
O little dark sloe-tree;
O watercress, O green-crowned,
at the well-brink.

O holly, holly-shelter,
O door against the wind,
O ash-tree inimical,
you spearshaft of warrior.

O birch clean and blessed,
O melodious, O proud,
delightful the tangle
of your head-rods.

What I like least in woodlands
from none I conceal it –
stirk of a leafy-oak,
at its swaying.

O faun, little long-legs,
I caught you with grips,
I rode you upon your back
from peak to peak.

Glen Bolcain my home for ever,
it was my haven,
many a night have I tried
a race against the peak.

Glen Bolcain

If I were to search alone
the hills of the brown world,
better would I like my sole hut
in Glen Bolcain.

Good its water greenish-green
good its clean strong wind,
good its cress-green cresses,
best its branching brooklime.

Good its sturdy ivies,
good its bright neat sallow,
good its yewy yew-yews,
best its sweet-noise birch.

A haughty ivy
growing through a twisted tree,
myself on its true summit,
I would lothe leave it.

I flee before skylarks,
it is the tense stern-race,
I overleap the clumps
on the high hill-peaks.

When it rises in front of me
the proud turtle-dove,
I overtake it swiftly
since my plumage grew.

The stupid unwitting woodcock
when it rises up before me,
methinks it red-hostile,
and the blackbird that cries havoc.

Small foxes yelping
to me and from me,
the wolves tear them –
I flee their cries.

They journeyed in their chase of me
in their swift courses
so that I flew away from them
to the tops of mountains.

On every pool there will rain
a starry frost;
I am wretched and wandering
under it on the peak.

The herons are calling
in cold Glen Eila
swift-flying flocks are flying,
coming and going.

I do not relish
the mad clack of humans
sweeter warble of the bird
in the place he is.

I like not the trumpeting
heard at morn;
sweeter hearing is the squeal
of badgers in Benna Broc.

I do not like it
the loud bugling;
finer is the stagbelling stag
of antler-points twice twenty.

There are makings for plough-teams
from glen to glen;
each resting-stag at rest
on the summit of the peaks.

The stag of steep Slieve Eibhlinne,
the stag of sharp Slieve Fuaid,
the stag of Eala, the stag of Orrery,
the mad stag of Loch Lein.

Stag of Shevna, stag of Larne,
the stag of Leena of the panoplies
stag of Cualna, stag of Conachail,
the stag of two-peaked Bairenn.

Oh mother of this herd,
thy coat has greyed,
no stag is following after thee
without twice twenty points.

Greater-than-the-material-for-a-little-cloak,
thy head has greyed;
if I were on each little point
littler points would there be on every pointed point.

The stag that marches trumpeting
across the glen to me,
pleasant the place for seats
on his antler top.

Sweeny travelling

O warriors approach,
warriors of Dal Araidhe,
you will find him in the tree he is
the man you seek.

God has given me life here,
very bare, very narrow,
no women, no trysting,
no music or trance-eyed sleep.

A year to last night
I have lodged there in branches
from the flood-tide to the ebb-tide
naked.

Bereft of fine women-folk,
the brooklime for a brother –
our choice for a fresh meal
is watercress always.

Without accomplished musicians
without generous women,
no jewel-gift for bards –
respected Christ, it has perished me.

The thorntop that is not gentle
has reduced me, has pierced me,
it has brought me near death
the brown thorn-bush.

Once free, once gentle,
I am banished for ever,
wretch-wretched I have been
a year to last night.

The man by the wall snores
a snore-sleep that's beyond me,
for seven years from that Tuesday at Magh Rath
I have not slept a wink.

O God that I had not gone
to the hard battle!
thereafter my name was Mad –
Mad Sweeny in the bush.

Watercress from the well at Cirb
is my lot at terce,
its colour is my mouth,
green on the mouth of Sweeny.

Chill chill is my body
when away from ivy,
the rain torrent hurts it
and the thunder.

I am in summer with the herons of Cuailgne
with wolves in winter,
at other times I am hidden in a copse –
not so the man by the wall.

———

Cheerless is existence
without a downy bed,
abode of the shrivelling frost,
gusts of the snowy wind.

Chill icy wind,
shadow of a feeble sun
the shelter of a sole tree
on a mountain-plain.

The bell-belling of the stag
through the woodland,
the climb to the deer-pass,
the voice of white seas.

Forgive me Oh Great Lord,
mortal is this great sorrow,
worse than the black grief –
Sweeny the thin-groined.

Carraig Alasdair
resort of sea-gulls
sad Oh Creator,
chilly for its guests.

Sad our meeting
two hard-shanked cranes –
myself hard and ragged
she hard-beaked.

————

Chill chill is my bed at dark
on the peak of Glen Boirche,
I am weakly, no mantle on me,
lodged in a sharp-stirked holly.

Glen Bolcain of the twinkle spring
it is my rest-place to abide in;
when Samhain comes, when summer comes,
it is my rest-place where I abide.

For my sustenance at night,
the whole that my hands can glean
from the gloom of the oak-gloomed oaks –
the herbs and the plenteous fruits.

Fine hazel-nuts and apples, berries,
blackberries and oak-tree acorns,
generous raspberries, they are my due,
haws of the prickle-hawy hawthorn.

Wild sorrels, wild garlic faultless,
clean-topped cress,
they expel from me my hunger,
acorns from the mountain, melle-root.

————

Terrible is my plight this night
the pure air has pierced my body,
lacerated feet, my cheek is green –
O Mighty God, it is my due.

It is bad living without a house,
Peerless Christ, it is a piteous life!
a filling of green-tufted fine cresses
a drink of cold water from a clear rill.

Stumbling out of the withered tree-tops
walking the furze – it is truth –
wolves for company, man-shunning,
running with the red stag through fields.

———

Ululation, I am Sweeny,
my body is a corpse;
sleeping or music nevermore –
only the soughing of the storm-wind.

I have journeyed from Luachair Dheaghaidh
to the edge of Fiodh Gaibhle,
this is my fare – I conceal it not –
ivy-berries, oak-mast.

———

All Fharannain, resort of saints,
fulness of hazels, fine nuts,
swift water without heat
coursing its flank.

Plenteous are its green ivies,
its mast is coveted;
the fair heavy apple-trees
they stoop their arms.

———

There was a time when I preferred
to the low converse of humans
the accents of the turtle-dove
fluttering about a pool.

There was a time when I preferred
to the tinkle of neighbour bells
the voice of the blackbird from the crag
And the belling of a stag in a storm.

There was a time when I preferred
to the voice of a fine woman near me
the call of the mountain-grouse
heard at day.

There was a time when I preferred
the yapping of the wolves
to the voice of a cleric
melling and megling within.

Moling's tribute to Sweeny

Here is the tomb of Sweeny!
His memory racks my heart,
dear to me therefore are the haunts
of the saintly madman.

Dear to me Glen Bolcain fair
for Sweeny loved it;
dear the streams that leave it
dear its green-crowned cresses.

That beyant is Madman's Well
dear the man it nourished,
dear its perfect sand,
beloved its clear waters.

Melodious was the talk of Sweeny
long shall I hold his memory,
I implore the King of Heaven
on his tomb and above his grave.

Sources

1: THE STUDENT

'Ad Astra', *Blackrock College Annual,* 1930.

'Memories of the L.&H., *RTV Guide,* 11 Dec. 1964.

from *Centenary History of the L.&H.,* ed. J. Meenan, 1956, The Kerryman.

'The L.&H. from the earliest times', *Comhthrom Féinne,* I/1, 1 May 1931.

'Graduate Cut to Ribbons by Express-train', *Comhthrom Féinne,* IV/3, Summer 1932.

'Lionel Prune Comes to UCD', *C.F.,* IV/1, 23 April 1932.

'Lionel Prune Must Go', *C.F.,* IV/2, 30 April 1932.

'Kameradschaft', *C.F.,* V/1, 25 Jan. 1933.

'The Bog of Allen', *C.F.,* V/3, March 1933.

'Academic Enterprise at Ballybrack', *C.F.,* IV/2, 30 April 1932.

'Sensational Libel Action', *C.F.,* V/3, March 1933.

'Are You Lonely in the Restaurant?', *C.F.,* V/3, March 1933.

'Let Us Be Your Fathers!', *C.F.,* IV/2, 30 April 1932.

'We Announce An Congar', *C.F.,* V/3, March 1933.

'Rumoured Closing of Earlsfort Terrace', *C.F.,* IV/1, 23 April 1932.

'Should Pin-money Girls be Sacked?', *C.F.,* VI/3, Dec. 1933.

'A Brass Hat in Bannow Strand', *C.F.,* VII/1, Jan. 1934.

'Scenes in a Novel', *C.F.,* VIII/2, May 1934.

'What is Wrong with the L.&H.?', *C.F.,* X/3, March 1935.

'The L.&H. Controversy' (By James FitzPatrick), *C.F.,* XI/1, April 1935.

'Tidying the Garden', *C.F.,* XI/2, May 1935.

2: THE ROMANCE OF *BLATHER*

All sources are *Blather.*

Editorial – '*Blather* is Here', I/1, Aug. 1934.

277

Book Reviews, I/4, Dec. 1934.
'The Romance of *Blather*', ibid.
'Threepence for 20 Pages!!', I/2, Oct. 1934.
'Friday Night at the *Blather* Offices', ibid.
'Whither Bettystown?', ibid.
'The Shan Van Vocht', I/1, Aug. 1934.
'Answers to Correspondents', ibid.
'Answears to Correspondents', I/4, Dec. 1934.
'Balm for Battered Hearts', I/3, Nov. 1934.
'Our Growing Pains', ibid.
'Our Wretched Rimes', I/4, Dec. 1934.
'An Impudent Scoundrel Unmasked', I/3, Nov. 1934.
Editorial: 'Four weeks Old Today!', I/2, Oct. 1934.
'Our Tottering Circulation', ibid.
'Hash', I/1, Aug. 1934.
'Our Sports Club', I/3, Nov. 1934.
'Rugby', I/2, Oct. 1934.
'Listen in to 2BL', I/3, Nov. 1934.
'More about our new Wireless Service', I/4, Dec. 1934.
'Has Hitler gone too far?', I/2, Oct. 1934.
'£30 in pin-money for Readers', I/5, Jan. 1935.
'The Abbey Theatre Subsidy', ibid.
'Is there a Santa Claus?', I/4, Dec. 1934.
'Our Handy Vocabulars', I/3, Nov. 1934.
'Beware of B.A.!', I/4, Dec. 1934.
'This is Angela. Form of Bequest', I/1, Aug. 1934.
'Balm for Ireland's Ills', I/5, Jan. 1935.
'The *Blather* Bounty', I/1, Aug. 1934.
'Is Your Son an Ignoramus?', I/4, Dec. 1934.
'Your Ignoramus of a Son?', I/5, Jan. 1935.
'Cavalcade', I/1, Aug. 1934.

3: FROM THE IRISH

'The Irish Question: An Old Tale from an Old Lad', *Blather,*
    I/2, Oct. 1934.
'An Insoluble Question', *Irish Press,* Christmas 1932.
'Good Luck and Bad Luck', *Evening Telegraph,* 29 July 1932.
'Woe to the Lovelorn', *Evening Telegraph,* 13 Oct. 1932.

278

'The Narrative of the Inebriated Man', *Irish Press,* 24 Aug. 1932.
'A Bijou: A Bon Mot', *Evening Telegraph,* 3 Oct. 1932.

4: *AT SWIM-TWO-BIRDS*

'A Conversation', From an early version of the manuscript.
'Memoir of the Pooka's father', ibid.
'Mail from M. Byrne', ibid.

5: HENRIK IBSEN AND PATRICK KAVANAGH

All from the *Irish Times* letters to the Editor column. On p. 202 is a section from a review by Patrick Kavanagh, 20 July 1940, in the same paper.

The Three Sisters
D. C. Barry, 30 May 1940.
F. O'Brien, 4 June 1940.
Lir O'Connor, 8 June 1940.
F. O'Brien, 10 June 1940.
L. O'Connor, 12 June 1940.
F. O'Brien, 13 June 1940.
Whit Cassidy, 13 June 1940.
H.P., 13 June 1940.
Paul Desmond, 15 June 1940.
Oscar Love, 15 June 1940.
Luna O'Connor, 19 June 1940.
Oscar Love, 20 June 1940.
Literary Criticism
P. Kavanagh review, 20 July 1940.
F.L.J., 22 July 1940.
N. S. Harvey, 25 July 1940.
Oscar Love, 27 July 1940.
Judy Clifford, 27 July 1940.
F. O'Brien, 29 July 1940.
Jno. O'Ruddy, 30 July 1940.
Lir O'Connor, 30 July 1940.

(Mrs) Hilda Upshott, 30 July 1940.
(The) O'Madan, 31 July 1940.
Ewart MacGonicle, 31 July 1940.
(Miss Lambkin), 31 July 1940.
'South American Joe', 1 Aug. 1940.
Whit Cassidy, 2 Aug. 1940.
Jno. O'Ruddy, 2 Aug. 1940.
F. O'Brien, 2 Aug. 1940.
'Lanna Avvia', 2 Aug. 1940.
Na2 Co3, 2 Aug. 1940.
F. McEwe Obarn, 3 Aug. 1940.
Miss (alas) Luna O'Connor, 5 Aug. 1940.
Patrick Kavanagh, 7 Aug. 1940.

6: *THE BELL*
'Going to the Dogs', *The Bell,* I/1, Oct. 1940.
'The Trade in Dublin', *The Bell,* I/2, Nov. 1940.
'The Dance Halls', *The Bell,* I/5, Feb. 1941.
'No, this is not from *The Bell*', *Cruiskeen Lawn, Irish Times,*
    31 May 1941.
'Bell-idiocy', *Cruiskeen Lawn, Irish Times,* 6 Oct. 1941.

7: POEMS IN TRANSLATION
'Standish Hayes O'Grady', *Irish Times,* 16 Oct. 1940.
'Scel lem duib', *Cruiskeen Lawn, Irish Times,* 20 Mar. 1941.
'Aoibhinn, a Leabhráin, do Thriall', ibid., 7 June 1941.
'Domforcai Fidhbaidae Fál', ibid., 9 Jan. 1941.
'ClochánBinn', ibid., 13 Mar. 1941.
'A Dhruimfhionn Donn Dílis', ibid., 19 Dec. 1940.
'Cridhe Hé', ibid., 30 Oct. 1940.
'Ach a Luin', ibid., 2 Nov. 1940.
'Int En Gaires Asintsail', ibid., 16 Jan. 1941.
'Sgíth mo chrob ón sgríbinn', ibid., 4 Aug. 1947.
'Do Bhulla, a Bhréagóg Fhallsa', *Cruiskeen Lawn,* quoted in
    Honest Ulsterman, No. 41, Nov. 1973–Feb. 1974.
'Protopolitics', *Cruiskeen Lawn, Irish Times,* 10 April 1958.
All succeeding poems from *At Swim-Two-Birds.*